Forgotten Citizens

FORGOTTEN CITIZENS

Deportation, Children, and the
Making of American Exiles and Orphans

Luis H. Zayas

OXFORD
UNIVERSITY PRESS

Oxford University Press is a department of the University of
Oxford. It furthers the University's objective of excellence in research,
scholarship, and education by publishing worldwide.

Oxford   New York
Auckland   Cape Town   Dar es Salaam   Hong Kong   Karachi
Kuala Lumpur   Madrid   Melbourne   Mexico City   Nairobi
New Delhi   Shanghai   Taipei   Toronto

With offices in
Argentina   Austria   Brazil   Chile   Czech Republic   France   Greece
Guatemala   Hungary   Italy   Japan   Poland   Portugal   Singapore
South Korea   Switzerland   Thailand   Turkey   Ukraine   Vietnam

Oxford is a registered trademark of Oxford University Press
in the UK and certain other countries.

Published in the United States of America by
Oxford University Press
198 Madison Avenue, New York, NY 10016

© Oxford University Press 2015

Cataloging-in-Publication data is on file at the Library of Congress
ISBN 978-0-19-021112-7

9 8 7 6 5 4 3 2 1
Printed in the United States of America
on acid-free paper

To
Mercedes and Luis Antonio Zayas who taught me compassion
and service

Once, I arrived a little early for one of our tutoring sessions,
Daniel was still playing Super Mario,
When his mother told him it was homework time
he whined and said he wanted to keep playing,
a smirk bullet-trained across my face
but her response derailed my smile in its tracks
she told him:
"*Mi hijo, tienes que estudiar, pa'que no seas como tu papá,
haciendo el trabajo que nadie lo quiere hacer*"
"*My son, you have to study so you don't end up like your father,
doing the work that no one else wants to*"

And I wanted to tell him 'no',
tell him your mother is a brick house *guerrera* of a woman
and I know what she's trying to teach you
but no *mi hijo*,

You be just like your father
learn to pick those locks like he taught ya'
let no rules written by men
tell you where you can roam on God's green earth
let no Uncle Sam Sandman tell you when you can dream
just rub those grains of the Sonora out of your eyes
and replace them with little bits of revelation

And if a classmate,
or a store clerk,
or a coward with a badge made of false courage ever calls you
"illegal"
you remind them that a few decades back
the gutter
       used to be the border
that kept black folk off the sidewalk
                   legally
You're a superhero to me *mi hijo*,

and just know
That one day you may find a brick house *guerrera* of a woman
that will hold you as tightly as her courage
and perhaps she will teach you to hold your son the same way,
he will have his grandfather's smile
and his mother's eyes
and if he ever doubts the fireballs in his palms,
she will tell him:
"*Un día mi hijo, tu vas a ser igual que tu papá*"
"*One day my son, you're gonna' be just like your Daddy.*"

Kane Smego
"Super Mario" (Abridged, 2012)

CONTENTS

A NOTE ON NAMES AND TERMS

The names of all citizen-children and their families that appear in this book have been changed to protect their privacy. I have not disguised their parents' originating countries and towns for authenticity. Children's ages have not been changed to present them within their developmental position. However, the locations of their homes and names of schools and other details of their lives have been "disguised, but" not to the extent of altering the contexts in which they live. The only real names that are used are those of children and parents whose identities have been revealed publicly by the news media. Professionals in public roles, such as our interviewers, expert witnesses, attorneys, and judges whose names appear on legal documents or news reports, are identified by their real names except in a few instances in which I decided discretion was best.

Quoted comments provided by the children during interactions with me or our project interviewers are drawn from transcripts and notes. They are the words actually spoken by the children. When I work from recollections of experiences with children or parents, I use paraphrasing. At times I condense the children's comments for brevity or I re-sequence them for clarity. Occasionally, I alter children's grammar to make their statements easier to comprehend. When they spoke in Spanish or interspersed their English with emotionally or socially laden terms in Spanish, I present the original Spanish and provide translations.

Illegal alien and *illegal immigrant* are official or legal terms for persons who enter the country without permission or who have entered with the proper documents but stayed beyond their allowable time. The terms *undocumented immigrant* and *unauthorized immigrant* are also in common usage. The two latter terms emerged in reaction to the legal terms that connote criminal behavior and stigmatize. You will see these four terms in this book, but generally I use the terms *undocumented immigrant* and *unauthorized immigrant*. It is essential to note that not all undocumented immigrants are from Mexico. Nor are they only from Latin America. It is true that about 81 percent of the unauthorized immigrant population is from Latin America, mostly from Mexico (Hoefer, Rytina, & Baker, 2009). The other 19 percent—nearly a fifth of all illegal immigrants—come from countries such as China, the Philippines, India, Korea, and Canada, and assorted countries of Europe, Africa, Asia, and Oceana. The situations of citizen-children of undocumented immigrants from countries outside of Latin America are in some ways similar to and in other ways different from their counterparts with Latin American parents. My use of examples of US citizen-children and their unauthorized-immigrant parents from Latin America is based on their sheer numbers and my greater familiarity with their situations.

I refer to unauthorized immigrants by their national origin rather than as part of an ethnic group. When referring to them as a group, I use the term *Latin American* rather than *Latino* or *Hispanic*. These last two terms typically represent a broader political grouping that includes foreign- and US-born people of Latin American heritage, not all of them immigrants.

PREFACE

In this book, I try to put a human face on the predicament of children who are born in the United States to parents who have immigrated to this country without permission or who have decided to stay in violation of the law after their permission officially expired. This is a book about citizen-children—and, to some extent, their undocumented brothers and sisters—who have not chosen their legal status. Citizen-children are born in the United States. They may have siblings who were born in another country and brought here by parents seeking brighter futures for themselves and their children. These sibling groups do not enter the world expecting that their parents will live under a cloud of deportability from the United States. Yet in communities all over the United States, citizen-children grow to learn the constant fear of losing parents and siblings, or being uprooted from the lives they know. Living under the threat of their parents' deportation colors how citizen-children view the world and how they move about in it, even how they perceive and judge themselves. They are affected psychologically by this constant worry. The citizen-children of unauthorized or illegal immigrants are the collateral damage of the laws and policies, and immigration enforcement practices that our government enacts. Their situation seldom rises to the critical attention of legislators, other policy makers, and the enforcers of immigration laws.

It is a deep empathy that fuels my passion for seeing justice done for the children and parents who live beleaguered lives for the decisions they made to emigrate from other countries. Many are brave people who decided to undergo the harrowing routes of coming to America by foot, boat, or raft, or on top of trains. They have been smuggled in the trunks of cars or in the oven-like trailers of eighteen-wheel trucks. They have crossed international borders and over state lines like livestock destined for auction or pallets of commercial goods destined for shiny supermarkets. Under these conditions their decisions and determination are no less vital than the decisions and grit of our country's earliest immigrants. Today's illegal immigrants encounter legal systems and public punishment and humiliation and possible arrest, detention, deportation and repatriation that affect them and their children. Deportation can fracture families and leave children without the rights to which they are entitled. These results, as unintended as they might be, go against important human rights conventions, such as the American Convention on Human Rights (Organization of American States, 1969) signed by the United States in San Jose Costa Rica on November 21, 1969. Article 17 of the Convention states that: "the family is the natural and fundamental group unit of society and is entitled to protection by society and the state." Article 19 addresses the rights of minor children: "Every minor child has the right to the measures of protection required by his condition as a minor on the part of his family, society, and the state."

In these pages, I try to depict and analyze the general and the unique about the lives of citizen-children of unauthorized immigrants, truly a narrow sliver of all the many facets of immigration and deportation. To accomplish this, I must present the situation of citizen-children and their parents and their brothers and sisters with the respectable efficiency of the scholar. That means pulling from research findings in economics, demography, psychology, sociology, anthropology, other social sciences, and abundant collections of studies, theories, biographies, histories, memoirs, and anthologies. It means reviewing history, policy debates, news accounts, and legal decisions, and integrating these with my research and professional experience to arrive at cold, clinical inferences and conclusions. The synthesis must yield intellectual and technical contributions to our knowledge base. It must render the situation of citizen-children accessible and understandable to the reader.

But mostly I seek to portray citizen-children as people, their illegal immigrant parents as fiercely protective and loving. I want to reveal them as I have experienced them: as individual human beings with aspirations and personality quirks, with flaws and with moments of great dignity and nobility; as individuals with complex motivations of love, duty, desperation, greed, and envy. I want to portray them at times when they show really poor judgments, and at times when they act with stunning courage. Their story should be told with compassion to touch on the deeply human. The story needs to show the impact of living as a citizen-child on human attachment, loss, trauma, nostalgia, yearning, and family unity. And it needs to show what happens when parents and children are torn apart by deportation.

Having been trained in the social and behavioral sciences, my natural inclination is to write with the terseness and objectivity of the scholar. But I know as a reader that scientific writing can cause us to lessen our grip on the emotional, the deeply human, and not be stirred to action to right a wrong. Therefore, I've chosen a first person voice both to facilitate communication of the children's and families' humanity and to reflect the personal nature of their information. This book relates my experience as a clinician and academician. It communicates the conclusions and opinions that I have reached in a career in youth development and mental health that spans 40 years. Throughout the book, I refer to anecdotes from my practice and findings from my research, especially my most recent work on citizen-children, to illustrate these assertions.

Robert Coles (1961), the prolific and noted child psychiatrist, has observed about scientific writing that "Our journals, our habits of talk become cluttered with jargon or the trivial . . . As the words grow longer and the concepts more intricate and tedious, human sorrows and temptations disappear, loves move away, envies and jealousies, revenge and terror dissolve. Gone are strong, sensible words with good meaning and flavor for the real" (p. 111).

Coles is correct. We know that data strengthen the arguments for legislative change and lend support to social movements. However, it is the human testimonial, the compelling story that changes minds, the account that leaves the enduring image. To convey then the real human tragedy that is our immigration and deportation policies and practices—the forces that make vulnerable young citizens the collateral damage in a national war against their parents—the data cannot be allowed to eclipse the human. Another great documentarian of our nation's vulnerable children, Jonathan Kozol, wields human testimonials to great effect. His books have reflected to a nation's conscience, maybe even seared on that conscience, how our educational policies have all but abandoned poor urban children. Kozol doesn't dwell on the data but instead makes his point by narrating the lives of the most vulnerable among us. I am guided by Kozol's (2000) words in *Ordinary Resurrections: Children in the Years of Hope*.

> The lives of children in poor neighborhoods are studied, and their personalities examined and dissected, often with a good deal of self-confidence, by grown-ups far away who do not know them but rely on data generated by researchers to come up with various conclusions that are used to justify political decisions. This is inevitable, I guess. Societies and governments need to rely on generalities to organize their understandings and establish policies.

Sometimes, though, these generalities seem much too big, too confident, and too relentless. It feels at times as if the world of adult expertise is taking hundred-pound cement blocks, labeled "certitude" and "big significance," and lowering them down on the shoulders of a six- or seven-year-old boy, then telling him, "Okay, you carry this for ten or fifteen years. Then, if we learn something new, we will come back and give you some new labels you can carry." Sometimes the size and weight of all of this signification make it hard to see if there is still a living body underneath. (pp. 14–15)

The big, confident, and relentless generalities that obscure the humanity in children in poverty that Kozol so affectionately describes also apply to the world of undocumented immigrant parents, their undocumented and documented children, and the deportation policies that treat them as numbers and violators rather than individuals with personal everyday needs. To bring awareness, understanding, and compassion for citizen-children to a broad and thoughtful audience, I try to balance the academic and the evocative. I hope you will find that I have.

CHAPTER 1

Keeping Silence

The only way that Virginia knew to protect her parents and older siblings was to keep quiet. Virginia had been silent for many, many months in order to preserve a family secret and keep away the big, complex world that made her feel so fragile and scared. She was a perfectly normal 6-year-old girl born to an intact family in Missouri, and her silence was not a problem of language or speech. Her parents were undocumented immigrants from Mexico, and Virginia had to help conceal their illegal status as best she could. Like her older siblings, she was born in the United States and had full citizenship, a birthright given to her by the Fourteenth Amendment of the US Constitution. But her parents, like millions of other undocumented parents, did not have the same protection. At almost any time, they could be subject to removal from the country for being present illegally. It did not matter that her parents were raising three American citizens; this fact alone was not enough to give the parents any legal protection. All Virginia could really do at her tender age was to keep her silence and thus avoid uttering anything that might uncover her parents' tenuous status.

I came to know Virginia when I received a call in late 2005 from a pair of dedicated immigration attorneys asking me to conduct a psychological and social evaluation of their client's daughter. The request was part of the attorneys' effort to prevent the removal of her father from the United States through the legal avenues available to them. The lawyers wanted me to provide an assessment of what the *potential* impact might be on Virginia's mental health and general psychosocial functioning if her father were deported to Mexico. The lawyers' request was a tall order. To win the case, the evaluation would need to show not only that Virginia would suffer if her father were deported, but more so that she would suffer "exceptional and extremely unusual hardship."

In the mental health field, forecasting a person's future behavioral or emotional reaction to changes in geographic or physical circumstances that are not well known or that will occur in some unspecified future time is a very inexact science. The best we can do is study past and present adjustments. Then we take this background and superimpose it on the factors that the person will *possibly* face—new physical situations with new people, unfamiliar institutions, unique customs and rituals, and differing modes of behavior—and then arrive at an educated, informed presupposition. It is not the neatest or most refined aspect of mental health practice, yet we do it all the time when we predict children's reactions to custody decisions in family courts. In divorces cases, we operate with a good deal of background information from the parents and maybe therapists. In child welfare situations, we make predictions about children's reactions to being moved from one foster home to another or to meeting adoptive parents, and the evaluator can rely on files that have recorded children's histories of past disruptions and adjustments. The lawyers for Virginia's father, however, were calling about an immigration court case, and there was very little to draw from to make predictions about such a serious potential life change.

The uncertainty regarding these predictions led to another possible obstacle in the case. What if the results of the evaluation did not point to any hardship? What if my evaluation resulted in findings that showed a strong, resilient child and a family system that would not be gravely affected by the deportation and probable move of the entire family to Mexico? The request from the attorneys and the obstacles we encountered ignited in me an interest that influenced me for the decade that followed. This one case became a cause for me. I shifted my practice, teaching, and advocacy to work with immigrant families in deportation. My research turned in the same direction. Some of the case studies included in this book come from my practice and some cases are taken from a research project titled "Exploring the Effects of Parental Deportation on US Citizen Children." (Details on this project are presented in Appendix A.)

At the center of this book are the lives of US citizen-children of undocumented immigrant parents and what happens to them. Throughout this book, the term citizen-children refers to this population: US-born children of undocumented immigrants. There are estimated to be about 4.5 million such citizen-children in the United States today, and another million undocumented children who were born in another country and were brought to the United States at a young age (Wessler, 2011; Dreby,

2012). Two other categories of children are important to distinguish from citizen-children and undocumented children who arrived with their parents. Though they are not the focus of this book, the two groups are children of Legal Permanent Residents (LPR) and children who entered the country as undocumented and unaccompanied minors. The first group is the offspring of LPRs, that is people who are commonly thought of as "green card" holders and who have obtained this legal status through the sponsorship of family members (listed in the immigration law as "preference allocation for family-sponsored immigrants") or employers (listed as "preference allocation for employment-based immigrants").[1] The special legal status of LPRs allows them to reside in the United States permanently, though they are still considered immigrants and are subject to deportation if convicted of a felony.[2] The children born to them in the United States, however, are citizens.[3] In a report titled *In the Child's Best Interest?: The Consequences of Losing a Lawful Immigrant Parent to Deportation*, attorneys Jonathan Baum, Rosha Jones, and Catherine Barry (2010) discuss the consequences of children's loss of a parent who is a LPR through deportation due to a felony conviction. The results for the citizen-children of LPRs who are deported are very similar to those of the citizen-children of unauthorized immigrant: they either leave with the deported parent or stay in the United States, a decision often based on the children's ages and needs as well as the families' economic resources and social supports. Despite their deportability, however, LPRs do not live with the same threat as undocumented immigrants. Except for committing a crime, LPRs and their citizen-children do not have to worry every day that they will be arrested, detained, and deported, as they are not in the country illegally.

The other distinct group of children is classified as "unaccompanied minors," or minor children who enter the United States alone and unlawfully. In some cases, they come here in search of their parents who they have not seen in years, parents who left them years before in order to find work. In other cases, these unaccompanied minors are not trying to reunite with parents, but simply may be fleeing the abject poverty, crime, and violence of small villages or capital cities in Central America. Because these children are undocumented, they, too, face the threat of deportation, although they have some protections because of their minor status. (As I write this book in the summer of 2014, the number of unaccompanied minors entering the United States from Central America has reached staggering proportions.)

For the purpose of clarity, the words *removal* and *deportation* mean the same thing. Removal is the official or legal term for deportation and refers to expelling an alien after his or her unlawful entry into the country or unlawful extension of stay in the country (Reasoner, 2011). It is, in effect, the banishment and transfer of an alien to his or her country of origin. Unlawful presence in the United States is an administrative, or statutory, violation. Unless the undocumented immigrant is separately convicted of a criminal offense, his or her punishment for unlawful presence is removal.

By focusing on citizen-children and the removal or deportation of their parents, I have three objectives. First, I want to paint a portrait of the lives of citizen-children and their mixed status families. I refer to these families as "mixed-status," as they comprise parents and kids with different types of legal status. Because the impact of migration can influence a family for several generations, in Chapter 2 I discuss the forces that motivate people to take sometimes treacherous journeys to find a better place. In Chapter 3 I provide a brief history of the complicated relationship that the United States—a nation of immigrants—has with immigration, and put recent Latin American immigration in the context of this history. This description provides at least a partial answer to the question of why the parents from other countries choose to break the law and enter the country illegally, as well as how this act and its consequences affect their children for years to come.

The second objective is to shed light on the social and psychological experiences of citizen-children born to undocumented parents in the United States. Pulling from the extant theoretical and empirical literature, and from the research I have conducted, Chapters 4–6 will show the challenges facing citizen-children and their behavioral and emotional reactions to the situations they encounter in their lives. The point is to show the impact that their parents' lack of legal immigration status have on them; how citizen-children see and act on the world; how they navigate the many challenges of their parents' immigration status; and the part they play in protecting that status. In Chapters 7 and 8, I review how the wheels of immigration justice operate and the effects the process has on citizen-children in mixed-status families. To achieve this, I discuss our laws, national and local politics, and public reaction to illegal immigrants. To humanize the situations that parents and children face when they seek relief from deportation in immigration courts, and to demonstrate the legal process as well as the judicial rationale for decisions to grant or deny relief, I include in these chapters several real-life cases and judges' written decisions.

My third objective is to propose that our immigration enforcement systems create, in effect, two subordinate classes of children: *exiles* and *orphans.* The word exile refers to both a person and a state of mind. An exile is by definition someone *forced* by some reason or other to abandon her or his home country against her or his will. This concept of exile applies to the citizen-child who has left the United States for another country. By compelling parents to make the decision to take their US citizen-children to another country and abrogating the young citizens' rights, we are coercing them into a state of exile. As a state of mind, exile is the loss of a sense of belonging to a place and its people, the loss of an emotional connection to a group or national identity. The idea that when deportation forces parents to take their children to another country constitutes *de facto* exile of children has been discussed by legal scholars, notably Jacqueline Bhabha (2014) and David B. Thronson (2005-2006, 2011) in the context of the contradictions created by immigration laws, family laws, and the rights of citizens. My focus is on the deleterious psychological and social impact that deportation and exile have on citizen-children. In Chapter 9, I present the realities of citizen-children in exile who are in that position through no fault of their own.

The term *orphan* in this book refers primarily to the loss of the daily physical presence, love, and attention of a parent or both parents, even though the parents are alive but living in another country. When parents are forcibly separated from their children and unable to physically minister to their children's needs, as is the case when parents are detained and deported without their children, they are involuntarily orphaning their children. The very fact that parents may have no recourse other than to leave a child in the care of others does not diminish the child's sense of loss, even if the child remains in the community and home to which he or she is emotionally attached. Therefore, orphans by deportation are children who are unnecessarily deprived of parents' care and affection. In Chapter 10, I describe the lives of those who have become orphans through family separation by deportation.

These terms may seem provocative to the reader. That is my intention, to provoke thought and discussion. My argument for assigning these labels is based on the fact that impersonal laws and insensitive enforcement compel undocumented immigrant parents to make decisions that have devastating effects on US citizen-children, the very people our government must protect. Indeed, immigration law often contradicts family law and undermines the rights of citizenship. Forcing citizen-children into exile or making them orphans are two of the most extreme and harmful outcomes of immigration enforcement. Most often, the children are not included in the thinking behind the establishment of the laws or the implementation of the enforcement practices. These laws are designed to keep out undocumented immigrants, but they do not adequately account for the reality of mixed-status families. Legislators who promote increased enforcement effectively increase family disruption and separation; citizen-children are collateral damage. Exiling citizen-children or forcing them to endure an orphan's existence is not in our national interest, a topic I take up in Chapter 11.

WHEN BIRTHRIGHT CITIZENSHIP DOESN'T PROTECT

The United States, through the 14th Amendment of the Constitution, confers all the rights, privileges, and protections of citizenship to anyone born in the United States. This important right is based on the concept of *jus soli* or birthright citizenship that dates back to colonial English rule. Under common law, colonial residents born within lands owned by the English and who pledged allegiance to the English were English subjects even if their parents were not. The only exception was for any children born to a "hostile occupying force," or children of diplomats, who by definition owed allegiance to a different country (Congressional Research Service [CRS], 2010).[4] Despite this tradition, the United States had no real statute or Constitutional provision that defined citizenship until 1866.[5]

Birthright citizenship finally became part of the federal statute with the Civil Rights Act of 1866, which declared that all individuals born in the United States, regardless of race, were citizens of the United States. Notably, this Act overturned *Dred Scott v. John Sandford* (1857),[6] in which the US Supreme Court declared that anyone who was a descendent of a slave, free or not, was not eligible for citizenship (CRS, 2010). The Civil Rights Act of 1866 voided this decision and awarded citizenship to all African Americans born domestically. To prevent amendment or repeal of the Civil Rights Act, Congress passed the 14th Amendment in 1868, solidifying the right to citizenship for every person born in the United States (CRS, 2010). In modern US history, Puerto Rico reflects the English common law origins of *jus soli* in that persons living in this Free Associated Commonwealth (i.e., a territory of the United States) are, in effect, born on American soil and are, therefore, US citizens by birth. Birthright citizenship is an honorable tradition but it is not shared by all countries.[7]

In principle, each citizen enjoys protections. But, when we enter the realm of immigration law and mixed-status families it becomes very murky. Despite *jus soli*, children cannot fully exercise their rights as citizens; they encounter many inequalities. As legal scholar David Thronson (2011) points out, immigration law devalues citizen-children and works against their welfare by separating children not just from their parents in the case of deportation but also from the protection of the state. That is, the full benefits of citizen-children of undocumented immigrant parents are denied to them. Parents' citizenship rights extend to their children but, by virtue of their youthful status, citizen-children cannot extend their benefits to their parents. "The system," writes Thronson, "facilitates the assimilation of children's status to that of their parents but does not provide for assimilation of parents' status to that of a child" (p. 239). In nullifying the rights and privileges that come with birthright citizenship, immigration laws and enforcement practices undermine the protections of citizenship and, instead, harm citizen-children. In fact, argues Thronson, the very ties that our general structure of laws are intended to protect—families and the connection between parents and their children—are undone by one segment of our legal system, immigration laws. At their extreme, US immigration laws diminish the connection between children and the state rendering them, Thronson avers, to the status of noncitizen and "effectively stateless" (p. 237).

Another noted legal scholar, Jacqueline Bhabha (2014), makes a similar observation.

> The assumption that children's native citizenship cannot alter parents' immigration status highlights a striking divergence between foundational assumptions of family and immigration law. Where families are divided by marriage or relationship breakdown, courts traditionally allocated the family home to the party with custody of the children—home is where the children are, the custodial parent's residence deriving from the child's. But if families face separation because of immigration law, the presumption is that the anchoring role of the child must give way, their primacy evaporating. If children have no right to use their citizenship as a basis for exercising family reunion or shoring up family unity, then—if their parents face deportation—the children too risk constructive deportation, despite being citizens. (p. 71)

Both Thronson and Bhabha identify the inherent incompatibility between immigration law and family law. In this book, I show how the separation between citizen-children and the state, and between citizen-children and their parents, is produced by immigration enforcement and what the effects are on the physical, emotional, and psychological health of citizen-children in mixed-status families.

Long before I met Virginia, I knew some things about the angry debates surrounding immigration reform. I read the newspapers and watched the evening news anchors and correspondents as they reported on ordinances that small towns and large municipalities were enacting to prevent immigrants from moving into their areas. I knew that these were efforts to make life difficult for many people, not only immigrants, but also landlords and employers who rented to immigrants or hired them. Some communities tried to block immigrants' access to jobs, housing, education, and healthcare as a strategy to combat growth of the immigrant population. There were stories, too, of good deeds done by immigrants or acts of heroism, of communities thriving through the influx of hard-working immigrants who were restoring houses and starting businesses, and of employers whose businesses were jeopardized by the loss of a primary source of labor. I knew many mixed-status families who lived in our midst. I had provided *pro bono* clinical services to Latin American immigrant families at a local free clinic, but these requests were not for immigration-related services. Most of the clients who sought my services at the clinic were couples encountering marital problems and occasionally alcohol abuse by a husband or wife; young men, some married and some single, who were depressed from the loneliness and distance from their wives, girlfriends, and families back in their home countries; children with emotional or behavioral problems; women who had traversed deserts where they had been raped and victimized in their journey and now suffered from depression and posttraumatic stress; and immigrants with long-standing psychiatric problems who could not get services or medications through the local hospitals, mental health centers, or federally qualified health centers because they were undocumented and uninsured.

But until the day the lawyers called about Virginia, I had not conducted an evaluation of a child for the explicit purpose of providing a professional opinion to an immigration court. I accepted the challenge. Over several hour-long meetings in the course of a month, I interviewed Virginia and her parents, administered some psychological tests to her, and got to know her siblings. I looked over Virginia's educational records and read notes that her current and previous teachers made on her report cards. After gaining permission from her parents, I contacted two teachers and was able to spend some time on the phone asking them about Virginia. I gleaned additional information from her health records.

Virginia was the youngest of three children, with a brother, age 13, and a sister, age 11. The family resided then in a four-bedroom, single family home that the parents had purchased three years earlier. The children each had their own bedroom. The parents had been married 14 years and had lived in California and Kansas before moving to Missouri just months before Virginia was born. Both parents were restaurant cooks, although the father also had a small side business selling used cars. They had completed the equivalent of high school in Mexico and had stable employment histories in the United States. Virginia's two older siblings were English-dominant, although they all spoke Spanish at home. Although they understood spoken Spanish, like many other US-born and raised citizen children of foreign-born parents, they did not write or read their parents' native language. They had never traveled to Mexico and had never met their maternal grandmother or extended family. They had a maternal aunt, also undocumented, who lived nearby. Virginia's parents were caring, nurturing, and generous people who had provided considerable stability for their children. Teachers described the parents as exemplary and very involved with their children's schooling and extracurricular activities. (The older brother played tuba, the older sister played the flute, and both were in the school's orchestra). Virginia's father became a target for deportation when a resentful co-worker informed the local immigration authorities of his status, leading to his arrest and detention.

Based on the history given by her mother, it seemed that Virginia had met most developmental milestones normally. She entered preschool when she was 3 years old and spent 2 years there with the same teacher, Ms. Mellon. The preschool teacher and Virginia's parents told me that Virginia had not spoken in school—neither to adults nor other children—for over 15 months. She was extremely timid and would not talk with anyone, including the bilingual teacher who was brought in to work with her. During the first year, Ms. Mellon told me, Virginia attended morning sessions and never talked nor smiled. Her affect was described as flat and scared. Ms. Mellon made a note, however, that Virginia's parents were extremely supportive of their daughter and took Virginia's education seriously. During her second year with Ms. Mellon, Virginia began to speak spontaneously by repeating what her teacher had just said. Those were her only utterances. Thereafter, Virginia spoke more, but her verbal production continued to be low relative to other children her age. Her academic progress was uneven and Ms. Mellon was alarmed when Virginia would occasionally stay in a corner of the classroom and curl into a fetal position. Virginia completed the second year of preschool and moved to kindergarten.

In kindergarten, Virginia was described by her teacher, Ms. Joshua, as sweet, compliant, and very quiet. From the very beginning of the school year, Virginia again did not speak or spoke very little to others. Ms. Joshua reported that Virginia followed rules very well and got along with other children. Even at the point in which I met her, at least five months into the academic year, Virginia had barely spoken in school. She would raise her hand in class occasionally, struggling to be a part of the class. Virginia's reading and writing levels were low for her grade and she spoke and understood English but would not read it or write it. Ms. Joshua thought that it was likely that Virginia would have to repeat kindergarten.

In the interactions with me, Virginia was cooperative, deferential, and respectful, but almost always quiet. Though initially timid, Virginia gradually became more at ease. I asked which language she preferred and she nodded affirmatively to English. When I spoke to her, Virginia would give her reply by gestures. Virginia could not name simple items in Spanish such as hat, buttons, scarf, or shoes. Engaged in play with a coloring book, she could identify some items in English and few in Spanish. It was evident that English was her preferred language. Nodding for yes and shaking her head for no was how we interacted for hours. The few times she spoke to me, her speech showed no signs of impairment, she enunciated clearly although shyly, and her grammar and syntax were age-appropriate. When asked to reproduce some basic geometric shapes, Virginia did so with good results but the size of her renderings were constricted and were placed along the edge of the paper rather than in the middle of the page which is more typical of children her age. Virginia was small physically, but her motor and verbal abilities were normal for her age. The tests I ran indicated no perceptual-motor integration, cognitive, or language impairments. Throughout the four hours, Virginia demonstrated good impulse control, frustration tolerance, and attention span. Her motor activity and emotional state were modulated and well controlled. When her parents and I were in conversation, Virginia entertained herself with coloring books and dolls for long periods, showing no adverse effects of not being the center of attention.

The drawings of her family that I asked her to do were similarly constricted and placed on the upper margins of the paper rather than at the bottom, which would be more typical of a child her age. Her figures were basic and appropriate to her age and were assigned corresponding gender characteristics. Her father was drawn with a bald head, an accurate representation. Virginia placed herself closer to her father than to her mother in the drawing. Asked what the family was doing in the picture, Virginia stated, "The family is taking a picture. They wanted to do fun stuff." A picture of a girl was similarly basic and age-appropriate and its accompanying story was of a girl making a snowman with a carrot for a nose, playing with dolls, and watching television. The girl was alone because she had been stealing stuff from her brother and parents. The girl did this because "she wanted a lot of stuff. She wanted to win everything." Virginia also drew a house, which took up much of the page and was placed appropriately on the bottom margin. It was a happy home, with a picket fence, curtains in the windows, flowers in the garden, and a dog named Sparky in the yard. Virginia, I saw, was just like any other American child who wanted a stable, familiar home with parents, siblings, pet, and neighborhood.

But when I asked her to describe who lived in the house and what the family was like, Virginia's narrative turned from that of the average American kid to that of a citizen-child fearing her father's deportation. Virginia began the list of the inhabitants of the home with her father and in a reflection on him she added that the girl in the house would "cry if daddy didn't live with her." Virginia stated, "I don't want to go to another place or another school," and acknowledged that she was timid in pre-school and would not want to go to a new school because she is shy. She did not want to go to another school where all the children spoke Spanish. While telling, these statements were the result of a long, slow, laborious process. Still, most of what I learned from her was through her gestures, pointing to things, and nodding yes or shaking her head to signify no.

It doesn't take a mental health professional or early childhood teacher to recognize that Virginia was a child with a secure attachment to her parents and family. Most of us might also notice that she was very close to her father. Whether this closeness to him came about because of his pending deportation or was just their usual relationship would require that we know them long before the deportation case. Ultimately, the origin of the strong relationship does not really matter, except that it was affected by the deportation case against her father. Simply put, Virginia loved her father and felt safe being around him, her mother, and siblings in the familiar surroundings of her home. The possible separation due to the deportation order was like a dark cloud hovering over their lives.

Virginia was emotionally fragile, a child who reacted to changes in her social environment through regressive behaviors, shyness, and withdrawal. She remained mute although there was no indication of a receptive or expressive aphasia (i.e., the inability to articulate ideas or comprehend spoken or written language that often is a result of damage to the brain due to disease or injury) or any speech problems such as lisping or stuttering. Her condition was not a result of other mental disorders, like schizophrenia, autism, pervasive developmental disorder, or mental retardation. She spoke English without an accent, something that probably protected her from teasing by other children. With this picture, I concluded that her behavior at school met diagnostic criteria for "selective mutism," an anxiety disorder seen among children, especially girls, which typically interferes with educational achievement (American Psychiatric Association, 2000).[8] Selective mutism is frequently accompanied by excessive shyness, causing children to become socially isolated. At times, children with this emotional disorder talk to other children only or they may have no problem talking at home. Virginia fit the profile well: For 15 months she did not speak in school, even with other children. This is particularly notable because at school there is an expectation to speak; speech and communication are, after all, fundamental to learning and engaging in ideas. During the same period, however, Virginia talked at home with her family. That she spoke to me hesitantly in the evaluation was likely a result of her parents telling her that I could be trusted to help her and her father's deportation process.

Based on this history, I was concerned with the high probability that Virginia would regress to the kinds of behaviors that she had shown in school. She was a child with difficulty encountering novel situations, and would simply become too anxious and insecure. The long-term life impact that such a regression would have on Virginia could confine her to a future of psychological and behavioral pathologies preventing her from meaningful or productive participation in the social environment, mostly school and work that the average person must navigate. I concluded that it was very likely that the move to Mexico would be traumatic for Virginia and cause her to suffer substantial psychological effects. My report presented all these points to the father's attorneys, the government attorney, and the immigration judge.

The complex picture that Virginia presented bears strong symbolic meaning. Her silence was not a conscious decision, but a deeply psychological one. Virginia had internalized her parents' caution to protect their legal status to such an extent that she *would not* talk to anyone about anything lest she inadvertently reveal the secret. Her parents, like other parents of undocumented children, had taught her and her siblings very early in life about discretion and prudence when it came to talking about the family's legal status. Virginia was too young to appreciate the nuances of what her parents meant, and instead took it as a rule that she was to follow inflexibly. Although most of us take for granted that a child will speak about her family in school, children of undocumented immigrants do so only to an extent, and must be circumspect. It is difficult to explain to a kindergarten-age child that there are some things about the family that she cannot speak about to others. With a young child's concrete and often categorical form of thinking—right or wrong, good or bad, yes or no, black or white—it isn't surprising that a child like Virginia becomes so quiet as to be mute in order to protect what was most important to her. It is a necessary fact of survival among undocumented families that children must learn at an early age that their parents are *sin papeles* (without papers). They may not understand the full significance of what this means but they are reminded by parents and reinforced by older siblings that there could be dire consequences to everyone in the family. The communities that they participate in with other undocumented families reinforce this point to the children.

HIDING OPENLY

Children of undocumented immigrants, regardless of whether they are citizens, must constantly live in a marginal world, covered by shadows and remaining unnoticed. They must, like Virginia, keep silent a family secret that, if revealed, could cause the collapse of the life they have built in the United States. But children can live invisible lives for only so long since they must attend school and go to the doctor like their peers. Children make friends and are invited to parties; they go to playgrounds, church, and supermarkets with their parents. As a result, undocumented immigrants and their children must enter into the daylight of school, work, playgrounds, hospitals and clinics, soccer fields, stores and malls, churches, and other public spaces. They must engage with the world around them and conduct the interpersonal exchanges of everyday life. At the same time, they must either appear invisible or quickly recede into the shadows of silence and invisibility, and away from attention. Although the children and "paperless" parents must participate in the town square, they must always be ready at a moment's notice to blend in and conceal one critical aspect of their lives: their legal status.

The average American, whether sympathetic or not to the plight and experiences of undocumented parents and their children, sees immigrants and their children in his or her community nearly every day. But that average American may not appreciate that the lives of the undocumented must be conducted within walls of secrecy, shadows and reflections, presence and elusion. Further, most of us may not appreciate what this kind of existence can do to children. Like Virginia, the children of undocumented immigrants worry; they worry a great deal about their mothers and fathers and their brothers and sisters, and uncles, aunts, cousins, and grandparents. They worry for themselves and about what will happen if mommy and daddy are taken away. As average Americans, we see immigrant families in the mall or taking their children to school and we may look on them as we do all other families, attending to the business of raising children and putting food on the table. Yet we may not see the toll that living this way exacts on their bodies and minds. Parents and children show the mental distress of the fear of deportation (Human Rights Watch, 2009).

Although the average American may not see the effects that immigration laws and the constant threat of disclosure, of being found out, have on children, a 2010 story that aired on national and international television put a real face to the worries of citizen-children. That May, the First Lady Michelle Obama visited an elementary school in Silver Spring, Maryland. It was a big media event, as it is anytime her husband or she makes public appearances outside of the White House. With her on the visit was the then First Lady of Mexico, Margarita Zavala. Together the First Ladies met with a group of second-graders in a gymnasium like those in just about every school in America, with its wooden floors and retractable bleachers surrounding the basketball court. Mrs. Obama and Mrs. Zavala sat on a folding chairs chatting with children, and Mrs. Obama was taking their questions. Other students, school officials, and media representatives were present.

Then, as carried by CBS News (2010), a petite little girl identified by Britain's *The Telegraph* (2010) as Daisy Cuevas—sitting cross-legged on the school's gym floor—asked Mrs. Obama a question about immigration reform and how it would affect her family.

"My mom, she says that Barack Obama is taking everybody away that doesn't have papers."

Mrs. Obama replied to Daisy by saying, "Yeah, well that's something that we have to work on, right? To make sure that people can be here with the right kind of papers, right? That's exactly right."

But Daisy wasn't content with Mrs. Obama's response. As a US-born child of Peruvian immigrants who had entered the country without authorization, Daisy persisted with the innocence of the very young child she was.

"But my mom doesn't have any papers," Daisy told the First Lady.

"Well, we have to work on that," Mrs. Obama replied before that part of the conversation ended. "We have to fix that, and everybody's got to work together in Congress to make sure that happens."

With the speed of our digital, high-definition, media-driven world, the video was featured on local, national, and international television and played and replayed in the evening and late news. Pundits, commentators, Democratic spokeswomen, Republican spokesmen, and apologists analyzed the video while defending or justifying a particular doctrine, policy, or institution. The Spanish-language behemoths Telemundo and Univision aired it, it became a hit on YouTube, and Daisy became a star in her mother's home country of Peru.

Maybe Daisy acted in naïve innocence when she spoke to Mrs. Obama. But comments she made later to Univision expose the depth of her insight and understanding, capacities that seem beyond her age. They reveal the thoughts of a child who has pondered her parents' status and the implications for her and for them.

"I'm a big girl and I don't want to be left with nothing. I could almost die," she told Univision. "My mommy wants papers so that she can be here legally, so that she doesn't have to go to Peru."

The Telegraph (2010) reported that Daisy's parents had left Peru eight years before, leaving behind a 1-year-old daughter, July, to be raised by her grandparents. In Maryland, her father worked as a carpenter and her mother as a housekeeper, and together they sent money to Peru every month to support their child and parents. Though sisters, July and Daisy lived apart and were separated by citizenship in two different countries: July as a citizen of Peru and Daisy as a citizen of the US. The two sisters had seen each other only once in person but occasionally chatted by webcam, which is how they knew each other and developed their sisterly relationship. Back in Peru, July said on Peruvian television, "I hope that they give my mother papers, so that she will be calm and no longer afraid." Virginia, Daisy, and July are some of the small faces and worried voices of the children of undocumented immigrants.

PUBLIC REACTION AND PROPOSED REMEDIES
TO RECENT IMMIGRATION

Solutions to a policy issue that involves 12 million people, the families who depend on them, and the businesses that rely on them are political, social, economic, and extremely complex in nature. But the public's proposed remedies have often been simplistic. Some Americans believe it is simply a matter of deporting them all, ridding our country of undocumented immigrants the way we sweep away the sand that kids track into the house.

In the closing decade of the 20th century, the attacks on undocumented people reached new heights. In California, for example, Proposition 187 was introduced on the state ballot in 1994 to create a state-run citizenship screening system and prohibit illegal aliens from using healthcare, public education, and other social services. "Prop 187," also called the *Save Our*

State initiative, insisted that all law enforcement agents who suspected that a person they arrested was in violation of immigration laws had to look into the person's immigration status. If police found evidence that the person was undocumented, they had to report it to the state's attorney general and to the federal authorities. Local governments were prohibited from stopping police officers from following the rules of Prop 187. Moreover, if any government worker suspected that a person who was applying for benefits was an unauthorized immigrant, the worker also had to file a report to law enforcement. The proposition further stated that a person could not receive any public social services until it was verified that they were citizens or lawfully admitted aliens. Despite international recognition of health as a human right,[9] undocumented persons applying for publicly funded health care services were to be denied services and identified to the police. The same was required of public elementary or secondary schools, and any identified child of an undocumented immigrant would have to leave the school within 90 days. Notably, Prop 187 rested solely on there being "suspicion" that a person was undocumented. More often than not, this suspicion would be based on the person's physical appearance and the accent in their speech.

It was chilling, but the people of California voted in favor of it anyway. Immediately, lawsuits challenging the proposition were filed and a temporary restraining order was imposed to prevent its implementation. In 1997, most of its provisions were struck down as unconstitutional by a federal judge, and in 1999, the new governor killed the law by not appealing the court's decision and subsequent arbitration (McDonnell, 1997, 1999). Many Americans continued the call to rid the United States of the nearly 12 million undocumented immigrants living inside its borders, and some argued for the construction of a long, tall wall from California's Pacific Ocean shores through deep South Texas to the Gulf of Mexico. At a visceral level, the cry seemed to be "Deport the 12 Million."

In the first decade of the new millennium, states and localities instigated a variety of anti-immigrant initiatives. Hazleton, Pennsylvania, for example, went from a small, obscure town in the northeastern part of the state to a national phenomenon when it passed a local ordinance in 2006 that would penalize landlords who rented to illegal immigrants and employers who hired them. The law was immediately challenged, and blocked in 2007 by a federal district court. Hazleton leaders pursued the case to the US Supreme Court only to have their case returned to the US Court of Appeals in 2011, which upheld its earlier ruling that the law was unconstitutional (Finley, 2013). Vitriolic attacks against undocumented immigrants continue to flourish in the second decade. There is name-calling and pillorying of those who would raise their voices in support of humane treatment of undocumented immigrants, reaching new levels that bring shame on our nation.

Forgotten in all this yelling and rancor have been the human costs and suffering. Immigrants who enter the immigration enforcement system—from arrest to detention to deportation—are often treated in ways that simply do not match the high moral standards that the United States espouses and that international conventions call for. There is evidence that detainees are made to spend long weeks, months, and even years in facilities during which they are addressed with racial epithets and slurs as well as unnecessary physical force (Phillips, Hagan & Rodriguez, 2006). Even the US Department of Homeland Security's (DHS) own investigation by the Office of the Inspector General (USDHS, 2006) found many instances of neglect and mistreatment of the detainees, such as ignoring guidelines for confinement, inadequate health care, and lack of means for the detainees to report abuses or human rights violations.

In 2006 through 2008, DHS escalated its use of raids in workplaces in which undocumented workers were employed, garnering much attention in the press. A report on three of the largest raids implemented in 2006 and 2007 shows that, for the 900 adults arrested, about 500 children, some less than 5 years old, were left with relatives or in custody of local authorities (Capps, Castañeda, Chaudry, & Santos, 2007). Some of the children were held up to two weeks. Even the conditions that detained children are held in have not met our nation's well-regarded standards for child welfare practices (Thompson, 2008).

Through the first decade of the century, laws were proposed and passed by all levels of government, some struck down and some not, that added to the vilification of immigrants and put stress on communities who relied on undocumented people to sustain their local economies. Some of these reactions and initiatives occurred at the local level, sometimes meeting the resistance of the state, but in some cases, such as Arizona, the governor's office championed anti-immigrant legislation. There were state level laws targeting immigrants and those providing vital services to them, such as healthcare centers and social-service organizations. And there were federal acts to increase the detention and removal of the undocumented.

BREAKING HISTORIC RECORDS

It is understandable that after the September 11, 2001 terrorist attacks on US soil, our country would move to protect itself more. The federal government increased its efforts to remove undocumented people out of concern for public safety. After that fateful day, we became engaged in an unprecedented level of deportation activities against undocumented immigrants, a policy very vigorously pursued by the US Department of Homeland Security. It is instructive to examine the extent to which this spirited enforcement has grown.

Table 1.1 below shows the increasing numbers of apprehensions (i.e., arrests) and removals (i.e., deportations) since 2005, published by the USDHS (2013). These figures reflect the "record levels of enforcement" boasted by the Immigration and Customs Enforcement ([ICE], 2012b).

Very few of those apprehended, arrested, detained, and removed were threats to the public. Most were poor people seeking out economic opportunity in hopes of improving their conditions.

During the Obama administration, the number of deportations increased well beyond the numbers registered by his predecessors. It was good to hear a president tell the nation in his 2011 State of the Union Address that US immigration policy "makes no sense," but the fact is that his administration was deporting record numbers of people. Nevertheless, in 2011 and 2012, the Obama Administration implemented some reforms to moderate the negative impact of aggressive immigration enforcement actions. The reforms protected vulnerable immigrants, such as those who had to care for young or disabled children or who were victims of domestic violence, sexual assault, or other crimes. In that same 2011 State of the Union Address, President Obama made the following statement:

Table 1.1

Year	Apprehensions	Removals
2005	1,291,065	246,431
2006	1,206,412	280,974
2007	960,772	319,382
2008	1,043,774	359,795
2009	869,828	395,165
2010	752,307	387,242
2011	641,601	388,409
2012	643,474	419,384
2013	Unavailable[a]	368,644

[a] As of April 2014, the figures for apprehensions by the Department of Homeland Security had not been released.

I am prepared to work with Republicans and Democrats to protect our borders, enforce our laws and address the millions of undocumented workers who are now living in the shadows. I know that debate will be difficult. I know it will take time. But tonight, let's agree to make that effort. And let's stop expelling talented, responsible young people who could be staffing our research labs or starting a new business, who could be further enriching this nation. (Obama, 2011)

It was a theme he built on in his 2013 Inaugural Address. "Our journey is not complete," he said, "until we find a better way to welcome the striving, hopeful immigrants who still see America as a land of opportunity; until bright young students and engineers are enlisted in our workforce rather than expelled from our country" (Obama, 2013). President Obama seemed willing to protect those young immigrants in the high-tech and lucrative fields of science, technology, engineering, and mathematics, but he did not mention those immigrants in the fields picking fruits and vegetables, those landscaping gardens, or washing dishes in restaurants. He was not directing his call to action for the many undocumented children of undocumented immigrants. Sure, some could find in his words the inclusion of these children, their siblings, and parents. But, the fact of the matter is that President Obama singled out highly skilled entrepreneurs and engineers, a group of skilled immigrants that the sociologist Rafael Alarcón (2000) calls *cerebreros* or "high-tech *braceros*" after the infamous bracero program that began in the 1940s. Alarcón prefers "to call them 'cerebreros' because, unlike Mexican braceros in the past, who worked with their arms (brazos) with temporary contracts, cerebreros work with their brains (cerebros) on a temporary basis" (p. 302).[10]

When it comes to citizen-children, the escalation in immigration enforcement only makes their lives harder. Demographer Randy Capps and his colleagues (Capps et al., 2007) have shown us that attending to citizen-children of undocumented immigrants is not just an inconsequential moral issue or simply a matter of statistics about the number of people sent out of the country for being here illegally. It is fundamentally affecting families and communities. Through their computations, Capps et al. estimate that for every two undocumented immigrants deported, one citizen-child is directly affected. In this case, affected means that the citizen-child is separated from one or both parents suddenly for what could be several days to several months. If the parent or parents are deported, the citizen-child has to stay in the United States in the care of someone other than parents, enter the child-welfare system, or reside with the un-deported parent if that option exists. Alternatively, the child might eventually travel to another country and resettle there with his or her parents.

Table 1.2

Year	Removals	Citizen-Children Affected
2005	246,431	123,215
2006	280,974	140,487
2007	319,382	159,691
2008	359,795	179,897
2009	395,165	197,582
2010	387,242	193,621
2011	388,409	194,204
2012	419,384	209,692
2013	368,644	184,322

Only by applying the two-to-one ratio that Capps et al. proposed can we really appreciate the magnitude of what the numbers mean, of how many young US citizen-children have had to lose their parents or leave the United States. Taking the figures shown in the Table 1.1, I apply the Capps et al. ratio and find a staggering number of citizen-children affected by the removal of their parents. Table 1.2 shows the stark results of these estimates.[11]

In the span of eight years, our nation's decision to deport 3,165,426 unauthorized immigrants has affected about 1,582,711 citizen-children. Even if I were to be more conservative and apply a 4 to 1 ratio, we are still talking about 791,356 of our most vulnerable citizens, a number roughly the size of a large American city. Baum, Jones, and Barry (2010) supply some additional numbers to these already stunning figures. The writers estimate that over 100,000 children of LPRs—88,000 of them US citizen-children—have been affected by their parents' deportation in the 10-year period between 1997 and 2007. The authors' estimates include 44,000 children who were under the age of 5 at the time of their parents' deportation. It is clear from these figures that the implications for child welfare and our country in general are significant.

THE GARCIAS OF CALIFORNIA: A MIXED-STATUS FAMILY

Mixed-status families are those whose members hold different types of citizenship and residency status. Some family members may be US citizens, and some may be in the United States illegally. Some may have legal status such as legal permanent residency. There are myriad of constellations of mixed-status families that include undocumented members. The most common is composed of parents who are undocumented and children who are all US-born citizens. Then there are those in which one parent is undocumented and the other parent is a citizen, as are their offspring. Still, other families are more complex. A family might have two parents who are undocumented, older children who are undocumented and younger children who are citizens of the United States. Even among the undocumented siblings in a mixed-status family, some may be eligible for protection if they are detained and others may not be—based largely on their dates of birth and an executive order signed by the President of the United States.[12] I have also met families in which the couples brought their infant children into the United States illegally over three decades ago. These children have grown up as Americans for all intents and purposes and now have US-born children of their own. Yet, these young parents may not be eligible for relief from removal. Some undocumented children learn when they are teenagers that they are not US citizens. Many of these kids are first told when they ask their parents' permission to get a driver's license, that greatly anticipated coming-of-age milestone so much a part of an American adolescence.

The Garcia family is one such mixed-status family, comprised of undocumented individuals and ordinary American kids growing up under extraordinary conditions. Although Garcia is their fictional surname, it is an apt one. It emphasizes the extent to which the Hispanic presence in the United States has grown. You see, Garcia is the most common Spanish surname in the United States. Rodriguez is a close second. Moreover, according to the US Census Bureau, the surnames Garcia and Rodriguez are the *eighth and ninth most common surnames in the United States, regardless of genealogy* (Word, Coleman, Nunziata, & Kominski, 2000). It is a fact of American demography that the Hispanic population is and will continue to be a major part of the American citizenry.

We met the Garcia family in February of 2013 when an interviewer on our research team, Mariana Ruiz del Rio, visited them in their home in a single-family house in a working-class neighborhood about an hour's drive from Sacramento, California. As she pulled into the neighborhood on a cloudless day, Mariana could see young boys playing basketball in a schoolyard near houses with front porches, driveways, and slightly unkempt yards. Older boys, mostly in their late teenage years and early 20s, played soccer on the adjacent field. Not certain which of the unmarked houses was the one she was seeking, Mariana asked one of the soccer players to point her in the right direction. A young man stepped forward and pointed to the house. "That's where I live," he said.

Mrs. Garcia was cooking when Mariana arrived. She wiped her hands on her apron as she opened the door for Mariana to enter. Bearing a broad, friendly smile, she greeted Mariana and led her to the dining room table. Mariana was impressed with the size of the home. It had a fireplace in the living room, a kitchen, dining room, and bedrooms on the second floor. There was a garden in the back and Mariana glimpsed a man stooped over working on the plants. Mrs. Garcia tapped the window overlooking the garden and waved the man, Mr. Garcia, in to meet Mariana. He greeted Mariana in Spanish but didn't offer a handshake as his hands bore the soil from his work. He welcomed Mariana, made small talk about hoping that she had found her way to them without problems, and then excused himself to return to his gardening. A television could be heard from another part of the house.

The Garcias are a Mexican immigrant family made of an intact couple in their mid-40s and 5 children. The child who was eligible to be in our study was their 10-year-old daughter, Valerie. She is the fourth of five children, three older brothers and a younger sister. On that day, Mariana met Valerie, her parents, two of the three older brothers, and Valerie's sister. By the look of their home, it became apparent that the Garcias are a religious family. They had an altar to the Virgin of Guadalupe in the common living area. There were paintings of the Last Supper and stamps and pictures of Pope John Paul II. Family portraits were everywhere, celebrating each child, parent, and the family as a whole. Mr. and Mrs. Garcia spoke Spanish to each other and did so with Mariana. The children responded to their parents in Spanish but spoke English with each other. Their English, Mariana noted, was flawless, unaccented American vernacular.

Both of the parents and the two older sons—one 21 and the other 19—are undocumented. Mr. Garcia was the first to immigrate to California and soon after he was able to send for his wife and two sons. Valerie and her 17-year-old brother and 8-year-old sister were born in California. Early on, the family moved from place to place until they were able to purchase this house and establish a home. Before conducting the interview, our research team was told that all of the Garcia children are fully aware of the unauthorized legal status of their parents and older brothers. Valerie knows that her parents are from Mexico and that she has extended family there. She does not know exactly what state in Mexico her parents are from. "I've never lived there," she told Mariana.

The young man who had directed Mariana to his home entered with his brother and they were introduced to Mariana. Their expressions showed wariness and they did not reply to the greeting. The brothers left the dining room to go upstairs to their bedroom. Rock music could be heard coming from their rooms. One brother returned to the kitchen and stood near the dining room, watching over Valerie as Mariana spoke to her. After a bit, the brother left his watch, only to be replaced by the other brother. Finally, Mrs. Garcia intervened and pulled her son away to let the interview continue without distractions.

Mr. Garcia works in the fertile fields of the Sacramento Valley for the agricultural businesses that grow citrus, almonds, walnuts, olives, and rice. He also holds a part-time job as a cook in a local restaurant. Mrs. Garcia told Mariana that her husband had been arrested and deported several times but each time has managed to re-enter the country to be with his family. The last time that he was deported was two years before. In that episode, Mr. Garcia was arrested for driving under the influence of alcohol and was kept in jail when it was discovered that he had been deported previously. Valerie is aware also of her father's precarious situation because of the multiple violations. Mrs. Garcia said that Valerie had been emotionally affected by her father's long detention and the time it took him to find his way back across the border. She "became very irritable and wouldn't speak to anyone." It took about a year after Mr. Garcia's return for Valerie to feel more at ease and become "herself again." Now the parents try to comfort Valerie when the topic of deportation comes up. Mrs. Garcia said her two daughters know that if she and her husband are ever detained and deported, the girls will remain in the United States with Valerie's *madrina* (godmother) and their brothers.

Mrs. Garcia continues to be scared that she will be deported, or that her older sons might get deported and have to live in Mexico. Like Valerie, the boys do not know Mexico because they had both been brought to the United States as infants. Given this, Mrs. Garcia's main concern is that they will not like Mexico and will have a hard time adjusting to it or feeling like they belong there. Worst, she fears that they could be lured into gangs and other bad influences. The sons are, however, applying for Deferred Action, a program that grants temporary work authorization to eligible undocumented immigrants who entered the United States as minors.

With all the external pressures related to their different legal statuses, the Garcia family is a closely knit one and Valerie says they spend a lot of time together. Their affection for one another is very evident. All the children volunteer at church, and Valerie does very few activities that don't include her family. She does not attend sleepovers unless it is with extended family in the Sacramento area.

Mariana completed the interview as the afternoon sun was waning. As she bid her farewell to the family, she overheard one of the brothers asking his mother who Mariana was and why she was asking Valeria all those questions. The mother explained the project and he seemed assuaged when he said, "Okay." Mariana saw it as an example of the family's closeness and the extent to which each member protects the others. As she was getting into her car, Mariana glanced back to see the eldest brother with one arm around Valerie and the other holding the younger sister's hand. She heard the brother say, "Valerie, you did a good job answering the questions" and promise to take his two sisters to the theater to see whatever movie they wanted. With his right arm still on Valerie's shoulder and his left holding his other sister's hand, he turned and went into the house, the screen door closing gently behind them.

NOTES

1. For detailed definitions and other information on legal-permanent-resident applications, see the United States Code, 2011 Edition, of the United States Code Title 8, Aliens and Nationality, section 1153, Allocation of Immigrant Visas. It is retrievable from http://www.gpo.gov/fdsys/pkg/USCODE-2011-title8/pdf/USCODE-2011-title8.pdf.
2. Baum et al. indicate that the most common felonies for which LPRs are convicted and deported are driving under the influence of alcohol, drug possession, and simple assault (i.e., when a person tries to strike or strikes another person physically, or acts in a manner that is threatening and puts the victim in fear of immediate bodily harm).
3. These groups are not mutually exclusive because some LPR parents may have noncitizen children. LPRs from Central America, for instance, often leave children behind when they immigrate. As these children age and determine to migrate north themselves, they often do so as unaccompanied children. In many cases, they either don't know where their parents are or their parents may not be aware of the child's travel plans. For example, in the years following Hurricane Mitch, which devastate Honduras in October 1998, unaccompanied Honduran children were intercepted along the US border. Often their LPR parents had no idea the children were in the country. The parents immigrated to the United States under temporary protected status after the hurricane and later were able to transition to LPR (Amy Thompson, personal communication, June 12, 2014). Often, parents in such situations either are unaware of any pathway to apply for their non-US citizen children or do not have the resources to do so. LPR status does not confer any benefits to offspring born elsewhere prior to receiving legal status in the US. Thus, noncitizen children of LPRs may be found in the United States living in mixed-status families or in removal proceedings, if apprehended.
4. In modern times, it is still the case that children of foreign diplomats born in the United States are not entitled to this birthright.
5. The Naturalization Act of 1790 discussed citizenship opportunities for individuals who were born in other places, but said nothing of automatic or ascribed citizenship to those born domestically (CRS, 2010).
   The first case regarding birthright citizenship to children of noncitizens came in 1844 with *Lynch v. Clarke*, a case in which an Irish couple gave birth to a child,

Julia Lynch, while temporarily residing in New York. The couple returned to Ireland with Julia six months after her birth and did not return. The child's uncle, however, moved to the United States and became a naturalized citizen. When the uncle died, he named Julia as a potential heir to his property. Because no individual could inherit property unless he or she were a US citizen, the New York Circuit Court of the Southern District heard the matter of whether the property should go to Julia or another naturalized citizen family member. Ultimately, the court upheld the traditional English standard, stating that without a Constitutional provision, it was necessary to use common law to determine the issue of citizenship. Interestingly, the presiding judge, Judge Lewis H. Sandford, drew from the Constitution's provision regarding eligibility for the presidency. He cited the requirement that one must be a "natural born citizen" or "a citizen of the US at the time of the adoption of this constitution," implying that "natural born citizen" was part of this common law principle (*Lynch v. Clarke*, 1844, p. 246). Accordingly, Judge Sandford stated in his decision that every individual born in the United States is a citizen regardless of the status of his or her parents (*Lynch v. Clarke*, 1844, p. 250).

6. According to Vishneski (1988), the respondent's correct surname in the Supreme Court case known as *Scott v. Sandford* was "Sanford" but it was kept in the records as Sandford. A clerical error resulted in the misspelling and it was never corrected.

7. In the United States, we are protected by the Fourteenth Amendment of the Constitution, which confers citizenship as a birthright to anyone born in the United States. It is a right, privilege, and protection, but not one that all countries provide. No European country, for example, has conferred unconditional citizenship to those born on its soil since Ireland amended its birthright citizenship law in 2004. Nineteen European states presently offer some type of conditional citizenship to those born in the country, including to children who were abandoned or would otherwise have no state to which to belong. Countries such as Spain and Greece offer automatic citizenship at birth, whereas those such as the Czech Republic and Hungary offer naturalization after birth (Baubock & Honohan, 2010). But perhaps the most appalling example of a retrogressive and inhumane legal decision was one issued in the Dominican Republic in 2013. The law, which was affirmed by the Dominican High Court, states that individuals born in the country to undocumented parents and registered as Dominicans may not receive Dominican citizenship. The law was aimed particularly at persons of Haitian descent born in the Dominican Republic. Haitian Dominicans are now excluded from being or ever becoming citizens: They cannot have Dominican nationality because their parents are considered to be "in transit." Even more abhorrent and glaringly discriminatory is that the law was applied by the Court retroactively, denying citizenship or rights to anyone born *after 1929* (Open Society Foundations, 2013). Therefore, parents, children, grandparents, and great-grandparents born in the Dominican Republic of Haitian heritage are effectively no longer Dominicans. They can't even appeal to be citizens, despite having lived their entire lives in the Dominican Republic. The United Nations' Office of the High Commissioner for Human Rights issued a response shortly after, stating that "the decision could have disastrous implications for people of Haitian descent in the Dominican Republic, leaving such individuals in a state of constitutional limbo and potentially leaving tens of thousands of them stateless and without access to basic services for which identity documents are

required" (Shamdasani, 2013). This attempt to revoke citizenship retroactively going back nearly a century is extremely rare, though many countries deny citizenship to those born to undocumented parents.

8. Selective mutism appeared as code 313.23 in the *DSM-IV-TR*.

9. The right to health has been formally recognized by several international human rights treaties, including the International Convention on the Elimination of All Forms of Racial Discrimination, Dec. 21, 1965; the Convention on the Elimination of all Forms of Discrimination Against Women, Dec. 18, 1979; the International Convention on the Protection of the Rights of All Migrant Workers and Members of Their Families, Dec. 18, 1990; and the International Convention on the Protection and Promotion of the Rights and Dignity of Persons with Disabilities, Dec. 13, 2006.

10. The *bracero* program came about in 1942 after agreements were forged between the United States and Mexico to import temporary contract workers from Mexico to the United States. The term bracero comes from the Spanish term for a manual laborer, literally someone who uses his arms (*brazos*). A plan intended to provide jobs for Mexicans and labor for American industries during a time of war, the bracero program went on to have an ignominious history. What the Mexican workers sought was a means to a better life. What they found in time was poor living and working conditions, food shortage in farms and work camps, racism, dehumanization, low pay and long hours, low quality food, and no power at the workplace to advocate or negotiate for better conditions.

11. Human Impact Partners in Oakland, California estimated that about 152,426 children had been affected by parents' deportations in fiscal year 2012 (Satinsky, Hu, Heller, & Farhang, 2013). The differences in our figures are a matter of different approaches to the calculations. Regardless of whether it was 209,692 based on my computations or 152,426 based on theirs, the number of children affected remains significant.

12. The details of this executive order will be discussed in subsequent chapters.

CHAPTER 2

Migrating for Life's Sake

Migration is as old as humankind. We see migrants and refugees in the Book of Exodus of the Old Testament, when Moses led the Israelites out of Egypt to avoid the pestilence of nature and the political persecution of the Pharaoh. After journeying through the wilderness, they finally came to Mount Sinai, where they were offered the Promised Land. Going back a million years even before Moses and the Israelites, our earliest ancestors, the *homo erectus* and then *homo sapiens,* were migrants, too. They primarily subsisted by means of scavenging, hunting, gathering food, and developing tools to survive. And they migrated from place to place as part of their subsistence strategy. If droughts or enemies imperiled tribes or groups, they moved to places where sustenance was plentiful and living conditions were safe and more favorable. They traveled long distances and faced constant dangers: they forded rivers and lakes, competed or cooperated with other clans for the same resources, and fought off fierce animals and poisonous insects that threatened their existence. In sum, humans have migrated to protect their families, escape from hardship, and find safe, prosperous lives in new promised lands since the beginning of time. Whether it was the Israelites of the Bible, our earliest human ancestors, our American forefathers, or today's border crossers, all of these groups display the commonality of moving about the earth to find better lives.

Migration is not so different today except that nations have created stricter political borders and laws that govern entry and exit. Today, passports, visas, and proofs of citizenship regulate the flow of individuals across borders. In postindustrial countries, instead of scavenging or foraging for our necessities, we labor in sophisticated systems called employment markets and we do our "hunting and gathering" in stores, markets, and malls. Some people migrate to avoid persecution and find stable places where they can establish or re-establish their lives. According to the United Nations Population Fund (2013), about three percent of the world's seven billion people are migrants, refugees, or asylum seekers. The International Organization for Migration (IOM) (2013) estimates that 214 million of the people on the earth live in a place other than the country they were born in, and more than half of these individuals are women. Most migrants seek better opportunities for themselves and their children, or even future children, places in which better economic and social conditions exist, and sometimes more political stability. In fact, only about 10.5 million migrants in 2011 fled national circumstances of armed conflict, persecution, or natural disasters such as floods, droughts, and famines. These are refugees getting away from life-endangering situations, often leaving involuntarily so as to protect their families and preserve their lives. The majority, however, migrate voluntarily.

Depending on one's vantage point, migration is defined as *emigration* (i.e., leaving one's land or country for another) or *immigration* (i.e., entering a country of which one is not a native). Usually, emigrants or immigrants intend to establish permanent residence in a new country. Migration can also be diced into *internal migration* (i.e., the movement of people from one place to another within the borders of the same country) and *external migration* (i.e., crossing borders to enter another country). The motivations for migrating have been parsed into *pull factors* that draw people to leave one country for another (e.g., better economic conditions or more freedom of expression) and *push factors* that repel people from the places they call home (e.g., government violence; economic instability; lack or rule of law or stable institutions repression because of religion, ethnicity, or sexual orientation). Pull and push factors are commonly associated with two other adjectives applied to migration: *voluntary* (i.e., a personal decision made without duress) and *involuntary* (i.e., a decision made forcibly or under duress). Regardless of the type of migration or the particular circumstances, population movement fundamentally changes our world. The epic migrations of the 19th and 20th centuries involving vast streams of people coming from Europe and Asia transformed North and South America. The 21st Century thus far has seen major demographic shifts in Europe as large numbers of people migrate from the Middle East, Asia, and North Africa, whereas the United States continues to receive people from other parts of the world such as South Asia, China, Mexico, and Central and South American. We witness ever-changing demographics as new waves of migrants settle and establish roots in these countries.

Migration is a compelling and endlessly fascinating subject of study. It is a gripping topic when we contemplate the personal journeys that people make, the decisions they make, and how they make them. How are the migrants themselves, their minds and their worldviews, transformed on their passages from one place to another? What are the psychological effects of these journeys on immigrants? Especially for those undocumented immigrants who must face physical dangers in the migratory process, the physical, spiritual, psychological, and emotional experiences must be profound. What then do they transmit to their offspring in their storytelling and in their actions? What do the children of undocumented immigrants learn and how do they react to the lives they must live? What are the emotional sequelae and trauma that are passed on to their children (Kaitz, Levy, Ebstein, Faraone, & Mankuta, 2009; Schwerdtfeger, Larzelere, Werner, Peters, & Oliver, 2013)? Whether coerced by political, economic, religious, or other forces, migration is full of separations, departures, losses, leave-taking, farewells, and the eternal question, "Will I ever see you again?" Part of my fascination with migration is with the leave-taking that it requires, sustaining losses that are never easy. The decision to emigrate involves the profound decision to part from families, communities, customs, places, and everything the person knows. It is about a rupture with everything that is known and familiar. Even when it is voluntary, leaving for a migratory passage can be painful and perhaps unalterable. It is a decision that is rarely made lightly regardless of the motivations at play.

What must the emotional and psychological experience have been like centuries ago when people made the decision to immigrate to faraway places, when such a decision was almost always irrevocable? Returning home was not always possible a century ago or more. When it was possible, it certainly was not easy to do. The typical migrant in the late 19th century was poor, determined, probably uneducated, maybe wielding a marketable skill, such as blacksmithing or carpentry. Remorse about their decision to migrate was not an option—they could not just take the next flight or ship back because of homesickness, regret, or unexpected hardships. There was a finality to the decision to immigrate to lands that were oceans away, raising the stakes of such a decision to a life-or-death struggle. Such must have been the considerations of so many people in the dawning years of our nation, and the millions who left Eastern Europe in the late 19th and early 20th centuries made similar irreversible decisions.

Catherine Lewicki (nee Prosyck) was one of those millions who took that courageous step. She was born in November of 1910 in Lviv, a city that in that year was part of the Austro-Hungarian Empire. It was a city that had been fought over and held serially by Austria-Hungary, Russia, Austria-Hungary again, the West Ukrainian People's Republic (for just a few months), Poland, Russia again, and most recently as an independent Ukraine. Its name had also undergone various alternations: Lviv, Lvov, Luson, and Lemberg. Catherine was born under Austria-Hungarian rule and emigrated in 1924 under Polish rule. For a 14-year-old, the decision to emigrate was less an individual one than a family consensus. Poverty was widespread, withering the country and its people. Families had to send someone who could survive and maybe remit money so that others, too, could live. Catherine accepted an invitation from an uncle in Saskatchewan, Canada with the promises of employment and a better life. Whether she genuinely desired to go, felt ambivalently, or was compelled by her family, the decision was made, no doubt, with the recognition that it would be a long time if ever before the family would reunite.

The ascendance of railroads in Eastern Europe in the mid-1800s made it likely that, in 1924, Catherine would have boarded a train and waved farewell to her parents and brothers and sisters. Although she would be far away, they all promised to write letters. For a 14-year-old girl with brothers and sisters and maybe a boy in town who was smitten with her beauty, the joyful expectations of what the New World would have in store for her were certainly offset by the poignant sadness of leaving her loved ones. The train that carried Catherine might have headed toward a Ukrainian port of embarkation on the Black Sea or more likely traversed north through Poland and Germany to a port such as Bremen or Hamburg. At the port, Catherine would have then boarded a rapid-moving steamship that would head out to the North Sea to take her and another 1000 migrants in steerage class—the cheapest passenger accommodation near the rudder—to the shores of Canada in a week or more. She was like many of her fellow travelers, religious people of Eastern rite Greek or Orthodox Catholicism, part of the Byzantine rite. One can be certain that they prayed together for a safe journey, and one can only hope that some kind older woman befriended the scared young Catherine during those days of confining, uncertain travel.

Young Catherine's life in Canada was not the ideal that her uncle had promised. First, there were a few letters exchanged with her parents and siblings but the slow delivery of international mail in the 1920s made communication difficult. She became, for all practical purposes, an indentured servant to her uncle and his family, sleeping in a shed on his property without adequate heat or other comforts. After those first few letters, Catherine recounted years later, there were no more and she could not tell her family of her suffering and her uncle's deception. Her retellings were always voiced with a deep, sorrowful sigh, and a long gaze at the ground, shaking her head as if to be rid of the memories of her fateful passage.

Catherine Lewicki nee Prosyck eventually married a Ukrainian man in Canada, migrated again and settled this time in New Jersey, bore two children who in turn gave her five grandchildren. She was sheltered in her old age by her son and son-in-law. The grandchildren helped Catherine in her final years, and she died in July of 1996 at the age of 86, never having seen or heard again from her parents or her brothers and sisters.

We were there the day Catherine Lewicki nee Prosyck died for Catherine was my wife's grandmother. In the two decades that I knew her, I asked Catherine many times to recount those early years. I persisted in my curiosity because I could not imagine what it was like for someone I loved as much as I did Catherine to never touch or see or hear or speak to her parents again, or fuss with her brothers and sisters. It is still an unfathomable experience to me. Just as it is impossible to comprehend the infinity of outer space, I cannot imagine not ever seeing my family again. For me, it was personal: could I have survived with my sanity and my spirit the loss that Catherine Lewicki nee Prosyck had endured? Catherine's biography is emblematic of what a long-ago immigrant might have faced. To migrate was a decision that people so many decades ago had to make, knowing that the goodbye could be permanent.

Today, most of us live with the comforts of the modern world. We seldom have to say permanent goodbyes to our brothers and sisters, our mothers and fathers, our churches and communities, never to see them again. Air travel and global communication networks mean that most immigrants do not necessarily lose touch with their loved ones. When someone contemplates emigration, it may not result in the permanency that Catherine and others like her encountered. In an international Gallup poll conducted several years ago, about 13% of the world's adults—roughly 640 million people—indicated that they would leave their countries permanently if given a chance (Clifton, 2012). A good 150 million of them said they would choose to move to the United States and another 90 million would choose Britain or Canada—three of the most technologically advanced nations on earth. Most of these would-be migrants were primarily from China, Nigeria, India, Bangladesh, and Brazil, some of the most populous countries on earth. Even if these hypothetical migrants move permanently to the one of the advanced countries, they will have use of telephone lines and Internet-based telephone connections to keep in touch with families in their countries of origin. They can buy web cameras to "visit" with relatives through the Internet, or they can keep up with everyone back home via Facebook, e-mail, cell-phone texting, or other rapidly changing technological innovations. In short, they don't have to lose contact permanently with their loved ones; even if they can't afford, or risk, traveling back home in the economy class seats of one of the major international airlines, they can remain connected. Emigrants today may make agonizing decisions almost like those of centuries ago but without the permanence or the disconnection. Still, they do not leave without melancholy, nostalgia, or yearning.

These are life-changing decisions that illegal migrants, or those without valid documentation, make in leaving their places of origins (Suárez-Orozco & Suárez-Orozco, 2001). Knowing that they face enormous risks, possibly death en route to new horizons, emigrants take those risks in crossing borders to escape places with sometimes intolerable conditions. We have grim reminders every day of what can happen to desperate emigrants who make these kinds of momentous decisions. Consider some recent events. On October 3 and October 11, 2013—within the span of a week—two ships overloaded with migrants and asylum-seekers from Africa and the Middle East capsized in the Canal of Sicily. In the first tragedy, only 155 of 500 people on board survived the roughly 70-mile sea passage. In the second tragedy, 221 were rescued but 27 people perished. When people face impossible conditions of unrest and persecution like those that overwhelm Africa and some Middle Eastern country, many migrants believe that even treacherous escape routes to Europe are worth the risk. In the Caribbean, a similar situation exists. Many people from the Dominican Republic have lost their lives in makeshift or poorly maintained boats crossing the 80 miles of the Caribbean Sea that separates their country from Puerto Rico. Puerto Rico, a US territory, is a destination place for them or a stepping stone to the US mainland. These Dominican migrants willingly risk their lives crossing the Mona Passage, some of the most turbulent waters in the Caribbean. Adding to this danger are the great sand banks that extend for miles from the islands of Hispaniola and Puerto Rico. The migrants place their faith in their gods and their fate in the hands of unscrupulous boat owners. Worldwide, there are probably many more such incidents occurring monthly or weekly that the US media does not report.

One detailed account of migrants entering the United States from Central America was written by Oscar Martinez (2010). Martinez's work covers not just the violence and extortion wielded by the people who smuggle immigrants but the full spectrum of dangers that migrants must navigate through Mexico. "A migrant passing through Mexico is like a wounded cat slinking through a dog kennel," writes Martinez, "he wants to get out as quickly and quietly as he can" (p. 93). Migrants in Mexico are just as invisible to the native population in Mexico as in the United States. This invisibility mixed with their inherent desperation and unprotected status makes them vulnerable to an unfathomable range of criminal activities and abuses. From Tapatuala to Juarez, migrants are targeted for rape, brutal robberies, forced conscription into sex or trafficking industries, and mass kidnappings that often end in death. As a priest in Ixtepec who runs a migrant shelter told Martinez, "this land is a cemetery for the nameless" (p. 61). Martinez reports that kidnapping migrants for profit has become a preferred business model for gangs as they diversify. Migrants rarely report crimes against them to the police, either because of their status or because the local authorities may be involved. This fact combined with the sheer number of migrants and the constancy of the population make them a safer, more profitable, and more sustainable target for extortion than local businesses. Threats await migrants in Mexico at every stage of their journey from local bandits, corrupt officials, and international gangs that exercise military control over vast regions. Martinez's description of migration through Mexico leaves no doubt that anyone capable of surviving such dangers would not see detention and removal from the United States as a deterrent.

There are riveting literary accounts of migrants making land crossings from Mexico to the United States and being smuggled by *coyotes* (paid human smugglers, seldom honest or trustworthy). Luis Alberto Urrea (2004) describes the gruesome yet determined quest by 26 men to cross into Arizona, braving the desert, cactus spines, mountains, and the intense heat of the sun. In great detail, Urrea describes the group of men, including a father and his sons, who faced the deadly odds to find a better life for themselves and their families. Of the 26, just 12 survived to tell their story. This tale of travelers who set out from Mexico to cross into Arizona and traverse the desert is a powerful reminder of the extent to which need and love can drive people. Urrea's account of the father and son pair is as painful as it is loving. Reymundo, Sr. was motivated to go north toward Florida to pick oranges during a long summer, where he could earn enough money to build an addition to his small house as a gift to his wife. "A summer of orange picking was all he had in mind," writes Urrea (p. 51). Reymundo, Sr.'s meticulousness comes through in the list of the materials he needed to expand the house: concrete bricks, aluminum roofing, and several bags of cement. He would have gone alone, Urrea writes, but his 15-year-old son Reymundo, Jr., his *tocayo* (Spanish for namesake), pestered him to go along. The younger Reymundo argued that he should go along because "two strong backs could earn more money in a short time than one. And if they both worked like burros all summer, they'd make double the money. They might buy his mother furniture to go in the new room. For them, the planned trip was a gesture of love" (p. 51). Despite his better judgment, Reymundo, Sr., relented. But we can only envision Reymundo, Sr.'s regret when he found himself two days into the journey in 108° F heat and blazing sun of the desert watching his son die in his arms. Without water or help, Reymundo, Sr. held Reymundo, Jr. until his son breathed his last breath. Father and son were found dead just yards from each other. It was told by the survivors that after seeing his son die, Reymundo, Sr., in utter resignation, walked a dozen steps to where he would die. As their trip was undertaken in love, their lives ended in acts of love for each other.

Then there is the account of the tragedy that occurred in May of 2003 when 74 immigrants, mostly Mexicans, Salvadorans, Nicaraguans, and Hondurans, were found in Victoria, Texas in the wretched, broiling trailer of a truck (Ramos, 2005). Nineteen of the "human cargo" were found dead, suffocated in the back of the truck; among the dead a 5-year-old boy. Not deterred by hardships such as this, many Central American immigrants set out from their home countries to seek a better future in El Norte. For those who do not make the crossing successfully, there are thousands more who do and enter the United States, live in anonymity and fear, and are vulnerable to exploitation. Sonia Nazario (2006) provides one such account of a young Honduran boy's determined trek by foot find his mother in the United States, a tale that is both harrowing and sad when the boy finds tragic disappointment in the United States.

The stories of the tens of thousands of undocumented immigrants who have made the decision to cross land borders or troubled waters that separate countries and continents evoke the immortal words of Emma Lazarus' 1883 poem "The New Colossus"—words so foundational to our country that they are engraved in bronze on the pedestal of the Statue of Liberty in New York harbor.

> Give me your tired, your poor,
> Your huddled masses yearning to breathe free,
> The wretched refuse of your teeming shore.
> Send these, the homeless, tempest-tost to me,
> I lift my lamp beside the golden door!

In today's immigration context, *these huddled masses, yearning to breathe free* may survive their trips only to be arrested when they arrive and expelled immediately, thwarting their dreams and plans. They may be forced back to the very places that led them to be *the wretched refuse, the tempest-tost, and the homeless* who sought a new place to live. For them, sadly, there is no lamp at the golden door, instead they are deported and repatriated to the places they fled.

Repatriation for some may be no more unpleasant than going back to the village or slum they fled. They will continue to do whatever they need to do to eke out an existence, waiting until the next chance they get to make another attempt at migrating. For some, deportation and repatriation to the places they fled may mean the fate of cruel imprisonment for taking flight from or speaking up against a repressive government. For others, it can mean death by execution at the hands of the government or the gangs they feared, or they might end up among the *desaparecidos* (disappeared) of ruthless forces.[1]

The majority of migrants are economic migrants, according to the International Organization for Migration (IOM) (2013). Alexander Betts (2013), a migration and refugee affairs specialist at England's Oxford University, calls them, more accurately, "survival migrants," people seeking livelihoods. If we consider that economic or survival migrants are people moving to places where a family can be fed, clothed, and sheltered, then we can say that, to some extent, those early hunter-gatherers and the Israelites of the Old Testament were, in part, economic or survival migrants. In contemporary times, these migrants are the fastest growing group of people going from one country to another, and frequently take the risks of crossing borders illegally to find more fertile life-opportunities and personal prosperity. Besides encountering dangerous journeys by foot or on boats across treacherous terrains and waters, unauthorized economic immigrants can easily be exploited by criminal smuggling networks and enslaved by unscrupulous employers who force them to work and live in difficult and dangerous conditions. Their undocumented or unauthorized status often leaves them helpless and afraid; they cannot turn to legal authorities when their rights are violated. Along with these dangers and indignities, immigrants may face the intolerance, discrimination, and rejection of the people whose country they have entered.

Still they migrate, several million of them every year without proper authorization into other countries (IOM, 2013). It is a matter of demand and supply: there are demands for labor in other countries and the migrants from underdeveloped nations are in abundant supply, often cheap and willing to do work that others don't want to do. Developed countries experiencing a decline in fertility rates and growth in aging populations are magnets for individuals in search of economic opportunity. Such demographics create a demand for workers from other countries in order to help sustain national economies.

We know why some countries attract migrants. But what makes some immigrants knowingly and willingly violate national laws to enter other countries like the United States without authorization? Emily Ryo, a sociologist, has sought answers to this and related questions. In her research, Ryo (2013) interviewed people in their home communities in Mexico, individuals who intended to migrate to the United States. Ryo understands the economic or survival motivations to migrate, but she dug deeper to understand the beliefs, attitudes, and social norms that her participants held about migrating, US immigration law, and legal authorities. Ryo found that even when women and men are nearly certain that they will be apprehended and that they will be punished, they are not deterred from migrating illegally to the United States. When the availability of Mexican jobs is very low, the dangers associated with crossing the border to earn a livelihood are worth facing. To these individuals, the risks outweigh living a life of poverty and starvation. The dangers of apprehension by US immigration and law enforcement do not alter significantly a person's determination to migrate or not.

But there is more that Ryo learned. The prospective migrants she spoke to felt that disobeying the law is sometimes justified, such as when the individual migrates for economic opportunities that go beyond basic survival.[2] Moreover, Ryo's Mexican informants recognize that the United States follows "procedural justice," that is, the American laws and the processes for resolving disputes (what we know as due process) are fair and transparent. Although the journey across the border carries with it great physical dangers, the interviewees say they feel safe in the hands of the US legal system. And though they know they are breaking the law to migrate to the United States without authorization, the prospective immigrants say they will obey the laws of the land once inside its borders, a point that gains credence in light of the fact that incarceration rates are lowest for undocumented immigrants, especially young men, who make up the largest proportion of unauthorized groups (see, for example, Rumbaut & Ewing, 2007). Ryo notes that "all else being equal, procedural fairness may produce greater deference to US immigration law" (p. 574).

It is an interesting juxtaposition: Prospective migrants willfully trespass international borders in violation of the law, but then obey the domestic laws of the land they enter. That is, immigrants will break one law to obey another. Survival needs override acquiescence to laws that seem unjust when one is desperate to provide for one's family. As the opportunity opens for employment in the new country, the individual agrees to follow the laws. There is inherent in this thinking a moral decision-making process, one resembling the dilemma that the psychologist Lawrence Kohlberg (1973, 1981) addressed in his studies of how humans justify their actions in critical times.

Ryo's description of prospective immigrants embodies a moral calculus like the one Kohlberg posed in the well-known hypothetical story of Heinz and the stolen medicine. Heinz, a fictional European man, was married and his wife was near death from an unusual cancer that required a specific, exotic, and expensive medication. It was a drug so unique that the apothecary who discovered it was charging a high price for a life-saving dose. No doubt it was expensive to the wife's poor husband, but the husband had done his research and knew that the druggist was marking up the drug by 100 percent—an outrageous amount of money since the basic ingredients cost mere pennies. The husband did not have the money. He borrowed money legally from friends and associates, but could only come up with half the cost of the drug. When he appealed to the druggist for a discount, the druggist said no. Offended by what he perceived as the druggist's greed and his insensitivity to Heinz's situation, and driven by his own growing desperation, Heinz waited until he could break into the pharmacy and steal the drug to save his wife (Kohlberg, 1973, 1981).

Was Heinz right to do what he did? Why? Why not?

Kohlberg was not so much interested in the right or wrong decision as he was the justification that people give for making decisions. Their reasoning would, according to Kohlberg, reveal their level of moral development. In the story, Heinz made a moral decision about taking the druggist's discovery illegally. His moral dilemma is between stealing and saving a life. What, then, is the justification for the illegal act? The prospective immigrants that Ryo interviewed entertained a similar dilemma about entering a country illegally. For undocumented immigrants, the dilemma weighs violating the law against remaining in poverty. What is the justification for breaking international laws? The question the prospective immigrant has to answer is "Should I migrate and how do I justify violating another country's laws?" Following Kohlberg's approach, immigrants face the same type of moral dilemma as Heinz did. The justification that people give for their actions is what is central to Kohlberg's theory, and for our purpose in this chapter, it is the justification that immigrants might give for crossing into a country without documentation. In Kohlberg's theory, there are six stages in the moral-reasoning trajectory of the human being, a range that starts at the basic and concrete and progresses to the complex and abstract. The stages can be applied to decisions to immigrate illegally.

In Stage One, the individual engages in a very rudimentary decision that looks at it as a matter of obeying the law or being punished. The person knows that disobedience will be punished and, therefore, places the responsibility for the decision on an external, objective force rather than his subjective intention. Thus, the person may wish to immigrate illegally but fears being caught and punished. Therefore, the conclusion might be "I should obey the law no matter what. To immigrate without papers is plainly illegal. I will not migrate."

Stage Two is similar in that the person is still concerned with being caught, but takes a different view of the moral decision. Rather than making it a matter of simple disobedience and punishment, the person takes the position that it is not justifiable for a migrant to break the law if it is being done only to, say, make fast money for gambling or go on public welfare. Whereas in Stage One the person externalizes the decision because it simply violates a man-made law that brings penalties, this stage rationalizes that violation of the law should be done for something more than self-aggrandizement or pure selfishness or greed.

In Stage Three, the person is concerned primarily with meeting the expectations of others; it is based on keeping good interpersonal relations. The decision is once again externalized as it is in Stage One, but what matters now is the opinion of others. The decision to migrate illegally or not to migrate at all is made on the basis of whether others would judge one favorably or unfavorably. In other words, the justification comes from pleasing someone else. A son may migrate illegally if he expects to earn the love, empathy, trust, and caring of other family members. The primary moral concern is with living up to social expectations that others have of us. The person may migrate to be nice, to conform, and to please others. He may be told that he is a better son if he crosses the border illegally and sends money back and maybe that it will impress the neighbors that his parents have such a generous son. In this moral stage, the individual makes a decision in order to get approval from others rather than because of a profound personal desire or need.

The next three stages reflect higher-order processes of justification. In Stage Four, the immigrant's reasoning might be focused on maintaining the social order, a moral concern with society as a whole. What if everybody broke the law and migrated? The reasoning might be that he cannot immigrate and break the law of a country because if everybody did it there would be chaos in the new country. And what would become of the country you're leaving? It, too, would fall into chaos if everyone violates international laws, because society cannot function if we do not follow laws. The justification, then, is to maintain the social order for its own sake.

Indeed, many Americans who oppose providing immigrants any opportunity to stay in the country through amnesty or paths to citizenship argue that we are rewarding people for violating the social order. Their question might be, when will it end and are we sending the wrong message that it is okay to immigrate illegally?

In Stages Five and Six, we see more of the kind of reasoning that Ryo's interviewees seem to use to violate the law. Stage Five of Kohlberg's moral development theory deals with balancing the social contract and the individual's rights. As hypothetical migrants, we might consider *how society should be* rather than how society *actually is*. In essence, we make a subjective evaluation of what is truly right or moral rather than what the specific law says. As prospective immigrants we might, like Heinz, argue that it's okay to migrate illegally (or steal the drug) because a person's life is of much greater value than anything else, even though the law tells us we may not cross into another country (or steal the drug). This moral choice is about human rights that say, in effect, "I can disregard the law because it is a fundamental right of all persons to choose to live, seek a livelihood, and provide for their families." A human rights argument may include beliefs that we all have the right to affordable housing and healthcare, a good education, and to be protected by the law no matter one's station in life.

Stage Six takes this thinking and moral decision-making to its ultimate level, one in which we observe certain universal human principles. What is of primary concern in this stage is, "What is just?" Justice as a universal principle overrides the objections about breaking laws. At this level of Kohlberg's moral stages, we invoke superordinate principles and use higher-order abstract reasoning. Universal human ethics are summoned to preserve life and justify that a human life or lives are far more important than anyone's property rights, no matter if it is the pharmacist's or a nation's. There is a philosophical, maybe even divine belief in an overarching universal ethic that humans are of this earth and no man-made laws should inhibit the human spirit and human rights. The person may believe that universal ethics protect our rights to make a living, to have a state to which we belong, to have clean water and a healthy environment, and to live in peace.

Applied to the decision-making of immigrating and violating a nation's laws, these moral issues take on great meaning. The Mexican respondents to Ryo's (2013) questions, as well as many immigrants who tell their stories about why they immigrated illegally, follow similar patterns of thinking. They justify their actions because of the desperate lives they live, the conditions they want to escape—conditions of hunger, unemployment, violence, danger, crime, government instability, drug trafficking, squalor—and for which they will take any risk, even the ultimate one, death. Yet, it seems to me, that although there may be individual choices that include self-interest, disobedience, conformity and simple lawlessness, collectively migrants make their decision to migrate without authorization on the basis of human rights and a universal human ethic. Is it wrong because a human-made law says it is wrong or is wrong because it violates moral principles such as those of human and universal rights? Ryo places her research participants' responses about breaking immigration laws in the context of legal philosophy.

> Immigration law is in some ways the quintessential example of a morally ambiguous law. Legal scholars typically refer to noncompliance with immigration law (i.e., unauthorized entry and presence) as a *malum prohibitum* offense (an act that is wrong solely because it is prohibited by law) rather than a *malum in se* offense (an act that is wrong because it is morally wrong). Consequently, tension exists not only between would-be migrants and U.S. citizens, but among various stakeholders within the U.S., about what kind of policy is appropriate when it comes to unauthorized migration. For many would-be migrants, as well as U.S. citizens, there is a lack of moral credibility to a law perceived as preventing individuals from working to support their families. For many, there is also no moral credibility to a law that seems to punish individuals for satisfying the demands of U.S. households and corporations for cheap foreign labor. (p. 594)

Escaping poverty may propel Ryo's migrants to do their own cost-benefit analyses and justify their decisions on moral grounds. But, as sociologist Jacqueline Maria Hagan (2008) observes, relying on economic and labor-force models to understand immigration fully is short-sighted. Many scholars, notes Hagan, view immigration exclusively through the lenses of neoclassical economic theory or economics of labor models. According to this theory, a person conducts her or his own cost-benefit analysis about leaving home and traveling to a new country. This personal analysis weighs the possibility of a new and profitable job, educational opportunities, and a better standard of living with the psychological costs of leaving his or her family, the possibility of being caught at the border or in the United States, and the dangers of the journey. Then the decision is made in terms of cerebral and rational models. But, as Hagan argues, this cognitive process occurs within a social context as well. Family members who have migrated and those still at home also participate in a collective analysis of the pros and cons. Ask most immigrants and you'll hear a version of this: they consider the costs and benefits and discuss it with spouses, parents, and friends, and sometimes community elders. Hagan (2008) argues that the decision-making process includes a spiritual component as well:

> While economic considerations may trigger the motivation to migrate, and family, trusted friends, and a community tradition of migration may contribute to the decision, other religious factor, embedded in strong cultural and local practices, ultimately guide and support decision-making and leave-taking . . . At some stage, the decision-making moves from a rational, real world level to a very private, religious, and even mystical plane. Moreover, individuals do not make these decisions in isolation or only in consultation with family and friends in sending and receiving communities. Prospective migrants reach this religious space through prayer and consultation with trusted clergy who provide for their spiritual needs. Decisions to migrate are often sanctioned by religious institutions that support the undertaking. (p. 23)

The dialogues and spiritual support that migrants engage in during the preparatory stages of the journey, which may include discussion about the morality and ethics of breaking laws, often provide the psychological and emotional resources to "make the monumental decision" (Hagan, 2008, p. 23), or the leap, if you will, to emigrate.

WHAT IT MEANS TO BE DEPORTED

After fighting and clawing their way to a new land, to a safer society, it can all come apart for the desperate immigrant and her family when the order of removal is issued. Then the deportation and repatriation that follows can ruin the immigrant's life, that of her citizen-children and all that the family has attained. Deportation can even end in death.[3] This outcome is something that Supreme Court Justice Louis Brandeis understood when he wrote the decision in *Ng Fung Ho v White* in 1922. The case involved five Chinese men who were held on the basis of having gained admission into the United States fraudulently, in violation of the 1892 Chinese Exclusion Act signed by President Chester A. Arthur that prohibited immigration of Chinese laborers. The men faced deportation. Two of the men, brothers Ging Sang Get and Ging Sang Mo, insisted that they thought themselves to be citizens of the United States because they were the foreign-born sons of a US citizen. The brothers were able to show that their father had testified in 1909 in his citizenship hearing that he was married and named his US-born children but had omitted these two sons for reasons lost to history. The brothers were given a chance to produce the testimony of their father but, although he was known to live in the San Francisco area, he could not be located. They appealed to the US Supreme Court which found that they had provided evidence of being entitled to citizenship but the final determination would be decided in the district court. Surely the Ging Sang brothers felt the disappointment that they might not see their father again or have families of their own in America.

In rendering the majority opinion for the Supreme Court, Justice Brandeis left us with some immortal words, words that are as apt today as they were nearly a hundred years ago. "Deportation," wrote Brandeis, "may result . . . in loss of both property and life, or of all that makes life worth living" (*Ng Fung Ho v. White, 259 US 276* (1922))

NOTES

1. *Desaparecidos* is the Spanish word for "the disappeared," referring to the forced disappearance of dissidents by state or political operatives. *Desaparecidos* are people who vanish without a trace. The forced disappearance of people for political reasons in Latin America, in which the term first used, occurred primarily in Argentina, Chile, Colombia, El Salvador, and Guatemala. However, forced disappearances have been documented in Africa, the Middle East, and many other areas.
2. This may explain the work ethic and ambition of most immigrants: if they wanted to earn just enough to survive or subsist, they might be able to do that in their home country. But the ambitious, determined migrant who seeks for her or his family a higher standard of living, better education and healthcare, and greater opportunities will face the risks, known and unknown, to find this life.
3. Such was the case of 16-year-old Edgar Chocoy who begged an immigration judge in Denver to let him stay in the US because he would be killed by his former gang if he were sent home. He was deported anyway on March 10, 2004 and was shot dead 17 days later in Villanueva, Guatemala. To read more see http://articles.latimes.com/2004/may/09/news/adfg-deport9

CHAPTER 3

Immigration Wars

The needs of immigrating individuals and of a changing American society have shaped the complicated relationship of the United States with immigration. From its inception through the 19th century, the United States had virtually no restrictions on immigration and relied heavily on migrants to help design and build a new state with successful economic, political, and social institutions. Like present immigrants, the colonists and later waves of immigrants to the new nation migrated for a variety of reasons, including seeking religious or political freedom, representing colonizing interests, promoting religious ideals, pursuing economic opportunity, or purely searching for adventure and a new beginning. Some came tragically or against their will as slave labor.

In this chapter I provide a brief history of immigration in the United States, a long and complicated relationship, starting in the 19th century. It was then that Europe began experiencing large-scale economic and social changes. In the 1800s, its massive population increasingly looked to the Americas as a new place to settle. During this time, the majority of immigrants came from Germany, Great Britain, and Ireland. These three countries alone comprised 70 percent of immigration to the New World from 1820-1840, then steadily decreased to 50 percent in the 1880s and 1890s when the immigrant surge came from Eastern and Southern Europe. Our country has a long tradition of taking millions of foreign individuals who become successful and loyal Americans and their children and grandchildren pledge allegiance to the US flag.

PAROXYSMS OF HATE

Then, the initial warm embrace of each wave of immigrants would often turn into mistrust, resentment, rejection, xenophobia, outright attacks by the public—comprised largely of descendants of immigrants—and the threat of exclusionary legislation. The many fears that the populace expressed resulted in Americans—themselves the children and grand-children of immigrants—becoming increasingly uncomfortable with the booming immigration that had begun to take shape in the late 1800s. It was this growing anti-immigrant sentiment that, in 1882, saw two land-mark laws that were anti-immigrant. On May 6, 1882, President Chester Arthur signed into law the Chinese Exclusion Act of 1882, a law that prohibited immigration from China and did not allow legal residents of Chinese origin to become US citizens. (I return to the topic of Chinese exclusion in the next section of this chapter.) Then on August 3, 1882, the 47th United States Congress passed the Immigration Act of 1882, consid-ered the first general immigration law. The Immigration Act taxed each new migrant 50 cents, barred convicts and other "undesirable" individu-als, created the first requirements for national origin, and declined admis-sion to those over the age of 16 who were illiterate. Fortunately, many Americans continued to defend the tradition of keeping our doors open and providing a home for any seeking a better life. In attempting to repeal the 1882 bill, President Woodrow Wilson (1915) cited the values on which the nation was founded. He concluded that the literacy requirement was a paradox. In this bill, he said, the irony was that, "Those who come seeking opportunity are not to be admitted unless they have already had one of the chief of the opportunities they seek, the opportunity of education." The legislation favored those who already enjoyed a certain privilege, edu-cation, and Wilson's belief was that we should make room for those less privileged who could contribute to America, too.

Although the literacy requirement was ultimately repealed, the national origin quotas became a key part of the Immigration and Nationality Act (INA) of 1952. As the first major act passed in reference to immigration, this bill finally consolidated various immigration statutes into a sin-gle piece of legislation. Forged in the growing post-World War II fear of Communism and desire to maintain some kind of national "identity," the bill reflects the nation's struggle to reconcile domestic security concerns with its history of welcoming victims of international strife. In drafting the 1952 INA, Congress also sought to ensure the unification of mixed families of US citizens and immigrants, a bow to the importance of keep-ing families together as Americans. Though the bill abolished exclusion of Asian immigrants, unfortunately, the quotas still promoted an overt preference for immigrants from Northern and Western Europe, reserving 131,000 visas for them and automatically filling 85 percent of the entry quotas. In contrast, Asian countries received just 100 visas each, counting toward a 2,000 visa cap for the entire "Asia-Pacific Triangle," including individuals of Asian descent living anywhere in the world. The bill pacified anti-Communist sponsors but generated concerns over discrimination for others. Congress passed the bill and overrode President Harry Truman's veto. The president reminded the nation of the benevolent tradition it seemed to have forgotten.

> Today, we are "protecting" ourselves as we were in 1924, against being flooded by immigrants from Eastern Europe. This is fantastic. The countries of Eastern Europe have fallen under the Communist yoke—they are silenced, fenced off by barbed wire and minefields—no one passes their border but at the risk of his life. We do not need to be protected against immigrants from these countries—on the contrary we want to stretch out a helping hand, to save those who have managed to flee into Western Europe, to succor those who are brave enough to escape from barbarism, to welcome and restore them against the day when their countries will, as we hope, be free again . . . These are only a few examples of the absurdity, the cruelty of carrying over into this year of 1952 the isolationist limitations of our 1924 law. (Truman, 1952, p. 443)

In 1965, in the midst of the Civil Rights movement, Congress amended these provisions in the INA to eliminate the quotas based on national origin and race, specifically. Under President Lyndon B. Johnson, the 1965 law shifted preference from Northern and Western Europe to immigrants who already had family in the United States, now prioritizing family unification and abolishing a much-criticized system. At the signing of the bill, which took place at the foot of the Statue of Liberty, President Johnson reflected on prior injustice in the quota system and its violation of American values, stating, "We can now believe that it will never again shadow the gate to the American Nation with the twin barriers of prejudice and privilege" (Johnson, 1965).

The immigration system that today creates impediments for immigrants has its roots largely in the trends that began in the 1970s, a period characterized by refugees and immigrants coming to the United States outside of the law. With the widespread presence of repressive dictatorships and authoritarian regimes in Latin America, emigrants traveled in large numbers to the United States to escape the disastrous economic conditions that followed and the persecution that was typically employed by dictators and tyrants. This sudden wave prompted yet another evaluation of immigration policies and the intensification of two camps of thought—those in favor of a stricter attempt to protect the nation's interests, and those seeking to stick to the tradition of immigrant integration. Cultural fear generated against Asian immigrants through the 1950s emerged again, this time in the form of concern over the large numbers of Latin Americans migrating north. As a result, immigration-related legislation in the 1970s included specific provisions limiting immigration from countries in our own hemisphere. President Gerald Ford (1976) specifically voiced concern over the resulting effect on the US's historic relationship with Mexico, but lamentably, he went on to sign the Immigration and Nationality Act Amendments in 1976.

It was not only at the national level that the enmity against immigrants from Latin America was galvanizing. At the state level, some lawmakers targeted the defenseless children of immigrants as a means of getting at their parents. One example of such a law arose in May 1975 when the Texas Legislature revised its education laws to withhold state funds from local school districts that were educating children who were not legally admitted into the United States. The law also authorized local school districts to deny enrollment in their public schools to children not legally admitted to the country. The Texas law fell hardest on the most vulnerable, the children of a very small subclass of illegal aliens. It was challenged in September 1977 in a class action suit filed against the Tyler Independent School District on behalf of school-age children of Mexican origin (*Plyer v. Doe* (457 US 252 (1982)).

In the US District Court for the Eastern District of Texas, the defendants argued that the law was intended as a financial measure to stop a drain on the state's budget. Besides, they argued, the immigration of Mexican families was crowding the public schools of Smith County that were unprepared for the numbers of children and the complexities of their learning needs. The District Court, however, determined that the increased school enrollment was made up of children who were legal residents. Maybe some savings would be achieved by barring the undocumented children from the schools but the quality of education would not necessarily be improved. In fact, the school district would lose state and federal funding if its enrolment numbers declined. It would, therefore, be to the school district's advantage to keep the children enrolled rather than exclude them. Furthermore, the District Court saw through the Texas law's intent: "the state's exclusion of undocumented children from its public schools . . . may well be the type of *invidiously motivated state action* for which the suspect classification doctrine was designed"[1] [emphasis added]. Presciently, the District Court stated that under current laws and practices "the illegal alien of today may well be the legal alien of tomorrow, and that without an education, these undocumented children, [already] disadvantaged as a result of poverty, lack of English-speaking ability, and undeniable racial prejudices . . . will become permanently locked into the lowest socio-economic class" (*Plyer v. Doe* (457 US 252 (1982)). US Supreme Court struck down the Texas statute in 1982.

As the Texas law aimed at mostly Mexican immigrants found its way to the Supreme Court of the United States, President Ronald Reagan was recognizing that Mexican migrant workers in the US benefited both Mexico by earning income for their families back home and the US economy by providing a large labor force on which it relied. During his presidency, Reagan argued that this important contribution justified the reward of citizenship, a point of contention that quickly emerged at the forefront of the next major comprehensive immigration reform. Family unity and reunification was reinforced in 1981 by The Select Commission on Immigration and Refugee Policy, a group appointed by Congress to study immigration policies and recommend legislative reform. The Select Commission (1981) stated that

> Reunification . . . serves the national interest not only through the humane-ness of the policy itself, but also through the promotion of the public order and well-being of the nation. Psychologically and socially, the reunion of fam-ily members with their close relatives promotes the health and welfare of the United States. (pp. 112–113)

After nearly 15 years of consideration, in 1986 Congress passed the Immigration Reform and Control Act (IRCA). This was the first legislation amending the Immigration and Nationality Act with the specific intent of addressing undocumented immigration. Notably, the bill made it illegal for employers to knowingly hire undocumented immigrants and imposed sanctions on employers who failed to make a good faith effort to verify the legal status of their workers. In an attempt to control the border, IRCA increased Customs and Border Patrol personnel by 50 percent. Finally, the IRCA contained a sweeping amnesty provision that offered three million undocumented individuals status, in line with Reagan's previous recom-mendations. While amnesty was acceptable in 1986, today in the sec-ond decade of the 21st century it is the "scarlet letter" of immigration reform among conservatives, the very people who see Reagan as a great Republican conservative (Nowrasteh, 2013). Amnesty conjures a stigma so strong that conservatives who favor any provision of legal status to undocumented immigrants have taken steps to distance themselves from Reagan's amnesty. They delineate very carefully the differences between Reagan's amnesty and their proposals to establish pathways and require-ments for citizenship.

Under the George H.W. Bush presidency, the United States expanded the number of immigrants allowed in each year in an Act that maintained the nation's historic commitment to family reunification (Bush, 1990). In contrast, many of the most aggressively anti-immigrant policies facing migrants today were signed into law by President Bush's democratic successor. In 1996, Congress passed the Illegal Immigration Reform and Immigrant Responsibility Act (IIRIRA), adding to an executive order by President William J. Clinton preventing federal contractors from working with businesses that hire undocumented workers. In his statement on the executive order, President Clinton noted that "For too long . . . the Immigration and Naturalization Service (INS) has lacked the resources needed for vigorous enforcement. My administration has provided the INS with the resources it needs to enforce the law" (Clinton, 1996).

The IIRIRA imposed some of the strictest sanctions against undocumented immigrants in decades, combating undocumented immigration with tougher penalties and again increasing border patrol activities. Under IIRIRA, undocumented immigrants present in the United States for six months or more received a 3-year or 10-year bar on re-entrance after leaving the country. But rather than containing illegal immigration, IIRIRA had the unintended effect of forcing them to stay in the United States once they had entered. Instead of coming for seasonal work then returning to their families during the off-season, migrant workers now had to stay in the United States year-round in order to avoid triggering this new bar, which, when violated, would prompt a lifetime ban on returning to the US legally. Separated from loved ones without the ability to go back and forth with the ebb and flow of seasonal work opportunities, many undocumented workers stayed. They then brought their families to live in the US with them, increasing the overall population of undocumented immigrants in the country. Further, IIRIRA increased resources for immigration enforcement, bumping apprehensions up to numbers not seen since 1986. In 1996, Immigration and Naturalization Service (the precursor to ICE and CBP now under DHS) apprehensions grew to 1.6 million, and continued to increase. In the year 2000, agencies apprehended over 1.8 million immigrants in a single fiscal year.

THE "YELLOW PERIL" AND THE "BROWN PERIL"

The progression of immigration laws reflects the historical context and contemporary issues facing the nation. Increasingly harsh federal and state laws have been propelled by the increasing and largely irrational fear of the effects of immigration in general. Despite America's legacy as a nation of immigrants, recent waves of immigration from Latin America, mostly from Mexico, have encountered a growing climate of unease fanned by misinformation and prejudice spreading throughout the United States currently. And, as we saw earlier in this chapter, this is not the first time in US history that racial fear and hatred have surfaced to influence policy. In the late 1800s, Asians were vilified in media and public discourse, leading to the passage of the Chinese Exclusion Act of 1882. Reference to the "Yellow Peril," a derogatory term for Asian immigration and immigrants, began in California in the 1870s as working-class, white laborers (descendants of immigrants) feared that Chinese immigrants would take their jobs during a time of economic decline. The idea of an Asian menace was later applied to the Japanese when Japan defeated Russia, a Western power, in the Russo-Japanese War of 1904–1905. The Chinese Exclusion Act was followed by the Immigration Restriction Act of 1917 and the National Origins Act of 1924, both of which continued the prohibition of nearly all Asian immigrants from legally entering the United States and prohibited immigrants already in the United States from attaining citizenship. Then, after the December 7, 1941 attack on Pearl Harbor by Japan, Americans reacted with even more fear and anger not just at the sudden power and audacity of Japan but also against Japanese-Americans who had long lived in the United States, primarily California. Japanese-Americans were herded into internment camps by Executive Order 9066, issued on February 19th, 1942. While immigrants may no longer face categorical exclusion through laws expressly based on race, as Asian immigrants once did, anti-immigrant legislation continues to reflect race-based fears in the United States.

By "Brown Peril" I refer to the continued tradition of racism against immigrants from Latin America, a racism that parallels some of the same racist sentiments emblematic of the Yellow Peril from the late 1800s to the mid-1900s. As historian John Dower (1986) wrote, "the vision of the menace from the East was always more racial rather than national. It derived not from concern with any one country or people in particular, but from a vague and ominous sense of the vast, faceless, nameless yellow horde: the rising tide, indeed, of color" (p. 156). The nameless, faceless horde of today is perceived as brown, and this is not a recent phenomenon. It goes back to the US annexation of Texas and California in the wake of the Mexican-American War, when the US citizenry became significantly less homogenous almost overnight.

With the ebb and flow of economic-migration and refugee populations from Central America and Mexico fear of a brown horde rises in connection to any migrant population from Latin America. It is evident today in our anti-immigration sentiments and policies. Just as cartoonists and journalists and demagogues alarmed the US of the horrors that would be wrought upon the nation by the Yellow Peril, recent hate-mongers use the same arguments recently against undocumented immigrants from Latin America. For example, in 2004, Samuel Huntington published "The Hispanic Challenge," an alarmingly dramatic representation of Latino immigration that uses fear as a tool to create anti-immigrant sentiments. In the article, Huntington (2004) paints a portrait of an America created and run by white Protestants who still embody the very heart of what it means to be "American." By using key words like "peril" and "clash" and alluding to the "end of America" as we know it, Huntington paints Latin American immigration as a "Reconquista" of the American southwest by Mexicans. In contrast with previous waves of immigration from countries like Ireland and Italy, Huntington highlights the Latin American immigration as unique due to the sheer magnitude of immigrants, the proximity of Mexico and United States, and the status of Mexico as a third-world country. These factors, Huntington proposes, constitute a vicious threat against American society and culture, disintegrating the foundation of American doctrine and contaminating American values with Latin American culture. Huntington's words are inflammatory, divisive, and racist.

Huntington's anti-immigrant model has been popularized in many sectors of the United States, precipitating a push for more conservative immigration policies that are more harmful to citizen-children. His language has been very attractive to a large portion of Americans who identify with Huntington's (2004) declaration that "There is no Americano dream. There is only the American dream created by an Anglo-Protestant society. Mexican Americans will share in that dream and in that society only if they dream in English" (p. 9). By subscribing to this obsolete definition of American culture while simultaneously associating Latino immigration with drug trafficking, protests, economic decline, and a lack of education, xenophobic Americans succumb to immigrant stereotypes. However, these prejudices and misconceptions extend beyond undocumented immigrants to their citizen-children and to legal immigrants of Latin American descent, labeling the entire population as one big problem.

These perceptions and the people who hold them play a crucial role in the policy-making process through their influence on representatives and senators. For instance, a groundswell of talk among conservatives emerged in 2008 and reached a fever pitch in 2010 about repealing the Fourteenth Amendment, in particular the part that guarantees birthright citizenship to persons born in the United States, including the children of illegal immigrants. Senator Lindsey Graham, a Republican from South Carolina articulated the source of the furor, a pernicious stereotype. "People come here to have babies. They come here to drop a child—it's called drop and leave. To have a child in America, they cross the border, they go to an emergency room, have a child and that child is automatically an American citizen. That shouldn't be the case. That attracts people here for all the wrong reasons" (Kahn, 2010). His comments were made on television, ensuring a national audience.

Then, two Arizona legislators who had a hand in sponsoring that state's infamous anti-immigration law, State Sen. Russell Pearce and Rep. John Kavanagh, proposed that birth certificates issued to children of illegal immigrants include an annotation—an asterisk, if you will, like those used in sports to denote a compromised or tainted record—indicating that their parents are illegal immigrants. The goal of the legislation that Pearce and Kavanagh proposed was to trigger reconsideration by the US Supreme Court of the interpretation of the section of the Fourteenth Amendment that allows for any child born in the United States to be given American citizenship (Wing, 2010). Like many other extremist and short-sighted solutions that the majority of Americans ultimately reject, this one too enjoyed a very brief shelf-life. Regrettably, this kind of bigotry and provincialism has been a powerful deterrent to substantial progress with immigration reform.

In the 2004 election, President George W. Bush won with 44 percent of the Hispanic vote, and quickly made comprehensive immigration reform a priority. In his 2007 State of the Union address, the President called for an ultimate resolution to the nation's immigration debate.

> We need to uphold the great tradition of the melting pot that welcomes and assimilates new arrivals. We need to resolve the status of the illegal immigrants who are already in our country without animosity and without amnesty. Convictions run deep in this Capitol when it comes to immigration. Let us have a serious, civil, and conclusive debate, so that you can pass, and I can sign, comprehensive immigration reform into law. (Bush, 2007)

In a strong bipartisan effort, Senators Edward "Ted" Kennedy (D-Massachusetts) and John McCain (R-Arizona) designed a blueprint for legalization, border security, and work visa programs in S.1033, the Secure America and Orderly Immigration Act. Most impressive was that it was created and endorsed by a group of reasonable politicians with different political orientations: a Republican president and former border-state governor with conservative credentials, a moderate Republican senator who was also from a border state, and a liberal Democratic icon in the US Senate from New England. It was an excellent example of how persons from different political orientations could come together on an issue of national and human importance.

However, the bill never made it to a vote after its introduction in 2005. The saving grace is that it served as an important outline for comprehensive reform proposals in 2006 and 2007. Both senators subsequently co-sponsored the Comprehensive Immigration Reform Act introduced in April of 2006 and then assisted with the design of the Secure Borders, Economic Opportunity, and Immigration Reform Act considered the following year. The 2007 bill emerged from the collaborative effort of 12 senators—known as the Gang of 12—and further incorporated input from President Bush. Once again, the bill died in Congress, eliciting a statement of regret from President Bush in which he urged Congress to work together to find a viable solution. "The American people understand the status quo is unacceptable when it comes to our immigration laws," he stated, reminding Congress of its obligation to come together on issues of importance (Bush, 2007). But the United States was riding a wave of entrenched conservatism that would not allow for significant strides on immigration reform or related social and economic plans.

After this failed attempt, several states began to take immigration enforcement into their own hands, citing the federal government's inability to properly ensure security for the American people. Arizona Senate Bill 1070, known as the Support Our Law Enforcement and Safe Neighborhoods Act, was one of the first state-level anti-immigrant bills transparently founded on prejudice. Signed into law on April 23, 2010, the bill required that all immigrants carry proper documentation at all times, and charges those unable to do so with a misdemeanor. Law-enforcement officials who felt an individual was, with "reasonable suspicion," in the country illegally were further permitted to detain the individual until their immigration status was determined. Finally, it granted individuals the privilege of suing the federal or state government in the event that they felt that immigration laws were not being enforced, generating additional pressure to apprehend and detain individuals. After extensive legal debates, the US Supreme Court struck down a number of provisions, including the clause making unauthorized presence a criminal offense. However, the court upheld the notorious "papers please" provision.

Arizona S.B. 1070 quickly sparked over 20 copycat bills in state legislatures. Georgia, Alabama, South Carolina, Indiana, and Utah all enacted similar enforcement-focused bills, some even more stringent than the

Arizona law. In addition to the "papers please" clause from Arizona, Alabama's H.B. 56 made it a misdemeanor for any unauthorized individual to seek work or enroll in any postsecondary institution. More controversial still, the 2011 Alabama law required public schools to collect information on the status of its students, prompting immediate withdrawals and absences among Hispanic students across the state. The Alabama law also penalized any individual who rented, hired, harbored, or transported an undocumented immigrant, imposing a tremendous burden on both immigrants and those inclined to help. Good Samaritan citizens could be arrested and prosecuted even if their intent was as simple as giving the undocumented person a ride to the supermarket or hospital. Taxi drivers, whose job it is to transport people and earn a living by it, would have been subject to this law. Similar to Arizona S.B. 1070, H.B. 56 met immediate legal challenge. Both the 11th Circuit Court of Appeals and federal district court blocked nearly every controversial provision, including the verification requirement imposed on schools.

DREAMERS, DACA, AND IMMIGRATION REFORM

As anti-immigrant sentiment increased, immigration advocates countered with an immigration reform movement. Shortly after Arizona Senate Bill 1070 was signed into effect, a contrasting bill seeking to alleviate some of the effects of immigration law was considered in the US Senate. The Development, Relief, and Education for Alien Minors (DREAM) Act was first introduced in 2001 as a means of preventing the punishment of undocumented children for their parents' actions. The act was targeted at the 65,000 undocumented children who would graduate from high school without the ability to attend college in order to further their education and contribute to American society. The DREAM Act would provide a six-year path to citizenship to any undocumented immigrant child who either achieved a college degree or served in the military for at least two years. Any undocumented immigrant child who was 15 years old or younger at the time of entry into the United States would be eligible, provided that they were residing in the United States for at least five years before the bill passed (DREAM Act Portal 2010). After years of support, the DREAM Act finally passed in the House of Representatives on December 8, 2010 by a vote of 216-198, only to be defeated in the Senate by just a handful of votes (Foley, 2010).

Despite this failure, the issue of immigrant minors reemerged during the second term of President Barack Obama's administration in the form of Deferred Action for Childhood Arrivals (DACA). Unlike the DREAM Act, DACA does not provide a path to citizenship to registrants, but does provide work authorization and removes the threat of deportation. Recipients do not gain legal status but they can renew their authorization every two years, dependent on developments in immigration reform. Notably, work authorization allows many students and young adults to obtain a social security number, obtain a valid state I.D., and attend college. DACA was an opportunity for the 2.1 million undocumented children and young adults who would have been eligible for legal status under the DREAM Act, had it been passed (Batalova & McHugh, 2010). Secretary of Homeland Security Janet Napolitano (2012) stated that although immigration laws must be enforced firmly and sensibly, "They are not designed to be blindly enforced without consideration given to the individual circumstances of each case. . . . Discretion, which is used in so many other areas, is especially justified here" (p. 2).

Deferred Action represents another stop-gap measure that is part of a patchwork approach to immigration reform. It holds limited weight as an executive order and is only a temporary fix for a problem that needed to be solved by comprehensive immigration reform. In 2013, President Obama again echoed this sentiment, appealing to Congress to put together comprehensive reform that will focus on dire problems with the current immigration system:

> Real reform means establishing a responsible pathway to earned citizenship—a path that includes passing a background check, paying taxes and a meaningful penalty, learning English, and going to the back of the line behind the folks trying to come here legally. And real reform means fixing the legal immigration system to cut waiting periods and attract the highly-skilled entrepreneurs and engineers that will help create jobs and grow our economy. In other words, we know what needs to be done. And as we speak, bipartisan groups in both chambers are working diligently to draft a bill, and I applaud their efforts. So let's get this done. Send me a comprehensive immigration reform bill in the next few months, and I will sign it right away. And America will be better for it. Let's get it done. Let's get it done.

Some in Congress acted. Groups of Congressmen in both the Republican-dominated House of Representatives and the more Democratic Senate began drafting separate comprehensive bills to address the nation's immigration needs. In the Senate, a group of four Republicans and four Democrats comprised the bipartisan task force known as the Gang of Eight. Ultimately, the Gang of Eight presented the first draft of comprehensive immigration reform, SB 744, also known as the Border Security, Economic Opportunity, and Immigration Modernization Act of 2013. On June 27, 2013, two and a half months after its introduction, the Senate passed the bill 68-32. Despite this accomplishment, the House of Representatives did not vote on SB 744, making it another victim of fundamental conflicts over what a good immigration policy should entail.

The sheer partisanship that plagued immigration reform during the Obama administration resulted from a host of different political, social, and economic factors that have shaped how the American people think and talk about certain issues. When a nation is stable, distinct parties are better able to work together and approach subjects from a common ground, but in the midst of economic and political upheaval, the drawing board is already polluted with preconceived notions and bias. The Obama administration is no exception to this rule. Inheriting the worst economic recession since the Great Depression, President Obama began serving his term in a state of conflict. (Furthermore, his administration made conditions worse for itself by having no coherent policy or approach—or political will—for handling immigration and the number of undocumented youth and their parents). It is no surprise, then, that fears over the economy continue to bleed over into other areas of reform, from healthcare to immigration. In times of heightened unemployment, there is an increased concern about immigrants taking the scarce jobs that do exist, regardless of whether that concern is justified by the historical record.

RHETORIC AND RAGE

The history of immigration from the early decades of the United States until today is one of repeated failures to follow moral arguments even when eloquently articulated by the nation's leaders. It is a history of defying presidents, from Woodrow Wilson to Barack Obama. It is a history of the self-defeating desire to reject and punish those who wanted to be Americans most as well as a history of an internal struggle about the US identity as a nation of immigrants. It is also a history of patterns of anti-immigrant sentiments during times of increased immigration caused by economic crises and violent conflicts in different parts of the world. An interesting paradox of this history is that many immigrants broke the law in order to live under the laws of the country. In Chapter 4, we will see how this paradox relates to the burdens that modern migrants face and the significance of their approach to resolving them.

In state and federal debates, the rhetoric of enforcement continues to rage on, with many supporters insisting that securing the border must be a significant part of any new reform. In the interim, deportation and detention levels have continued to soar as we've seen in Chapter 1. One major problem with this enforcement-focused approach is that it has failed to take into account a demographic reality that has come increasingly to our attention: mixed-status families. Despite a call for increased enforcement, deportation and detention not only affects the undocumented immigrant but also his or her family members, many of whom may be legal residents or US citizens. It is messy, complicated issue, but it requires action if we are to truly protect all American families equally. We can assert with confidence that the life of a citizen-child today is not equivalent to his or her counterpart born to American parents. The restrictions and legal hardship faced by the family members of the citizen-child are not like those of the average American family. As with past immigration laws, the United States is now in serious need of a new system that accounts for the growing reality of these children and provides them with the protections and privileges to which all US citizens are entitled.

NOTE

1. The suspect classification doctrine refers to situations in which a presumptive unconstitutional distinction is made between individuals on the basis of race, national origin, alienage, or religious affiliation, in a government statute, ordinance, regulation, or policy. The US Supreme Court has held that certain kinds of actions taken by federal and state governments are discriminatory and inherently suspect because they may violate the Equal Protection Clause of the Fourteenth Amendment and others (e.g., Fifth Amendment protection of due process; ownership of private property; protection against double jeopardy and self-incrimination).

CHAPTER 4

The Lives of Citizen-Children

In Chapter 1, we met Virginia and Daisy, who were both living the lives of citizen-children. Virginia wouldn't speak to anyone for fear that, if she did, her father's legal status would be revealed and his deportation ensured. She did not want to lose her father. Daisy Cuevas spoke guilelessly to the world to convey her concern about her mother. She wanted to protect her mother from having to worry. These two girls are normal American kids who attend school, make friends, speak English, watch cartoons, do homework, collect stickers, go to church, sneak a forbidden piece of candy, and do all the things children do. Both critics and supporters of US immigration and deportation policy recognize the averageness of US-born children of unauthorized immigrants, and agree that they will grow up as Americans (Haskins, Greenburg, & Fremstad, 2004, p. 1).

Citizen-children speak English as their first language, pledge allegiance to the US flag, engage in authentically American traditions like Thanksgiving and Fourth of July, abide by the laws of the land, aspire to college and affluence, and want a happy life. However, their parents' undocumented status is where their averageness ends. They witness the vituperative public pronouncements by politicians and neighbors against their parents, siblings, and themselves, and face a constant fear that their parents will be deported. Although they are the US-born citizen-children of mostly Latin American immigrants, they are told by other children in school to "go back where you came from." On television, they hear vocal arguments against immigrants and for deportation and see footage of arrests and protests. The fear creeps into nearly every waking moment and they are made to feel illegitimate and flawed. They might hear around the neighborhood about the growing courage of undocumented teenagers and young adults brought into the country as infants who are challenging the laws and social structures that label them as illegal.

Still, with undocumented parents and very little relief on the horizon to protect their parents and families, citizen-children are not average. With respect to concerns for their family's integrity, they do not enjoy the freedom from worry of other American citizen children. Those other citizen children don't have to worry about their parents being ejected from the United States. The reality is that citizen-children and their siblings suffer privations, challenges, hardships, and stresses that put their health, mental health, and educational progress at some risk. In this chapter and the next, I focus on the social issues facing average citizen-children and the psychological effects. Then, in Chapters 6–10, I turn to the effects on citizen-children when their parents are caught in the immigration enforcement system and deported. For these discussions, I draw on the research that illuminates the lives of citizen-children, including my own study which is described in Appendix A.

GROWING UP IN ENGLISH

In terms of cultural and national identity, US-born children of undocumented immigrants grow up to be regular American kids. Even undocumented, foreign-born children who are raised from a very young age in the United States identify themselves as Americans, the most notable being the group known as "DREAMers" (i.e., those who would have been eligible for legal status under the DREAM Act). They are now young adults who have been in the United States from such a young age that they are, for all intents and purposes, Americans. Citizen-children and their siblings who grow up in American cities and towns speak English primarily (sometimes exclusively). Organically, English is their native tongue. The children of immigrants from any part of the world may possess skills in their parents' original language to varying degrees of fluency but in general they are English-dominant, the language of their socialization and education, and of the media they consume. It's the language that has helped them integrate effectively into the social fabric of schools and communities, and form friendships across ethnicities and race. As language is linked to national identity, English adds to their self-definition as Americans, and is the language of their social references and personal identities. Although citizen-children and undocumented siblings may speak their parents' native language at home, it is not the predominant language of their peers, their schools, or their communities.

Most immigrant parents encourage their children to master English. They know that English is the gateway to success in the American economy and to all the advantages that English confers for navigating our complex world. This reality is reflected in a 2011 Pew Hispanic Center survey, which shows that Hispanics hold strongly to the perception that English is the language for their children's success in the United States (Taylor, Lopez, Martinez, & Velasco, 2012). Eighty-seven percent of Hispanics surveyed agree that adult immigrants need to learn English to succeed in the United States, a fact not lost on unauthorized immigrants who work to learn English whether it is on the job, through English as a Second Language (ESL) classes, or purposefully engaging with their children in English. From the second generation onward, the Pew survey confirms, immigrant families make English the primary language of their homes, a fact that has been shown to occur with every wave of immigrants to our shores.

Although English becomes the mother tongue for subsequent generations, parents know the importance of maintaining Spanish fluency. Spanish prevents the loss of the culture of origin and enhances participation in the United States and global marketplace. Ninety-five percent of respondents in the Pew Hispanic survey agreed that US Hispanics should keep Spanish alive in the home. Being fully bilingual is part of the path to economic success and civic participation.

I've seen first-hand how important it is to immigrant parents (with and without legal status) to have their children schooled in English while maintaining the family's language of heritage. In 1994, while on the clinical staff of a community health center in the South Bronx that was part of Montefiore Medical Center, the university hospital of the Albert Einstein College of Medicine, several Spanish-speaking immigrant parents with children in bilingual classes approached me. They were concerned that their children were being kept in bilingual classes longer than the parents felt was necessary (Zayas, 2004).

"You see," the parents told me, "we want our children to be mainstreamed and to take all their classes in English." But the parents encountered a resistant school bureaucracy, stemming from what they saw as bilingual education program teachers and directors entrenched in the protection of school turf. The school officials argued that children were better off staying in the bilingual program and learning many of their courses, such as mathematics and science, in Spanish because it was their first or dominant language. They argued that to switch Spanish-speaking children into all-English programs would pose unnecessary challenges for the students and possibly set them back. This seemed odd since most of the children were born in the United States or migrated with their parents at a young age. Besides, the Spanish they spoke at home was often rudimentary, as basic a level as their parents' own limited education. Many of these parents had completed only four to six years of education themselves in their native countries and spoke a similarly limited idiomatic and vernacular Spanish. It was hardly the case that their children were speaking such fluent Spanish that they needed to remain in bilingual classes in order to learn advanced concepts. But these were only my impressions; I listened to the parents as was my clinical and ethical obligation.

When the parents approached me, they were exasperated, but not angry. They stated the problem very clearly: they knew in the future their children would be living, studying, and working in the United States, and they were determined to make sure their children were as ready for this future as they could be. With the craftiness of people who have lived in marginalized, disempowered communities and have had to find clever ways to get institutions to respond to them, the parents felt that the school might listen if they leveraged the influence of another institution. It seemed to them that if they brought evidence of their children's readiness for regular classes from an independent source such as the community clinic of a highly respected hospital in the community, they would be negotiating from a position of strength. These parents were determined to enhance their children's future in the United States, and they wanted to give them all the resources they could. Besides, they added, they would always keep Spanish in the home to maintain their heritage and give the children the advantage of two languages, not just one.

Their determination to have their children master English, maintain a second language, and reap the associated benefits in school and in life in the United States was impressive. Limited in what I could really do for them, I agreed to administer standardized vocabulary and language tests to their children in both English and Spanish to see if we could find differences in their performance on the tests. We made an agreement: if a child did better on the English than on the Spanish tests, or if the child showed equal proficiency in both languages, I would write a letter of support explaining my findings to the schools and recommending that the child be considered for mainstreaming. If, however, the child's English scores were below those in the Spanish tests, then I would not write a letter of support but instead encourage them to keep the children in bilingual classes for at least another school year (Zayas, 2004). It seemed a reasonable arrangement to these parents. After testing, a few of the children appeared to be ready to be moved into mainstream classes, whereas others were obviously not ready. The school system responded sensitively. This experience underscored for me the value that immigrant parents place on both languages. They understood that with proficiency in two languages their children would eventually enjoy an advantage in American society.

Research supports these parents. First, heavy involvement in English-intensive contexts helps Hispanic youth with their language competence and has the added benefit of facilitating relationships with others (McKay-Semmler & Kim, 2014). Hispanic teenagers who learn English well enough to engage in friendships and activities with members of mainstream US culture are more likely to succeed in school and feel better about themselves and their futures. Mastery of English helps raise their level of engagement in extracurricular activities. Language competence also helps citizen-children and undocumented siblings to gain access to resources, social supports, and information that prepares them for participation in the educational system and in occupational roles. If citizen-children feel alienated from other youth because of their parents' legal status, English makes them feel less alienated from others and more satisfied with their sense of belonging.

Second, even among disadvantaged children, bilingualism helps some areas of cognitive maturation and executive functioning (i.e., the mental processes of organizing, planning, strategizing, paying attention, remembering details, inhibiting inappropriate behaviors, and managing time and space; Engel de Abreu, Cruz-Santos, Tourinho, Martin, & Bialystok, 2012; Kalashnikova & Mattock, 2014). One area in which two languages is beneficial is in what is known as attentional control, children's ability to select what to remain focused on even when there are conflicting perceptual cues (Kalashnikova & Mattock, 2014). This bilingual advantage is thought to confer through the individual's ability to activate both languages as they formulate their thoughts and then selectively suppress one of them to produce speech. Stated another way, they can draw from two languages to communicate their ideas but when speaking they use only one language at a time. It is a complex process that helps bilingual people inhibit attention to conflicting information more than monolingual persons. Regularly using more than one language enhances executive functions, such as attention-switching, short-term or "working memory,"[1] creativity, and problem solving (Adesope, Lavin, Thompson, & Ungerleider, 2010; Bialystok, Craik, Green, & Gollan, 2009). Functional magnetic resonance imaging (fMRI) research also supports the idea that managing more than one language on a regular basis exercises the brain's executive functions, particularly the skills of language switching and resolving conflicts between languages (Luk, Green, Abutalebi, & Grady, 2011).

Despite their socioeconomic status, low-income children benefit from being bilingual, particularly with regards to their attentional control

(Engel de Abreu et al., 2012). The more difficult or demanding the cognitive task a child faces, the greater the likelihood is that the bilingual effect will surface. Another way to look at it is that the child can draw from a reservoir of linguistic and mental abilities from two languages rather than one to solve mental tasks because of the cognitive flexibility that is needed. The parents I met in the South Bronx who asked for my help with their children's bilingual schooling did not know of all the cognitive advantages that bilingualism gave their children, but they were certainly very aware of the practical and tangible effects.

KNOWING LEGALITY FROM ILLEGALITY

When they learn that their parents are undocumented, very young children (5 and 6 years of age) do not quite grasp what not having papers or being in the country illegally means. Then, when you ask 7, 8, and 9 year-olds the same questions about what it means not to have papers or to be undocumented, they demonstrate a better understanding of their parents' legal status but still not full comprehension. They understand being a citizen versus not being a citizen but the concept of what the papers are that distinguish the two legal statuses remains fuzzy. In the minds of young citizen-children and even some adults, being an immigrant is synonymous with being illegal. For children, citizenship is an abstract concept that they may just begin to understand, but the distinctions between different types of "papers" are not yet clear. For example, a 9-year-old girl we interviewed in California learned that her father was undocumented when she was about 7 years old. It happened when her mother was planning a trip to Mexico with the girl and her sister. They were all US citizens but her father was not. He stayed in the United States. The girl explained to us that her father "couldn't have a passport because he is not from here. He is from Mexico." He told her he didn't have a passport because he didn't have some important or official papers like her mother and her sister did. To get a passport, she understood, her father must have very important papers "like the ones that my mom has in the folders in our house," papers she did not understand but that held some magical power. These were precious documents that her mother took great care to protect.

Most interesting, though, is that younger children see legal status as a private family matter. That is, they make sense of it by learning that *their* family cannot go visit members in another state or another country; it may not yet be generalized to other families and the explanation for it is still an ego-centric construction, how it affects "me" or "us." This is not surprising, since younger children operate with a relatively concrete and self-centered form of thinking. They may define lawlessness in more obvious ways, like stealing and killing. But they may not understand how someone can come to this country, work and pay taxes, and not commit crimes but still be considered to have committed an illegal act. With growth and maturity, the older child understands legal status as an issue that is more pervasive, public, and part of a system of laws that govern people and institutions (Dreby, 2012). In time, they come to understand the structural determinants that affect their parents and how people and institutions discriminate against immigrants without papers (Gonzalez, 2011). And citizen-children of undocumented parents understand this reality and its implications to a degree that most adult US citizens outside of mixed-status families do not.

This is the more sophisticated thinking that occurs in adolescence, the "formal operations" in the mind that entertain complexities that are not binary or that require physical evidence (Piaget & Inhelder, 1950). The adolescent mind uses sophisticated hypothetical, deductive, and propositional thinking to make verbal assertions and evaluate the logic of these assertions without having to have the concrete evidence before them. Through this inferential reasoning, the adolescent mind can integrate ethical and moral factors with philosophical legal principles and judicial actions, capacities that require abstract thoughts. The teenager understands what not having papers really means. To illustrate the point of the evolution of how citizen-children make sense of the idea of "papers," I present the description given by a participant in our research, "Exploring the Effects of Parental Deportation on US Citizen-Children," of how she first learned of and now processes her parents' illegal status.

Felicita

Felicita was 11-and-a-half years old when our project director, M. Andrea Campetella, interviewed her in Austin. Felicita is a loquacious girl who connected trustingly with Andrea. She said she had found out that her parents were undocumented from a cousin. Her cousin told her that her parents did not have papers but Felicita did not understand anything about what the "papers" were and why they were so important. Felicita narrated the story of how she found out with the deportment of an older woman, encouraging her listener to sit back and relax because this would be a very interesting story that might take some time to tell.

"Well," she said, "at first it was this rumor. Well, I mean, I thought it was a rumor made up by my cousin, because she lies a lot and I don't trust her much, and she was like, well your parents came here illegally, and I was like wait, illegally? What does that mean? And she told me and I was like, wait. I was little. I didn't even know anything. I was like wait, illegally? And she said they didn't have papers. And I said what? I don't get it. I thought she meant papers, like those right here [pointing to Andrea's note paper]! I was little I didn't know what was going on."

"So how old were you when this happened and what did your parents say when you talked to them?" Andrea asked.

"I was like 7, and then, that's when my parents told me. I asked them and they told me. They are like . . . I told them that my cousin says that you all came here illegally. And they are like, wait, she told you that? And they got mad at her because they were like you were not supposed to tell her that, but they didn't like tell her, they were just mad at her, like just thinking about it. And so then I was like yeah, and they are like, oh, well, I don't really remember much of what they told me. But like they told me, well, we did come in a plane with a visa, and I was like what's a visa? So, I was like, oh forget it, I don't get this. I'll wait until I grow up to get this better. That's what I remember."

"And when did you feel that you understood it better?"

"Well, at first I thought they meant like in paper-paper, but then they told me like a visa, and then I remember like in second grade my, well, she was sort of like a friend of mine, and she was like, oh yeah, they deported my aunt because she didn't have a visa, and I was like visa? Is this like visa, the [credit] card? And then she was like, oh no, I mean like papers, and I was like papers? Oh my God, what's going on, I don't get you all! Because first my cousin tells me about the papers, and she says 'no, not that type of papers,' and she does not really explain it to me and so I say, 'Now you tell me about papers. I don't get it.' She is like it means that you came here illegally. And I was like what does illegally mean? It means that . . . like they broke the rules. And I was like I don't get it. And so then I asked my parents again, what does undocumented mean? And they were like oh that means that we don't have documents to come, like to travel to a different country. And then I was like, oh, I get it. That was when I got the point . . . and so I was like so you all could not get here, so when you came it was sort of like breaking the rules . . . because they put it in sort of a basic way so I could understand it."

Felicita's story is like those of many other children though perhaps told with more chattiness than most. Her story, all the same, provides a glimpse into the cognitive and emotional maturation process from the age of 7–12.

Undocumented parents' deportability has a pernicious effect on their families' use of healthcare, their involvement in early childhood education, and their children's development and well-being. Not all the situations that mixed-status families face are the same or have the same impact, though they do have a cumulative effect. In an impressive presentation of how deportation affects children of immigrant families, sociologist Joanna Dreby (2012) organizes the various pressures into six levels that make up what she calls the *pyramid of deportation burdens* (see Figure 4.1). Dreby's interviews with study participants reveal that the deportation itself—the most dreaded of all outcomes—is not the only pressure that the undocumented immigrants feel. Catastrophic as an actual deportation can be to families, she characterizes the state of deportability as the relentless pressure of persistent threats, insults, stresses, and instability. Although deportation devastates a number of families every year, deportability wears on all undocumented immigrants every day, constantly. "The threat of deportability," Dreby notes, "[inspires] fears of separation among children regardless of their own

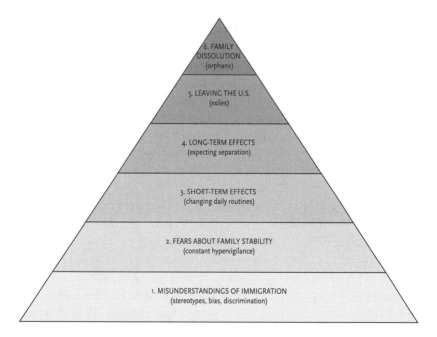

Figure 4.1:
Dreby's Pyramid of Deportation Burdens
Source: Adapted from Dreby (2012) with permission.

legal status or family members' actual involvement with immigration officials" (p. 830). Dreby's pyramid of deportation burdens is a useful heuristic model for grouping the pressures that citizen-children of undocumented immigrants live with. To be clear, the pyramid represents a continuum not a hierarchy of individual pressures or burdens that children and families can experience, sometimes simultaneously, because of their state of deportability. Each level may affect some people and not others but taken together the burdens are oppressive and weaken the child's and family's functioning.

On Level 1, Dreby locates the burden of dealing with the widespread misunderstanding about immigrants: the stereotypes, biased depictions, and discrimination against them (e.g., micro-aggressions of everyday life, misinformation, insults, and innuendos; media reports of anti-immigrant sentiments and legislation). This level contains the erroneous associations made between legal and illegal immigration, and between criminals and immigrants. The myths that swirl around in public commentaries that demonize immigrants are part of an environment of micro-aggressions in everyday life. Although the barbs and mischaracterizations sting and may not be directed against individuals but rather at the group, the fact of being the child of an undocumented immigrant, a member of the target group, makes the citizen-child feel self-conscious, defensive, and self-doubting. Comments and myths about immigrants, such as, "They take jobs away from other Americans," "They come here to be on public welfare," or "They get pregnant just to have 'anchor babies'" [2] have their negative effects on the citizen-child that cumulatively can be malignant.

Whereas Level 1 can be characterized by discrimination, Level 2 is characterized by the burdens of being constantly alert—in fact, hyperalert—to the dangers in the environment. Undocumented immigrants and their children must remain vigilant at all times, always on the look-out for events and situations that can destabilize the family (e.g., when a parent is stopped by the police; when immigration enforcement patrols are within sight; Ayon, 2014; Brabeck & Xu, 2010; Chavez, Lopez, Englebrecht, & Viramontez Anguiano, 2012). Level 2 burdens may be related to the fear of how they will be treated if new laws are enacted and to living in a community in which the local police use aggressive tactics for immigration enforcement. We can see how when the first and second levels are combined: Undocumented people must be on high alert for signs that they might be discovered or attacked. This unremitting worry destabilizes families and has injurious effects on children's well-being and sense of security.

Levels 3 and 4 of the pyramid represent some of the short-term and long-term pressures that deportation or even the *threat* of deportation can cause families. Level 3 holds the short-term problems of changes in regular routines brought about by economic instability and avoiding detection by law enforcement. For example, the loss of a job due to a workplace raid or because a project has ended or because of seasonal fluctuations in the industry that mean a period of unemployment and less income, even if only for a short period of time. Economic insecurity and hardship calls for families to alter their daily routines to find means for survival while protecting against discovery by immigration enforcement. For young children, frequent moves and a general lack of stability can cause considerable distress. Particularly for children who have spent a significant amount of time in a specific home, the sudden loss of both a parent and a home can be devastating. As Adam and Chase-Lansdale (2002) explain, a sudden move to a new residence is not just the loss of a home, but a "loss of familiar physical environments, activities, and routines, [and] the loss of social support networks" (p. 793). Frequent moves, like those that many undocumented immigrants face in the aftermath of an arrest, are further associated with a wide range of detrimental social, educational, and psychological impacts. By constantly moving to new residencies to maintain a low profile and avoid future apprehension, the child is unable to maintain existing ties to teachers, friends, or other community members, exacerbating the feelings of loss and disintegrating a support system that may be especially necessary after the trauma of a parent. Working openly to survive and put bread on the table while avoiding discovery by immigration enforcement becomes part of the daily routine. Parents are under constant emotional distress and their children notice it. They worry about themselves and their families. From a mental health standpoint, worry and secrecy become part of the survival strategies for daily life. This daily survival mode is sporadically punctuated by more acute episodes of stress, such as apprehension by a police officer. These are, in Dreby's model, the less severe but more common or numerous afflictions that chip away at parents' and children's lives.

At Level 4 there are the pressures that come with separations from parents for short or long periods due to direct encounters with immigration officers. Unlike Level 2 in which it is the vigilance for law enforcement and Level 3 in which it is the changes that are wrought on daily life, Level 4 burdens are those that actually involve the arrest of parents by police or immigration officers. The worries are no longer about what was anticipated but by what has actually happened: the arrest and detention. The parent may be released and return home pending a removal hearing.

But the child's concern is what will happen if the parent is re-arrested or deported. The experiences of sudden emotional and social upheavals leave lasting psychological marks that alter their personalities, moods, affects, and worldviews. In Dreby's words, "to fully capture the impact of deportation policies on children, one must consider how children's lives are changed by both the relatively infrequent, more intrusive cases of deportation and the more common instance in which it is the politics of deportation that affect children" (p. 836).

The top two levels of the pyramid are the most virulent and damaging, corresponding to what I label the "exiles" and the "orphans." Social work scholar Cecilia Ayon (2014), writing in another context, captures the essence of these two levels of Dreby's pyramid when she states, "Families who have been disintegrated due to deportation are confronted with significant financial losses and emotional turmoil that take a heavy toll on the family. Families do not have the coping skills to deal with discrimination or the tools to discuss such issues with their children" (p. 21). Exiles, children who leave the country in the care of their parents, occupy Level 5. Although the children may still be with their parents when the deportation occurs, they are separated from everything else they know—friends, schools, neighborhoods, and so on. At the apex of the pyramid, Level 6, we find the deportation orphans. Due to the forced removal of one or both parents, couples make decisions to leave their children in the United States, resulting in the dissolution of the family units the children and parents once enjoyed. This disbanding of families as the *de facto* result of public policy is counter to the value of strengthening and preserving families that our government espouses.

CHILDREN SCALING THE PYRAMID

The cases of Armando and Veronica in California and Marcus in Illinois are examples of adolescents who live on the pyramid of burdens. Armando and Veronica were participants in my research project and Marcus was a teenager I evaluated for his father's deportation case before the immigration court. Armando and Veronica lived a carefree American life until it was upended by the discovery that their parents and eldest sister were undocumented immigrants. Armando and Veronica were put squarely in the middle levels of the pyramid, Levels 3 and 4. Marcus catapulted suddenly from feeling that he was not directly affected by his father's undocumented status (which put him on Level 1 or Level 2) to experiencing anguish from the uncertainty of whether his life would end up on Level 5 or Level 6 of the pyramid.

Armando and Veronica

Eleven-year-old Armando and his sister, Veronica, 15, were interviewed for our study on separate occasions at their home in an attractive condominium complex near an elementary school in Fresno, California. They are two of four siblings in the family. Their father works long hours at two jobs and their mother stays at home with the children. The parents speak Spanish to each other and to the children, but the children typically answer in English. The children communicate with each other in English. They know Spanish but seldom use it except when they are with extended family.

Armando and Veronica learned in the past year that their parents and the oldest sister are undocumented. One evening, Armando recalled, his parents and oldest sister were having a conversation in the kitchen in what seemed to be hushed tones about President Obama's deferred action program (DACA). He told Mariana Ruiz del Rio, our research interviewer, that whenever he or Veronica or his younger sister went near the kitchen where the parents and sister were talking, his father or mother shooed them away. After some time, Armando said, his parents called everyone together to the kitchen table. There they told the three younger children that their sister and parents did not have legal papers to be in the United States. Because they would be working on the DACA application for his sister, his parents decided that everyone in the family should know and understand what was going on. His younger sister did not understand fully but he did; and so did Veronica. Both parents emphatically told the children very explicitly that they were not to talk to anyone about their legal statuses. As Armando explained it, they can talk about it at home but they must not share it with anyone outside of the home, not even their best friends.

Until that night, Armando had not worried about his parents. He had been living a happy life—going to school and making friends. But when he learned that this parents and sister could be deported he became worried and tried not to talk about it. He tried not to talk about it but his worry was constant. To compound his worry, a few weeks after the family conversation about their legal status, Armando's mother got a speeding ticket while driving with him and his younger sister. Armando told Mariana that they all became very scared and that his mother "had to pay, like, a thousand dollars for the ticket." He said that since getting the speeding citation his mother has curtailed her driving and refuses completely to drive at night. Then, a few months later, the police stopped Armando's father as he was entering the condominium complex because of a broken taillight on this car. Armando and his mother watched helplessly as neighbors came out to speak with the police officers, intervening on behalf of his father. Neither mother nor son could go to aid the father. He was issued a ticket but fortunately was not questioned about his legal status.

Armando felt his safe world become more fragile; it was no longer the normal life he had so enjoyed before he learned his parents were undocumented. The reality of his family's vulnerability hit home when the two incidents with the police occurred. Since that time, Armando's anxiety has been high and he is easily moved to crying, according to his mother. It became evident to Mariana during Armando's interview. During the administration of the questionnaire with the standardized instruments, Armando answered enthusiastically and sometimes made jokes about the questions or his responses. But when the interview turned to his experience as the child of undocumented parents, Armando's demeanor changed and he became increasingly nervous. He bowed his head, mumbled his answers, fidgeted with his hands and legs, and spoke softly, almost inaudibly. It wasn't long before he began to cry.

When Mariana asked why he was crying, Armando replied, "Because I'm scared that my mom and dad are going to be arrested." He had never talked to his parents or his sisters about his worries, he told Mariana, "I kept it in so they wouldn't worry, too." As Armando seemed highly distressed, Mariana stopped the recorder to give him time to calm down. Once he acknowledged that he was scared of how he was feeling and that he really did not talk about this with anyone, he said he began to feel better. Armando told Mariana he was ready to resume the interview and that the recording could start again. But after the first question, Armando began to cry again and Mariana decided that it was sensible to end the interview.

Several days later, Mariana returned to the home to interview Veronica. Much like Armando, Veronica is riven with anxiety and worry. Veronica was frightened when she first heard that her parents did not hold the proper papers to be in the United States. "I was never worried before that night," she said. Now that she knew about the family's situation, she understood that getting stopped by police or getting caught in some other way meant that deportation was possible. It could mean that she and her two younger siblings could be left behind. "It still makes me scared," she admitted, "[But] I think I understand more about the consequences of not having papers and it makes me less scared than I was before." She bears the futility of her sister's and parents' situations stoically, but not without profound feelings. "It makes me feel bad for my sister especially because it's something that no one can really fix and it's not like it is up to her to change it," she told Mariana. "Maybe her application to DACA will help but we don't really know. I mean, I'm going to ask for her nationality and my parents' nationality when I'm 21, but before that there is nothing we can do. But it seems to me to be so unfair." (Veronica uses the term "national-ity" as a literal or direct English translation of the Spanish *nacionalidad*. The Spanish *nacionalidad* is a cognate of *ciudadanía,* citizenship.)

Mariana asked Veronica if she saw a difference between her parents not having papers and her sister not having papers.

"Yeah," Veronica said unhesitatingly, "I think, well, I guess that in a way it's the same. But with my sister not having papers, it's like she doesn't have the opportunity to do the things that she would be able to do at her age, like other people of the same age. I mean, like, not being able to get a driver's license or be able to get an ID to go out with her friends now that she is older. My sister doesn't really ever talk about it but I think she does get scared about the idea of being without papers. She doesn't talk to any-one. It's something that I just don't really talk about with anyone either."

Marcus

Marcus, a tall, well-built 14-year-old boy of Mexican father and white American mother, fits the average citizen-child profile except that his father was contesting an order of deportation. In every other way, Marcus was a remarkably well-adjusted American teenager. As part of the legal challenge to his father's order of deportation, Marcus agreed to meet with me. He arrived promptly at the appointed time, dressed in the attire of any other boy his age: blue jeans that sagged a bit, a loose-fitting rugby-type shirt, and the latest designer athletic footwear. He greeted me in English, establishing the language in which we would communicate, slumped in the chair in front of me, feigning some degree of boredom, or maybe it was a stance of nonchalance about having to talk to a middle-aged man. (I over-heard Marcus answering his father in Spanish before entering my office but it was not a fluent Spanish.) By his bearing that day, Marcus wanted to let me know that there were apparently much better and exciting things to do at his age than meet a shrink who wanted to talk with him about his father's pending deportation case. Still, he was polite and courteous, and likable. After decades of interviewing teenage boys of all social classes, races, and ethnicities, I recognized the overscripted self-confidence of a young man in the apogee of his adolescence. I took a liking to Marcus almost instantly for his apparent normality and adolescent swagger.

Marcus was born in Illinois to Francisco and Ashley after a normal pregnancy and birth. In infancy, Marcus exhibited some asthmatic symptoms but these may have been due to the smoke from his mother's cigarettes. Marcus's parents separated when he was about 4 years old and his parents shared custody for about three years. The arrangements were for Marcus to stay with one parent for three to four months and then with the other for three to four months. This back-and-forth seemed to disrupt Marcus' stability. Marcus developed behavioral problems that seemed to the parents to be a result of the constant moving from one home to another. Francisco and Ashley were thoughtful, caring parents and agreed that for Marcus' sake, Francisco should take full custody of their young son. In reality, Francisco had a more stable financial situation. And so, at the age of 7 Marcus went to live exclusively with his father; he would be able to see his mother whenever it was possible. Once he was not around her smoking, the asthma disappeared, never to flare up again. In the medical record, there were notes by a pediatrician of symptoms of Attention-Deficit/Hyperactivity Disorder (ADHD) that was diagnosed shortly before Marcus turned 9 years old. He was put him on medication commonly prescribed for this disorder and it was changed a month later to another similar drug. Marcus continued on that medication for about two years whereupon Francisco appealed to the pediatrician to stop the medication. Francisco set about carefully supervising Marcus, establishing rules, routines, and expectations at home and in school, and generally providing consistent and predictable parenting for Marcus. He never returned to the medication and his ADHD, like the asthma, disappeared.

Ashley subsequently remarried, but her life followed an unstable pattern of drug use and involvement in unhealthy relationships with men, landing her in a shelter for abused women by the time Marcus and I met. Marcus had very little contact with his mother; sometimes two years would go by without any contact with her. Marcus lived with his father, his father's girlfriend, Maria, and her three children. He shared a room with Maria's son, Felix, age 17, who Marcus considered to be "like a brother to me." In keeping with this theme of a new family, Marcus often referred to Maria as "Mom." His educational records showed Marcus to be an average student with some "ups and downs" in his academic performance. Otherwise, he was a well-behaved freshman in high school who was a lineman on the junior varsity football team.

On a clinical measure of self-esteem and self-concept, Marcus showed a generally strong positive self-appraisal and he evaluated himself as generally performing well but not without some unspecified difficulties. In other words, he was not so grandiose as to think he was without problems and limitations. In most other areas he was normal. He considered himself relatively intelligent, doing fairly well in school, average in his physical appearance and attributes, and somewhat popular among his peers. There was no indication of any anxiety or unhappiness. There was no depression or other symptom to give me cause for concern. In fact, Marcus had grown up fairly removed from the threat of his father's undocumented, deportable status. His father, of course, was aware of his precarious legal status. But with the regularity of a job that insulated him from the public and an intimate family life, Francisco did not exude worry about his legal status. This attitude freed Marcus to live as a regular teenage. Indeed, his father's success in his place of employment—a small family owned salvage business in which the patriarch and matriarch, and their only son, had promised employment to Francisco for as long as he wanted—was an inspiration and source of pride for Marcus. He went fishing with his father on weekends and watched his father play soccer. Occasionally, he accompanied his father to the salvage yard to help him wash tractors and other large vehicles. Marcus aspired to go to college to be an engineer. He earned some money mowing lawns and had a savings account with about $1000 in it. From his earnings, Marcus paid for his own cell-phone service. Francisco confirmed that Marcus had a list of chores at home (e.g., washing his clothes, making his bed, washing dishes, cleaning house) that he generally accomplished. Sometimes Francisco had to "get on him" when Marcus skipped or took short cuts on his responsibilities. Francisco said that in those instances Marcus would comply.

Francisco seemed attuned to Marcus, describing him as a "sentimental" child who freely expressed his feelings to his father. Francisco also recognized Marcus' compassion and empathy for others. In spite of his self-assured adolescent demeanor, Marcus became tearful when our conversation turned to his father's deportation predicament, and the impact this would have on him. During the few days of his father's detention that occurred about a year before, Marcus told me of his apprehension about whether and when he would see his father again. It was the first time he had confronted the reality that his father's legal status was not as protected as it had always seemed. It was when we talked about the possibility of his father's deportation that Marcus' nonchalance and detachment faded to fear and sadness.

"How am I going to live out my life without him? He is the only one out there for me. Without him, I don't know where I'd be." There was no hint in Marcus' words that leaving the United States with his father was part of his thinking or planning. His home is the United States and Marcus never said or entertained the notion of leaving the country with his father if the order of removal was enforced. In his hurried move to describe alternative solutions for his life should his father be deported, Marcus said that he would simply have to "go it alone and use my savings." He was correct in concluding that he and his father were alone in facing the world. Although he had an uncle nearby, Marcus could not live with him for the uncle was a low-wage laborer with few resources and in no condition to take in a nephew into the house he shared with three other men. Maria, his father's girlfriend, could not assume custody of Marcus both because the pair was unmarried and her own financial circumstances were precarious. Living with his mother was not an option owing to the unfortunate pattern of drift in her life. Mother and son were not close and had such little contact that Marcus did not know her address. He could not yet be an emancipated minor and would have to enter foster care. Even if he tried valiantly to live alone, pay rent, clothe and feed himself, and make his way through life on his own, Marcus would have to drop out of school and work full time. At his age, who would rent an apartment to him? If Marcus were to remain in the United States without his father or without a competent and caring adult, his future would be truncated. And the deportation of his father would very likely leave Marcus in a good deal of emotional pain and produce long-lasting psychological scars.

My report to the immigration court described Marcus as I have done here and concluded on an upbeat but realistic note.

> This is a remarkably well-adjusted young man. He is bright, engaging, respectful, and full of life (as an average, healthy 14-year-old should be). He shows great respect and admiration for his father. Since moving in solely with his father, Marcus's behavior has improved, according to his father. It is a tribute to Francisco that he has been a single father and has raised Marcus under hardship but with exceptional care and results. He is a very engaged father who has, even with the support of a mother-surrogate for Marcus, not relegated the care of his child to anyone else. His knowledge of Marcus's educational and medical histories, of Marcus's friends and whereabouts, and of his son's emotional states is indicative of the solid parenting he has provided.

The government attorney largely agreed with this assessment and did not challenge very vigorously Francisco's appeal for a cancellation of his removal orders. Likewise, the judge agreed that exceptional and extremely unusual hardship would ensue if Francisco were deported, and granted a cancellation of removal.

INSECURITIES ANTICIPATED AND ACTUAL

Like many parents in America, though perhaps more so than most, undocumented immigrant parents face challenges to securing financial and basic needs for their families. Unequal access to educational opportunities and healthcare, and housing and food insecurity can compromise the health and development of citizen-children. Enforcement measures exacerbate the challenges that parents face, putting citizen-children at even greater disadvantage and risk.

Developmental research has long shown the powerful links between economic hardship and children's behavioral and educational outcomes. Persistent poverty, indeed even transitory poverty, can have detrimental effects on children's measured intelligence, school achievement, and social and emotional functioning (Blair & Raver, 2012; McLoyd, 1989, 1998; McLoyd, Kaplan, Purtell, Bagley, Hardaway, & Smalls, 2009; Yoshikawa, Aber, & Beardslee, 2012). Children who live in unabated poverty or episodic poverty generally do worse than children who have never faced economic hardship. Unemployment and earnings loss often increase the stress of the primary breadwinner, resulting in irritability, tense interactions with spouse and children, and lowered self-worth. Children, in turn, may mimic their parents' behaviors and begin to display emotional and conduct problems, somatic problems, poorer school performance, and lowered aspirations. Psychologists Edward Zigler and Nancy Hall (2000) explain these effects, stating, "Living in poverty *can* . . . take a tremendous toll on the child's future by eliminating opportunities that facilitate success: Educational opportunities for children living in economically deprived areas are likely to be substandard, and health problems associated with poverty both challenge healthy development itself and interfere with academic performance" (p. 9; original emphasis).

Income has a higher association with a child's measured intelligence (that is, their IQ scores) than maternal education, ethnicity, or female-headed household (Aber, Bennet, & Conley, 1997). Children who live in poverty for an extended period of time tend to score much lower on tests of cognitive ability, showing large deficits in cognitive and socio-emotional development than children not in poverty. Poverty is one reason—another is wariness about revealing their legal status—that undocumented immigrant parents are less likely to have their young children in preschool than US citizens or legal permanent residents (Crosnoe, 2006; Hernandez, Denton, & Macartney, 2008; Kalil & Crosnoe, 2009; Matthews & Ewen, 2006). Child development researchers R. Gabriela Barajas, Nina Philipsen, and Jeanne Brooks-Gunn (2008) elaborate on this idea, stating that the "emotional, physical, and intellectual environment that a child is exposed to in the early years of life affects early learning, self-regulation, and perhaps brain organization" (p. 314). Children in low-income households show both cognitive and emotional effects. At age 2, low-income children demonstrated an average IQ 4.4 points lower than children from higher-income households. Poor children are more likely to show emotional or behavioral problems persisting later into childhood as a direct result of the stresses associated with poverty.

Living conditions associated with poverty provide additional threats to a child's developmental health. Due to the inability to pay for safe and healthy housing, children in poverty are often exposed to higher lead levels, toxins, higher noise levels, crowding, and greater risk of accidental injury or death (Aber et al., 1997; Evans, 2006). Hospitalization due to asthma, bacterial pneumonia, dehydration, gastroenteritis, and parasitic diseases are common for impoverished children; hospitalization for asthma alone is four times higher for poor children than for those at an economic advantage (Aber et al., 1997). Meanwhile, toxic household substances common in substandard living conditions can create additional complications. Lead poisoning, for example, is known to affect the neurological pathways of the child's brain, often resulting in learning disabilities and speech disorder. In addition to increased hyperactivity, impulsivity, and aggression following, lead poisoning has been found to reduce their measured IQ scores by three points per 10 micrograms of lead per deciliter of blood (Evans, 2006). Thus, these pollutants lead not to temporary afflictions, but rather to long-lasting ones.

Naturally, poverty affects a family's food security, which, in turn, can also impact the health of the child. Each year, the US government adjusts the poverty level to reflect the income needed by a family of three to provide each member with an adequate diet (US Department of Health & Human Services, 2011). Families that fall below this level are, thus, unlikely to provide children with the vitamins and nutrients necessary to support development. There is more food insecurity among children of unauthorized Latin American immigrants than U.S.-born children (Kalil & Chen, 2008). In 2003, children suffering from food insecurity were twice as likely to be in poor health, with approximately 30 percent higher hospitalization rates as higher-income children (Cook et al., 2003). A family's access to healthcare and insurance can be limited, further preventing a family from seeking medical care in a timely fashion. Although health inequalities in the United States have decreased over the past decade, poorer families are still less likely to stay up-to-date on immunizations and routine visits, preventing the child from receiving sufficient primary care and basic illness prevention measures. In 2007, only 76.5 percent of poor children had received the recommended immunizations, as compared with 84.1 percent of their wealthier counterparts. Furthermore, only 67.9 percent of uninsured children had a usual care provider, in contrast to 93.5 percent of privately insured children (Agency for Healthcare Research and Quality, 2009). As a result, fewer poor or uninsured children receive access to sufficient primary care, ultimately leading to higher rates of child hospitalization due to untreated affliction or deficient illness prevention (Aber et al., 1997; Cousineu, Farias, & Pickering, 2009).

Unauthorized immigrant parents face critical situations in their use of healthcare services for their children and themselves. The undocumented are less likely to use health services for lack of insurance and fear of encountering legal authorities who might report them. Even when their citizen-children are eligible for many public programs such as food stamps, child-care subsidies, and quality healthcare, undocumented parents may not use them. They often defer the use of healthcare until it is absolutely necessary for their children's safety. Fear of having their undocumented status discovered is one reason for not accessing these services (Yoshikawa, 2011). In one study comparing healthcare, use of services, and healthcare experiences of Latinos by citizenship and immigrant authorization status, undocumented Mexican immigrants had about 1.7 fewer physician visits compared to US citizens of Mexican descent, whereas other undocumented Latinos had 2.1 fewer visits to their physicians when compared to their US-born counterparts (Ortega, et al., 2007). Following a similar pattern, undocumented Mexican immigrants are less likely to have a usual source of care—a healthcare center that becomes their "medical home" or a steady primary care provider—and more likely to report having had negative experiences with their healthcare providers and institutions than US citizens of Mexican descent. This isn't surprising since children of Mexican heritage are more likely to live in families whose incomes fall below the federal poverty level compared to non-Hispanic White families (Ortega, Horwitz, Fang, Kuo, Wallace, & Inkelas, 2009). The proportion of children living in poverty among the Mexican families alone reflects the poorer situation of the undocumented: 56 percent of children with undocumented parents are below the poverty level compared to 27 percent of children with documented parents but who are not citizens (probably legal permanent residents or visa-holders), and 15 percent of those with parents who are citizens.

Cumulatively, economic hardship, unstable housing, food insecurity, and healthcare use affect the child's overall health status. These factors explain why just 39 percent of families near the poverty line rate their children's health as "excellent," while the statistic soars to 64 percent for those making at least $35,000 a year (Zigler & Hall, 2000).[3] Despite recent national efforts to reduce health inequalities, immigration raids and detention confound any effort to alleviate the impact of these trends on children, instead forcing thousands of children into harmful social and economic conditions.

According to an Urban Institute study of immigration raids (Chaudry et al., 2010), the arrests of the primary breadwinners often leads to quick declines in income, prolonged instability, and greater food insecurity for families. At three of the raid sites, families faced a partial or complete loss of income, as most of the apprehended workers held steady full-time jobs. In some cases, the parents had worked for many years and over time had earned higher positions within companies, successfully supporting their families while contributing to society. On average, family income after the raid was less than half of its income before arrest, causing the families to rely on private charities, informal support, and public benefits. Approximately two-thirds of the families reported difficulty paying bills and were unable to bounce back even after the release of a family member. Many of those who were displaced by the raids said they entered the country with the philosophy that they will work hard to support their families without "handouts," and thus they will take on extended hours rather than apply for aid (Chaudry et al., 2010). Although spouses often worked extra hours to manage finances, they often experienced difficultly obtaining additional employment or were reluctant to do so out of fear of future arrest.

Faced with high costs and little income, many of the families displaced by the immigration enforcement raids experienced housing instability for extended periods of time. One in four families moved in with relatives, and nearly one half of the families at one studied site eventually lost their houses (Chaudry et al., 2010). Unable to make mortgage payments, families often moved into already-crowded housing and moved frequently to avoid future arrests. For families lucky enough to have their loved one released, the detainee often returned with an Electronic Monitoring Device (EMD), entailing a variety of new challenges for the family. As EMDs function in conjunction with landlines, many families in one community that was studied (Van Nuys, California) were forced to incur the additional cost of landline installation, which in many cases can be extremely difficult for those with limited credit histories. To other members of the community, EMDs pose a different type of threat. Families with members who have been detainees may find themselves evicted by scared landlords who do not want scrutiny from police or neighbors. Others voluntarily chose to separate from their families even after release in order to avoid jeopardizing other undocumented family members.

As a result of lowered income, three out of five families in the Urban Institute sample (Chaudry et al., 2010) stated that they experienced difficulty paying for food "sometimes" or "frequently." In the sixth months after arrest, 72.5 percent of the families bought food, but did not have the money to buy more after it ran out. Past six months, this number increased to 82.6 percent, as compared with the vastly different national average of 12.4 percent. In up to 22 percent of the cases, the respondent "was hungry but couldn't afford to eat" in the first six months. After this period, the number increased to over 28 percent, while the national average lingered around 3.3 percent. In many cases, parents had to choose between necessities. While some parents go without to allow their children to continue eating, even these sacrifices rarely afford the child a healthy diet. Thousands of children of undocumented immigrants—many of them American citizens—find themselves plunged into impoverished conditions due to a sudden decline in families' financial resources, subject to all the deprivations and risks associated with these insecurities.

Research shows that public assistance and entitlement programs are far less likely to reach impoverished mixed-status families (Capps & Fortuny, 2006). Citizen-children of undocumented immigrants are eligible for public benefits regardless of their parents' legal status, yet often the parents may be unaware of this fact. Some families fear that information about public assistance will be available to ICE and that they will run the risk of losing their children. Beyond rumors and fears, the application process itself presents a number of barriers to assistance. Parents who are unable to speak English or even Spanish fluently may encounter language difficulties or may not understand eligibility requirements. Furthermore, due to their immigration status, parents holding jobs in the informal sector may be unable to document the income or employment information that applications require (Capps & Fortuny, 2006). Some parents simply may be opposed to assistance on principle. Others may fear disclosing their own nationalities and subjecting themselves to discrimination. There are other hardships that children of immigrant families confront, such as children being denied public healthcare owing to the parents' undocumented status (Ayon, 2014; Cristancho, Garces, Peters, & Mueller, 2008; Kullgren, 2003). Cecilia Ayon (2014) reports that immigrants in Arizona where her study was conducted recognize that their undocumented status—or, rather, the manipulation of their fears by others—prevents them from receiving services for their children although they know that their US-born children are entitled to health and other public services. "Scare tactics," Ayon notes, "are often used to prevent individuals from accessing care for their children. For example, parents are asked for their identification cards or documents, even though they are seeking assistance for their US-born children. Because participants fear that they will be reported to immigration officials they elect to pay cash for all medical care" (p. 18). To pay for medical care that they are entitled to without charge because of fear of disclosure adds to the misery. Government offices and public services become places to avoid.

Psychologist Kalina Brabeck and attorney Qingwen Xu (2010) report that as the legal vulnerability of undocumented parents increases so, too, does their report of the impact that detention and deportation has on their families. Brabeck and Xu interviewed 132 immigrant parents, mostly mothers, from Guatemala, Colombia, Dominican Republic, El Salvador, Mexico, and Honduras. About a fifth of their participants had been in the United States for less than five years and nearly 50 percent were long-term residents. Many of the mothers had had direct experience with the deportation system either through their own cases or those of people they knew. Consequently, they felt a great vulnerability to deportation and the effects it would have on them and their families. More than half of the parents felt that the policies and practices in immigration enforcement caused them to worry about their capacity to provide financially for their families if they were to be deported.

Sociologists Jorge Chavez, Anayeli Lopez, Christine Englebrecht, and Ruben Viramontez Anguiano (2012) interviewed 40 mixed-status families in north central Indiana about the stress and uncertainty of living in a mixed-status family. Among their findings, two themes emerged: the impending possibility of arrest and the social isolation that families felt. The theme of the looming potential of arrest, detention, deportation, loss, and separation fostered an equally constant stress (Level 3 on the pyramid). Stress and having to keep guarded and watchful for police and immigration enforcement was further heightened by the talk of state-level legislation that would intensify the restrictions and penalties for immigration violations. Understandably, this day-to-day life stress added strain on relationships between parents and children and between spouses. Chavez et al.'s findings align with other research showing that immigrant parents are often so confused and worn by the ongoing stress that they cannot truly help their children deal with similar stresses in their lives (Brabeck & Xu, 2010). In the same way, the parents that Ayon (2014) studied in Arizona find it difficult to talk to their children about the toxic political environment. It is a tough job for these parents "because they are unsure about how to present the topic to their children without frightening them, or they feel like they do not have all the answers" (Ayon, 2014, p. 17). The other major theme that Chavez et al. (2012) report is the social isolation imposed on mixed-status families. Families spoke of fear in their daily lives and the increasing isolation they feel. They devise new ways of coping and techniques to evade the new restrictions and harsher penalties for immigration violations. Families in these circumstances lose many of the social support and networks they relied on and report very little involvement with their communities.

Undocumented immigrant parents frequently live in marginalized communities with limited or inferior services with few places or people to turn to for help. The people around them are also disenfranchised and low-income and hence community resources are usually limited. I have seen, though, how the contexts of these communities can embolden undocumented immigrants to seek services. For example, in the Morrisania neighborhood of the Bronx, I met many undocumented immigrant mothers of Mexican, Dominican, and Central American origins who sought help freely for their young children in a community child development center that offered excellent services (see Hausmann-Stabile, Zayas, Runes, Abenis-Cintron, & Calzada, 2011). Two factors and possibly others appeared to help these mothers seek and receive these services. One factor was the density of the community, which offers essential buffers and safety. As an inner city neighborhood inhabited by thousands of other Hispanics—documented or not—its residents protected each other and shared information freely. Another was the credibility of the agency and its affiliated hospital and the trust that the community mothers had in these institutions. They knew they would not be reported to immigration authorities and there were no local ordinances or state laws that would force providers to disclose the legal status of the patients. These perceptions of how undocumented immigrant parents find and use services are supported by the work of Qingwen Xu and Kalina Brabeck (2012) who report that undocumented immigrants parents "learned about and navigated systems to access services for their children with the support of their social networks and through their community . . . they learned about services that would be available to their families, particularly free services that did not check legal documentation. Family members, friends, neighbors, and coworkers, especially those who have been in the United States for a longer period of time, speak English, and 'know the system'" (p. 215).

Vital connective networks offer valuable information on such things as enrolling children in school, finding clinics with Spanish-speaking staff, and accessing public programs.

Communities and organization that have a welcoming attitude for immigrants regardless of population density can have positive effects on the economic prospects and health and well-being of immigrants (Delva et al., 2013). In other places, there is no hiding. These are typically the cities and towns where the density of the Hispanic population is low and the visibility of the unauthorized immigrants is high. The newer or smaller the immigrant community, for that matter, the fewer ethnic agencies and trusted institutions that will be found. It is in situations like this, when there are few protections around them, that the children of undocumented immigrants are ceaselessly disquieted by the possible separations from parents.

GROWING UP AMERICAN

The children introduced in this chapter are doing well in life, generally speaking. Although the broad political, social, and economic issues surrounding immigration and the anti-immigrant debate affect them, they are American children, born, raised, schooled, and socialized as members of the United States The United States is not only their birthplace but also, for most of them, the only home they have ever known. They typically have good, strong parents and are in good health. They may choose to identify as Hispanic, Latino, or Latina. Or they may even state that their ethnic identity derives from their parents' heritage and identify as Salvadoran, Honduran, Mexican, or Dominican. But they more commonly think of themselves as Americans. They keep silent about their parents and their undocumented siblings and huddle in the shadows with parents who cannot attract attention. The children are average American kids but only to a point, because they cannot relax their vigilance in protection of their parents and themselves. The anxiety and fear of disclosure get communicated to children by the parents' words and actions and anxieties. As we see in Dreby's pyramid, carrying the burden of their parent's deportability has an erosive effect on children's mental health.

NOTES

1. Working memory refers to the brain's system for storing and managing information for short-term use. It is the capacity to hold many pieces of facts, or

transitory information such as visual images and verbal information, so that it can be manipulated for the purposes of application and communication. Language comprehension, reasoning, and problem-solving and mathematical abilities are thought to depend on working memory.

2. The term *anchor baby* denotes a child born in the United States who, because of birthright, becomes an American citizen and then makes it possible for parents to achieve legal status and to bring other relatives into the country. It gained traction in 2006 when it began to be widely used as a slur against undocumented immigrants, primarily. By 2010, Republicans and many on the conservative right had taken the term in their fight against illegal immigration. Senators Jon Kyl (R-AZ) and Lindsay Graham (R-SC) were among the leaders who argued for a short time that it was necessary to repeal sections of the 14th Amendment that grants citizenship to anyone born in the United States. The Canadian counterpart to *anchor baby* is *passport baby* and is associated with so-called "birth tourism" in which unscrupulous immigration consultants told women to prevent the detection of their pregnancies when entering the country and then give birth in Canada to take advantage of Canada's many benefits in health care and education.

3. In 1997, the United States was home to the greatest percentage of impoverished children than almost every other industrialized nation. Approximately one-half of these children lived in families whose incomes were under half of the poverty line, and the percentage of young children in extreme poverty was increasing even faster than the overall child poverty rate (Aber et al., 1997).

CHAPTER 5

Rules and Responsibility, Guilt and Shame

Undocumented parents may try to protect their children from all possible harm, but as we've seen, their tenuous economic situation and the threat of deportation weaken their ability to do so. Some parents feel that their children are too young to understand the nuances of what immigration policy means and what it can do to destabilize their families, and thus may avoid talking to their children about legal status altogether (Dreby, 2012). Parents often encourage their children to stay close to home and limit activities at school and in the neighborhood. To protect their children and provide as normal a life as possible, some parents try "to shield their children from the negative effects of changing immigration enforcement, often at great toll to themselves. Yet, despite their efforts, the constant fear of being detained by the police and the associated threat of deportation is too great to allow their children to properly integrate in the community" (Chavez et al., 2012, p. 646). Children start to wonder why their parents are so restrictive; they become keenly attuned to their parents' every anxiety, action, change in mood, and behavioral changes. Their parents' insecurities become theirs, too.

Near the bottom of Dreby's pyramid of deportation burdens, Level 2 is organized around the constant fear and worry of deportation and what it can do to the child and her family. Deportation burdens accumulate, building level by level. We saw in the last chapter how a parent's arrest, loss of job, and loss of income cascades into a series of problems that include financial hardship, food and housing insecurity, and compromised health and health care utilization, corresponding to Level 3 of the pyramid. The pathways from economic adversity to emotional anguish and negative behavioral outcomes can be as varied as is each family.

On Level 4, long-term effects on children come from the constant dread of disclosing their parents' legal status. Children live ever mindful of the fact that immigration officials can discover and deport one or both of their parents. Protracted stress occurs with the everyday micro-incidents at school and other public places that cause children's anxiety and fears to spike. Sometimes this spike isn't momentary; it endures for days, not giving the child enough time to recover. There is little respite from the constant vigilance they must keep. The lives and futures of undocumented parents and their mixed-status families hang in the balance every day, and every situation or incident that reminds them of the delicate state of affairs in which they live has a corrosive effect on their long-term well-being. In this chapter, I look at the psychological well-being of citizen-children living under the threat of deportation. What is the mental and emotional wear-and-tear that citizen-children experience in the course of everyday life? What are the physical and mental health consequences?

FRIGHT, FIGHT, AND FLIGHT

Undocumented children and citizen-children may be typical kids in many ways, but they live unique lives defined by their parents' status as unauthorized immigrants. Mostly they live in fear, that very human condition that motivates our learning and protects us from real or imagined threats (Hall, 1897). A state of constant negativity about legal status and daytime vigilance—at school, at the shopping center, at the playground—has its corrosive effect on the psychological status of citizen-children. The cumulative effects of everyday insults, micro-aggressions, and trauma, as well as less routine events like immigration raids and deportation of their friends' and schoolmates' parents take an extensive toll on them. Even voluntary departures that separate parents and children can result in the development of psychopathological symptoms (Henderson & Baily, 2013).

Worry and fear are normal responses to danger that help us survive. They warn us when danger is near and alert us to fight or flee. As with other emotional states, we cannot live in a state of fear for long before we begin to show its caustic effects: the ailments and breakdowns of our bodies, the tricks our minds play on us, and those peculiar behaviors that others often notice before we are fully aware of them. Our perceptual apparatus and problem-solving abilities are weakened and our memory is distorted (Mackie & Hamilton, 1993). The brain's capacity to store and process information is reduced. Fear can damage social interaction, lead to social isolation, and affect our sense of who we are (Gullone & King, 1993).

Fear is different from fright, that momentary startled response. As Sidney Stewart (1956) wrote:

> Fright is a thing of the moment, attacking as a cornered animal does, on a second's notice. But fear is an ulcerous growth, pulsating and alive, attached to you like a jungle leech . . . Sometimes it is not so bad, but then again it grips you and binds you as though it will not allow you the smallest movement. Again, at other times, through absolute weariness, you feel you can be free from it. But no, you can only hope to control it. It is always there. It lives with you . . . (p. 45)

Stewart's metaphoric description of fear as ulcerous and leechlike has a corresponding scientific explanation that comes from neuroendocrinology and stress physiology. Scientists have examined the underlying psychological processes that explain why childhood poverty has such pervasive ill effects on development and adult morbidity. Findings show that the unremitting stress that accompanies poverty damages children's biological and regulatory systems, leaving physical and psychological scars that lead to higher-than-average susceptibility to chronic diseases (Evans & Kim, 2013).

The human body wasn't built to sustain stress for long. Rather, our stress response system was intended to react to acute stress—those moments of fear and worry that are best managed when they are brief (Sapolsky, 1994). Our brains are geared to turn on and activate the fight-and-flight response in the face of threat. This natural defense response to fear and worry raises the person's heart rate and blood pressure, and turns on other cardiovascular systems. Then, when the danger is gone, the body turns off the stress response and returns to a less alert state. In the short term, the flight-fight response helps. But when adversity and stress is chronic, as is the case with children living in poverty, the stress response system is mostly "on" and seldom "off." The body and brain do not recover from the stress and our natural stress management system is, to use a term, overstressed. This chronic situation exerts damaging effects on our physical and mental health, creating symptoms of posttraumatic stress, increasing the risk for depression and other mental illness, and lowering life expectancy.

Immigrant parents' own state of worry and anxiety about the vulnerable legal status they occupy is transmitted to their young children through words and deeds (Yoshikawa, 2011) and, I add, by everyday-strains and tensions they subtly betray. Because children are so keenly attuned to their parents' changes in mood and anxiety, the children become anxious, too. Researchers (Dreby, 2012; De Genova, 2010; Talavera, Núñez-Mchiri, & Heyman, 2010) report uniformly that the lingering possibility of parents' deportation affects children, leaving them with constant anxiety and vigilance about the potential becoming real. To demonstrate the depth of the impact that this wariness has on the psychological functioning of children, I turn once again to participants in my study: Felicita, Alejandra, and Leticia.

Felicita

Felicita, the citizen-child we met in Chapter 4, lives with her two parents and a 17-year-old sister, all of whom are without papers. Felicita said her parents work long hours, her father in a cleaning company and her mother in a hair salon. They work very hard to provide as balanced a life as they can. Her pride in her parents (both are college educated) and the pleasure of family life is apparent in Felicita's lively descriptions—when they go to the cinema together, her parents always choose educational movies for their daughters, such as *Lincoln* and *Les Miserables*. Nevertheless, Felicita's tone and demeanor changed when she told our interviewer, Andrea, about the interior tensions and worry she felt.

> I feel frightened, sort of, that they are gonna come and deport them and send them back to Mexico, especially my sister, who I really, really need, because when my parents are not here I stay with her. They tell me "when we are not here anymore you are gonna need your sister." And I'm like yeah, and I thought, like my sister, when she was in my mom's, like in a bag right here [she makes a gesture as if holding a baby carrier], she too migrated, technically. So I was like, so my sister, my mom, and my dad can be deported. This can happen. I don't want that to happen. [A nervous laughter betrays Felicita.] When I was little I thought that when somebody came I would just, I would just grab some snowballs, I don't know, and throw them at them, at the ICE people. I would say, like no, leave my parents alone, leave my family alone! And they would get away.
>
> Once I had a dream that they were looking for me, and my parents, and my sister. It happened the night I was in my cousin's house for a sleep over. It was a very strange dream because first we were playing hide and seek. Then there were these buses that, umm, that they were riding around in, and they were looking for, they were looking for people, and I didn't know who they were looking for. Then they said or I heard people shouting "Show me your

papers!" I was like what's going on? We are just playing hide and seek, me and my friends, and I wasn't good at hiding at all. I wasn't good at it and so my friends they had black hoodies, and they could cover themselves well but I had a pink sweater. I was like, I don't get what the black hoodies are gonna help. And so then they covered themselves and they run. I was left out until they found me and they took me in the bus. And they took me to, I don't know, this jail. It was a nightmare and my mom was right there in the dream and her hands were covered in blood because she had scraped them on the grass. My dad was up to the very top, because it was a two-story bus. He was at the top because the boys and girls were separated, and my sister was there too, but she was at the very front. But I was sitting next to my mom. I was little and that's when I woke up at my cousin's and I was like "Oh my God."

We see the residue of a child's daytime worry in her dream. In her young mind, she entertains fantasies of how she can save her parents, including one in which she plans a little escape. In that fantasy, she goes to Mexico to visit her deported parents and to "try my best to get them out, or something. With my friends we make a fundraiser or something, like I remember that my friends and I wanted to make a lemonade stand or something to raise money, and so then I'm like well we could use that money to go get my parents. But I try not to think about it. I should not really go that deep into the future, because then that would really affect me and make me more sad or depressed."

The dream of being apprehended and jailed is also reflected in Felicita's fear of jails.

I try my best not to think about that or go near jails, because there is this jail close to my school, and I try not to look at it because I think that there might be deported people there, and I'm like, well, I hope that's not where my parents go . . . and so I try my best to stay away from it.

Alejandra

Disruption has been a constant in the life of Alejandra, a 14-year-old from Central Texas. As with other children in my study, Alejandra's scores on an instrument that measures children and adolescents' level of anxiety showed that she had clinical levels of separation anxiety. Loss looms greatly over Alejandra and her family as she told Marina Islas, a research interviewer. Her younger sister was diagnosed with brain cancer and underwent expensive treatment, ultimately forcing the family to leave a secure, two-story home in Austin. Although the cancer has gone into remission, the treatment expenses devastated the family and they have moved to a small trailer south of Austin. The trailer is dilapidated, with only a plywood floor and exposed insulation along the walls. Sheets hang at one end of the trailer's living room in an attempt to partition off sleeping areas. Despite these meager conditions, the home is tidy and smells of bleach, as though regularly cleaned. They are a loving, unified family, but Alejandra feels the stress of deportation looming over them.

> Knowing that they don't have papers, we cannot do nothing. At first I felt bad because my grandma, she was dying, and . . . [Alejandra began to cry, interspersing her story with sobs. Marina offered Alejandra tissues.] She talked to us. My grandma told my dad, like she predicted, that he wasn't gonna come to Mexico. Every time she came to Texas to see us and she told us hopefully, we could go to Mexico to see her. And my dad said he promised to go but she was really sick. My grandma called over the phone and said, "I thought y'all were gonna come?" And my dad said he would try. But the next day my dad's brother said that she passed away. And we felt really bad because we made her a promise that we couldn't keep.

Alejandra mentioned that she had nightmares, and told Marina about one in particular. In the most salient of her dreams, Alejandra was at school when some police officers came to her classroom. The police escorted her to the principal's office and told her that her parents were taken by immigration. The officers told her, "Y'all are gonna be sent for adoption. Something like that." When Alejandra told her favorite teacher about the dream, he was comforting and reassuring. "So that gave me a little bit of relief," Alejandra said.

Marina asked if her family "talked about what you would do if the worst case scenario was to happen and your parents were taken away? Do you have a plan or anything?"

> No. 'Cause we never thought that could happen so we never talk about it. If that ever happened I would stick with my siblings and not like protest but tell the person that is settling our case to let our parents live in the United States because they've lived here so many years that they should have rights to papers. So, my parents, my siblings, we'll stick to each other and just pray to God that they'll just give them the papers and just let us live happily ever after.

Leticia

This nearly 12-year-old girl from San Marco, Texas, is the child of a Cuban father and Mexican mother. Her father died of a heart attack while in jail; it is unclear why he was there and Leticia said she did not know. She is very aware that her mother does not have papers. Leticia told the project interviewer in our study, Marina, that she could not stop thinking about the possibility of her mother being deported. She said she finds it hard to go to school and concentrate when she is worried about her mother.

> My mom works hard and she has to work everywhere. And like what about any minute a police pulls her over and ask her for her like papers or something like that? And she doesn't have them! So like that's kind of hard to think of. Because you don't know if anything can happen during the day while you're away. Because that's exactly what happened to my friend. His dad was working and they pulled him over because he looked suspicious and then they asked him for his papers and he didn't have them and they deported him. So that's just like hard thinking that it could happen to my mother. Like what would we do if that happened? But I don't like imagining that. Like I like imagining that someday my mom will get her papers and that it will all work out.

Leticia said she has nightmares in which evil men capture her and her mother and she must choose between her mother living or surviving herself. She said she chooses to die for her mother. She said, "My mom and me were in a building I think. We were both like sitting there in desks and two guys with two guns came up to us. And they held them to our heads and they asked me, they asked that we had a choice if we wanted to live. And that they would let either one of us to go outside. And I told my mom she could leave me behind. I think about it all day.

RULES TO LIVE BY

From over 30 in-depth interviews with citizen-children whose parents had never been detained or deported, we learned about rules of conduct that their parents insisted they follow. Two rules that parents expected them to observe were most salient.

> Rule One is "Don't talk."
> Rule Two is "Sit still."

The rules were taught, maybe browbeaten or drilled into them by parents and siblings, often reinforced by the culture of their communities.

These are rules so important that they add to children's ongoing adversity: it means that their stress response system must always be "on," alert to dangers related to their parents' legal status. The kids did not always understand (depending on their developmental level) why their parents were insisting on particular behaviors or why the rules seem to change depending on where they were: "sit still," "watch out," "do not talk," "do not attract attention," "be careful who you speak to," "do not say more than you need to," and similar instructions. Citizen-children consistently told us that they did not talk to others about their parents' undocumented status and that they were always told to behave in public for fear of drawing attention to their parents.

Rule One: Don't Talk

The first rule that even the youngest children—as early as six—learn is to be quiet about matters related to the family but especially about their parents' legal status. It is a rule that pervades their lives and under which they must constantly operate. It is not a rule invoked only on some occasions or at a moment's call but rather it is a rule that regulates the children's conduct in all manner of public and semipublic arenas. Maybe they can ask questions at home and discuss it with siblings but that is the extent of it. Little Virginia, in Chapter 1, kept quiet entirely because she had not yet learned to judge when, where, and to whom she could speak. A number of our citizen-children did not want teachers and kids at school to know their parents' legal status. Only their close friends, most of whom were the children of unauthorized immigrants, were trusted interlocutors. What follows are examples from children in our research.

Rafaela is a 9-and-a-half-year-old girl in California with an undocumented mother and US citizen father. Her father has not been able to help his wife get her papers because she had entered the country illegally and would have to leave the country before she could file for residency. Her return could be delayed by months and possibly years. Rafaela's parents talked about their hopes that immigration reform will help them. Rafaela was also comfortable talking about her mother's status to Mariana Ruiz del Rio, our interviewer, because she understood the trusting, confidential nature of our project. Rafaela, according to Mariana, "wanted to make sure that I understood that she was 'normal' and that her mother's situation is not the best but not the end of the world." The worst-case scenario for Rafaela would be her mother's deportation, yet she knows her family "will find a way to be together," an important psychological comfort for children to have. Rafaela told Mariana that her mother had discussed being undocumented with her. Rafaela describes it this way: "It was just like a normal day and she, well, I don't know what happened, but we were getting in the car and she told me that I must always put on my seatbelt because she doesn't have any papers. If they stop us she could be sent to Mexico and we would have to stay here." Rafaela felt "really bad because I have seen many kids on TV news and stuff that lose their parents because they don't have papers."

Rafaela was perhaps the only child in our study who understood that having to go back to Mexico for many years was a form of punishment. In her naïve way, Rafaela told our interviewer Mariana, "I think it means that she can't, she can't be here until she gets her papers. She has to go to Mexico to get them and to do the *castigo* [punishment]. I really don't know what the *castigo* is but I think it's something like that she will have to stay in Mexico for like, well they are going to assign her how much. A few years, like five or seven." Like other children, Rafaela doesn't talk to anyone at school about her mom not having papers. "I just don't talk about it with anyone really."

Micaela recalls that she found out that her parents don't have papers when a conversation with her peers prompted her to ask her parents some questions.

"A bunch of my friends were saying that they went to Mexico," she began. "When I came home I asked my mom why can't we go to Mexico and she told me. I was like nine years old." Mariana asked her if she thought that her parents' lack of papers made her life different from other children. She responded, "Yeah. Like a lot of people are very racist at my school. And a lot of them say, 'Go back where you came from.'" Micaela explained that she had accidentally told the other children at school about her parents. "I was like talking to my friends about something and it came up. I don't really know why and I guess they overheard and that's how they found out." She had learned a lesson that was reinforced by her parents, and went on to say, "Now I only talk about it with my friends [whose parents are also undocumented]."

Several children provided painful accounts of living in silence, not simply because of the rule of keeping quiet but because of the constriction it caused in their lives. One girl, Lourdes, could not talk about her mother, someone she was obviously very proud of and loved very much. Another child, Orlando, also had to carry the responsibility of protecting his parents, something all kids seem to feel but which he voiced aloud.

Lourdes, a 10-year-old girl in California, left us with some of the most wrenching words of any of the project's participants when she lamented that she could not speak openly to anyone about her mother, the person she most admired. She could not tell anyone at school about her mother's wonderful, delicious cooking or how much fun they had together making up games to occupy themselves. She could not tell others how much she admired her mother. She always had to hold back. Her mother could not do some of the most basic things parents do at their children's schools. She could not attend Lourdes' school events or volunteer in Lourdes' classes like other class mothers. Her mother had to remain invisible, anonymous. Lourdes explained, "My mom has to act different from other families because she doesn't have papers. Like, she can't sign our paperwork for school or our homework. My dad has to sign. My mom can't drive me to classes. It makes me feel sad. [At the school] they don't know my mom's name and stuff. They only see my dad's signature on my homework and permission papers. I can't tell anyone about my mom because my mom doesn't want me to tell anyone. She told me that she could get in trouble if I talk to people about it."

Lourdes had to hold back on all the noble sentiments that a daughter can have about her mother for fear of exposing her mother. One can only wonder, for now, what the long-term impact will be on a child, such as Lourdes, of having to deny someone so precious, so beloved as her mother.

Orlando, a 12-year-old boy from outside Sacramento, California, like many other children voiced the sense of responsibility that hovered over him constantly. His mother is undocumented as is his younger sister. Yet, he and an older brother are US citizens. The parents are divorced and the younger child was born when the parents relocated to Mexico in an attempt to save their marriage. Asked if his family had to do things differently from other families because his mother and sister don't have papers, he replied, "Yeah, we take care a little more than other families." Neither his friends nor his teachers know of his mother's status.

"They don't know," Orlando told Mariana, "I've never told them. I don't talk to them about this . . . or to anyone really. My mom tells me not to tell anyone she doesn't have papers because I can get her into trouble."

Daniel is a nearly 12-year-old boy who echoed Lourdes' and Orlando's words. He, too, avoided talking about his mother. When asked why, he responded, "Because I don't want to get my mom in trouble, and she always tells me that I have to tell people that she does have papers because she doesn't want to get in trouble." To keep a secret, Daniel also has to lie.

Rule Two: Sit Still

The command, *"¡Quieto!"* (Sit still!), was often followed by "Behave," according to many of the children. Whereas the first rule was taught and observed in far-sweeping and ongoing ways, the second rule is most often invoked suddenly and without warning by parents. Children must obey quickly in response to an immediate or obvious threat. As they age, citizen-children know when they need to "sit still and behave," no one has to tell them; they have learned why. At home, on the playground, at family gatherings, and even at school they are allowed to loosen the constraints of this rule. But that can change abruptly. The constant vigilance of being uncovered is evident when the children in our study told of being admonished to avoid any behavior that would draw attention to them and their parents. They were to sit still and behave. They were not to argue, yell, or do anything in public that would bring attention to them and their parents, especially from the police. Public tantrums could simply not happen. Several children told of family car trips to the shopping center or mall a few blocks away or to other cities and states to visit family, and the tension of watching out for police cars and sitting still. Omar, a 12-year-old boy from San Marcos, Texas, who was interviewed by Eden Hernandez Robles, gave a remarkably interesting story of how he learned why he had to be well behaved.

Omar only recently learned that his parents are undocumented. He had become curious about his parents' behavior. Two things gnawed at him. The first was his parents' insistence on good behavior, which at times seemed excessive to him. He had grown up understanding that his parents wanted him to be well behaved in general and especially in front of police. As a result, Omar did his best to be a good and obedient son; it wasn't something that troubled him. But then he noticed something else about his parents: whenever they drove to family outings, his father and mother would be on the lookout for police cars.

"We go to a ranch a lot to be with our family and like my parents look out for cops. My dad and mom would keep saying, like, 'there they are.' Once, a police car came behind us and my father got scared, like nervous." He saw the same anxiety at other times when the family drove somewhere or when a police car came near to their car. On one such trip, Omar's father was pulled over by the police for some minor traffic violation or malfunction in the car. Omar did not really know what it was and the police let his father go because "my father had nothing on his record." But Omar saw an unusually high level of anxiety in his parents that day and kept quiet. He did not want to upset them any more than they were already. When the time felt right, Omar asked his father why he always got so nervous when the police were around, especially as he "hadn't done nothing." His father told him that the reason he and Omar's mother were nervous was because they were in the United States illegally, *sin papeles*. Omar now recognized the difference between the average driver, watching for the police to avoid getting caught speeding, and his parents' legal status. They had to watch for the police because of their legal status and the mighty implications of being stopped.

> Sometimes we go to Houston to see family members and then we see cops on the highway. As we get nearer, we just get still. Or sometimes we are just still the whole way. Like just behaving, just sitting there. My parents look out for cops. *But just not like regular people here.* Like they don't have papers. My parents don't have papers [he repeated]. Every time they see cops stopping someone they say like "Omar, be still, to be like . . . calm." They want me to keep still, like quiet so the police don't have to look over at us. 'Cause probably the cops would stop us and probably send my parents back to Mexico. They tell us before we leave, like to behave during the car ride. Like if we see cops or something just, like, be still. Just sit.

He had to behave like this virtually every time he was in public.

"Even like when there are festivals, like you know there is a lot of police everywhere, so I behave better than I behave [*sic*]." When there are no police around, then he can relax.

Until his father was stopped by the police, Omar had seen it as just a routine thing and that his father's anxiety was natural, he did want to get a ticket. Discovering his father's and his mother's legal status changed Omar's perspective on the past and present. It wasn't that his parents thought he was behaving badly. They were worried about the consequences of discovery. This made him feel better; he felt they truly trusted him. Still, he dug back into his memories to reconcile incidents and perceptions from the past with the knowledge that he now had—a process of cognitive and emotional restructuring. Eden wrote that Omar "came close to crying" several times as he narrated his story.

Once, Omar behaved just to be the good son. Now he behaved because he carried a heavy responsibility for his parents. Misbehavior could not be tolerated; it wasn't an option for Omar. Misbehavior could have deportation consequences.

Alejandra, the 14-year-old girl in Texas we met earlier in this chapter, remembers a time when her family was driving together, and an ICE patrol car pulled up next to them. Her father insisted immediately and with alarm in his voice that the children be still and behave. He then steered the car over a lane to put space between his car and the ICE vehicle. When Alejandra asked her father why he told them to behave and why he switched lanes, he pointed out that there was an ICE car driving next to them and they did not want to be stopped because mom and dad did not have papers. At the time, Alejandra did not quite understand the extent of the situation. Her father went on to say, "We're immigrants." Still, Alejandra didn't understand what *immigrant* meant.

"No. They told us that they came illegally to the United States—without papers. First I thought it was 'papers,'" Alejandra said, referring to sheets of paper. "But he said no, it was a certain type of paper that give 'em . . . that makes them official. That they're in the United States and they have the right to be there."

A RESPONSIBILITY TOO GREAT: GUILT AND SHAME

Leticia's dream—to save herself or to save her mother—and the two cardinal rules that were repeated by many citizen-children reveal the psychological trials of these young Americans. There are likely more than two rules that exist but that did not find expression in the narratives of the citizen-children we interviewed. It is possible that neither our researchers nor the children know they exist, that the children had not yet put other rules into words, or that they knew other codes but did not want to expose them. The fact that the rules to be quiet and sit still were so often repeated reveals how salient they truly are. We heard the same guidelines from children who had never met each other, children living in South or Central Texas, and those in Sacramento County, California, allowing us to easily deduce commonalities. Moreover, the fact that these lessons appear in the children's narratives denotes their significance in everyday life. These are proscriptions that they must live by every day and cannot violate even in moments of unguardedness. Choices they have to make on a daily basis, certainly not as tragic as the one in Leticia's dream, are part of a vital calculus designed, however unconsciously, to preserve the integrity of their family.

More troubling is that such rules and decisions reveal something much more profound than just obedience. Citizen-children feel that they hold their parents' fates—and by definition their own lives—in their hands. This is not a figment but a reality; what they do or say can have devastating consequences. We heard it time after time: follow the two rules to avoid getting their parents into trouble with the police or immigration officials. Misbehaving in the wrong place or talking too much to the wrong persons can rend apart their lives with disastrous repercussions for the entire family. Citizen-children must help keep their family members' unauthorized statuses secret. In some instances, they must make complicated moral decisions, such as whether to lie, to preserve the secret. This is too great a responsibility for any child to carry without repercussions.

It is easy to see the worry and the fear in the children's comments. Recall that Lourdes said that her mother "could get in trouble if I talk to people about it." Orlando's words were that "My mom tells me not to tell anyone she doesn't have papers because I can get her into trouble." And Daniel said he had to behave "Because I don't want to get my mom in trouble, and she always tells me that I have to tell people that she does have papers because she doesn't want to get in trouble." Most children behave because they have been taught to do so by their parents. And even if they misbehave the outcomes are not severe; they do not result in charges lodged by law enforcement against the parent. The child's bad behavior may lead to some form of punishment by the parents, such as time out or being grounded; maybe they have to use their weekly allowance money to replace something they broke, make restitution. In most every other family, a misbehaving child, even one that comes to the attention of the police, does not cause their parents to be arrested. This is an unusual responsibility, a heavy burden for any child to carry. To hold the fate of a parent in one's hands is utterly unthinkable for most children. Except in the rare physical crisis, like a fire or capsized boat, in which a child must act to save her parent or sibling—and make the decision instantaneously—the average child scarcely ever has to face this kind of anguishing situation.

What can we expect the psychological and somatic fallout to be from having this monumental responsibility as a child, at a time when social, emotional, and cognitive faculties are still developing? Worse still, what can happen when the child fails to observe the responsibility, hold it securely, or handle it properly? What happens if the child lets it slip through his or her hands in a moment of distress or carelessness? Probably guilt and its more malignant cousin, shame. Guilt and shame are both emotional reactions that children as young as preschool-age experience when they feel they have failed to do something or have done a wrongful act (Kochanska, Barry, Jimenez, Hollatz, & Woodard, 2009; Thompson & Hoffman, 1980). These two affective experiences sit on a spectrum that connects them but guilt and shame are distinct in some important ways, and they have different effects on people (Ferguson, Stegge, Miller, & Olsen, 1999; Roos, Hodges, & Salmivalli, 2014).

To elaborate the distinction, guilt comes from the awareness that one's actions can or have hurt someone. It is an internal and specific attribution of the harm it can do or did (Tangney & Dearing, 2002). It feels uncomfortable; it agitates with regret, worry, remorse, fear, tension, and anxiety. The other unique element that comes with guilt is empathy; we recognize and consider the victim's feelings after the wrongdoing. In reaction, we try to fix the situation. But we fear the results of our actions and admit culpability to ourselves and to others. Guilt has been linked to prosocial or positive human behaviors (Roos et al., 2014). The experience of guilt lowers aggression and negative social behaviors, regardless of the gender of the child (Thompson & Hoffman, 1980). In early adolescence, guilt reduces (and shame increases) the likelihood of experiencing depression and lashing out at the world.

The guilt of the citizen-child is mostly about what they *might* cause to happen to parents and siblings. Citizen-children may be consumed with the worry of doing wrong, or conversely failing to do the right thing to protect their parents and families. It shapes how they think and how they control themselves, which speaks to the positive aspect of guilt as well. This may be why so many of the citizen-children we interviewed were exceptionally well behaved. Perhaps they were not doing well academically, but they were kids who showed no signs of defiant, rebellious, discourteous, or petulant behaviors. They showed self-control, a behavior that guilt may help regulate.

"The difference between shame and guilt is far more than a matter of intensity," write psychologists Paula Niedenthal, June Price Tangney, and Igor Gavansky (1994). "Shame is not merely a more intense form of guilt. Rather, shame and guilt appear to vary along a range of cognitive, affective, and motivational dimensions" (p. 593). Shame has little curative value, and is generally more debilitating. Whereas guilt is a focused condemnation of an act or a failure to act, shame involves a condemnation of the self for some major failure or transgression (Niedenthal, Tangney, & Gavansky, 1994). Guilt is unstable, short-lived, maybe even transient, and specific (i.e., guilt for one or few wrongful actions), but shame is maladaptive. It is stable, enduring, and it condemns the person as a whole, not just as an actor, "resulting in a more severe threat to the self, compared with guilt" (Roos et al., 2014, p. 941). Shame brings with it humiliation, disgrace, and worthlessness, inducing the child to feel helpless and incompetent. The child wants to escape or become invisible and anonymous to the world because it seems that everyone knows the child's badness. Whereas guilt can stand for "I did something bad," shame stands for "I am bad," a more poisonous affective or emotional state. Research further shows that shame is strongly correlated with aggression (Roos et al., 2014).

To be sure, guilt has its good properties but only to an extent. The child may respond with empathy to the distress of the person they have harmed; the more distressed the victim the more guilt-aroused the perpetrator (Thompson & Hoffman, 1980). But it can cause harm in the long run, because guilt held too long can convert to shame. The sense of culpability and heightened, internal guilt erodes emotional functioning. Pathologies that come from unabated guilt can have an obsessive rumination that begins with "what I did was wrong" and progress to "what I did was awful" and conclude in the shame that "I am awful." Persistent thoughts like these underlie depression and other internalizing disorders (Ferguson et al., 1999).

HOW LONG MUST THEY LIVE THIS WAY?

Immigration law is fundamentally based on trauma and fear. The threat of ICE raids alone serves as a fear-arousing method of discouraging undocumented immigrants from moving about freely through the very prospect of trauma (Wilson, 2000). The threats are also demoralizing to the immigrant. ICE raids often occur in the early hours of the morning, quickly removing parents from workplaces or households in a swift event that emphasizes trauma. This strategy creates an intentional climate of fear for a heightened emotional impact on the immigrant and his or her relatives (Thronson, 2008). In a system so reliant on fear, practices that are traumatic to undocumented immigrants can be extremely detrimental to their children. Young children who are present at the time of their parent's arrest or apprehension frequently suffer flashbacks, recurring nightmares, and other signs of psychological distress centered on the event, effects of a painful early childhood experience that may lead to other problems later in life (Baum et al., 2010).

The recent intensification of immigration enforcement activities by ICE has put citizen-children of undocumented parents at "increasing risk for family separation, economic hardship, and psychological trauma" (Lamberg, 2008, p. 780). In the aftermath of an immigration arrest, children of undocumented parents often miss school, move away, lose their academic focus, and may eventually drop out of school (Chaudry et al., 2010). The child's family atmosphere may become tense, as might occur on Dreby's Level 4 of the burdens pyramid. The stress of reduced income and interrupted employment may lead to arguments. Parents' behavior toward their children may be changed, where warmth is replaced by constant tension. The child may feel a more insecure attachment, and may not receive the emotional support necessary to develop a strong sense of self-confidence and socially adept behaviors. As a deficit of affection or displays of love continues, the child may experience an increase in depression and dependence, conditions that can be difficult to reverse (Aber et al., 1997). Studies reveal that children of undocumented immigrants often display attentional deficits, withdrawal and depression, anxiety and depression, and rule-breaking behaviors (Delva et al., 2013).

There is an undeniable relationship between the undocumented parents' legal vulnerability and children's well-being (Brabeck & Xu, 2010). The children of deported parents consistently show more internalizing problems (i.e., withdrawal, depression, guilt, anxiety, social isolation) and externalizing problems (e.g., rule-breaking, antisocial or delinquent acts, aggression, and fighting) at significantly higher levels than children whose parents were challenging their deportation orders or children whose undocumented parents were under no deportation orders (Allen, Cisneros, & Tellez, 2013).

Children in immigrant families may be less likely to have behavioral problems than those with US-born parents, but the children of immigrant families are more likely to feel worthless and withdrawn compare to those with nonimmigrant parents (Degboe, BeLue, & Hillemeier, 2012). When others harbor negative stereotypes about immigrant children, they project these biases as we saw in the pyramid of deportation burdens. Immigrant children suffer from these stereotypes in their self-perceptions (Suárez-Orozco & Suárez-Orozco, 2001). People who feel they are perceived as negative are more likely to engage in poor or self-defeating behaviors, sometimes resigning themselves to hopelessness. In early life, a child must achieve a sense of autonomy and be encouraged to act freely on her environment or suffer shame and doubt when she is stymied or rejected (Erikson, 1950). If a child's initiative to succeed in his environment, a success that leads to a sense of purpose, is thwarted, belittled, or backfires, guilt from the sense of failure or wrongdoing is induced.

Fear, guilt, and shame are miserable emotions. Keeping quiet and behaving well under conditions of unceasing fear may be rules to live by, and may help social and emotional functioning. Citizen-children's responsibility to protect their parents by behaving enhances their self-control and emotional regulation (barring other unforeseen traumas). Yet, this self-regulation is motivated by fear and maintained by the sense of guilt. How long can children live with this responsibility before the signs of psychological erosion begin to show? Dropping their guard, missing a cue, making a mistake, looking the wrong way, or trusting the wrong person, just to name some possible moments of unintentional irresponsibility, might even move the citizen-child from bearing simple guilt to feeling agonizing shame if the parent is arrested, detained, and eventually deported. If detention and deportation happen to a parent because of a momentary lapse in the fearful vigilance and guilt-induced self-restraint, the citizen-child may be doomed to live in shame, humiliation, and disgrace. "How can I ever forgive myself," the citizen-child might ask. No child should be placed in such a predicament, yet our current immigration enforcement system is uniquely structured to do just that.

CHAPTER 6

Arrest and Detention, and the Aftermath

Social isolation and the chronic psychological strain of living in the diffused light of unauthorized status take their toll on citizen-children and their mixed-status families. Up to this point, I have focused on comprehending the varied motives for taking the bold steps to immigrate in spite of many dangers and examining the life of immigrants, in the shadows. To continue to the next steps in the sequence toward deportation, I now discuss what happens when undocumented parents are arrested by police officers and detained by the immigration system. Arrest is the dreaded event, the one that undocumented immigrants and their children anticipate wearily every day of their lives. This is a close look at the first steps in the process toward potential or eventual deportation.

APPREHENSION

Once in the United States, the moment most feared by the undocumented immigrant is a direct encounter with law enforcement agencies. That meeting can be with Immigration and Customs Enforcement (ICE) or Customs and Border Protection (CBP), both under the umbrella of the US Department of Homeland Security (DHS), or it can be with local law enforcement. An arrest[1] can occur while living and traveling domestically, or during ICE raids on workplaces or communities. Or the arrest can happen because of an encounter with CBP, the agency responsible for security and apprehension activities on the borders and other points of entry into the country, such as shipping ports, airports, and border checkpoints. In other circumstances, a run-in with local police and state law enforcement bureaus can initiate the process. If the local and state police are working in cooperation with ICE or CBP, the person apprehended can be funneled into the immigration enforcement system. Anytime an immigrant is unable to show proof of legal status, he or she is subject to being arrested.

Most apprehensions begin with a routine practice of law enforcement: a traffic stop. The majority of these are a result of minor driving offenses such as a broken taillight or making a lane change without signaling, though it can be a more serious event such as a traffic accident or suspicion of intoxication. During these routine or investigative stops, police officers will ask the driver for identification. In some municipalities, failure to carry a license may only result in a ticket, whereas other towns and cities adhere to policies that require automatic arrest and booking of an individual who cannot produce a valid state license. As of 2014, California, Connecticut, Colorado, Illinois, Maryland, Nevada, Oregon, New Mexico, Utah, Washington, and the District of Columbia allowed undocumented immigrants to obtain a valid state driver's license,[2] largely reducing the incidence of immigrant arrests that result from routine traffic stops. In other states, however, arrests and detention can be a frequent occurrence. The law enforcement agency that does the "booking" of the person arrested at the local level takes the individual's fingerprints, triggering an automatic crosscheck with the fingerprints in ICE databases. If it is determined that the individual is unlawfully present, ICE will request that a "hold" be placed on the immigrant.

In local municipalities, the rigor of immigration enforcement may also depend on the individual municipality's policies. As of 2014, there were 37[3] law enforcement agencies in 18 states[4] that had signed "287(g) Agreements," or partnerships with ICE that allow local law enforcement to effectively carry out federal enforcement activities. The agreement derives its name from Section 287(g) of the Illegal Immigration Reform and Immigrant Responsibility Act of 1996 that authorizes the ICE director to train local agencies on enforcement activities (ICE, 2014a). There are usually two models of the agreement: the task-force model and the jail-enforcement model. For task force agreements, local officers are allowed to inquire about the immigration status of any individual they believe to be present in the country without papers, and can arrest individuals based on suspicion alone. Under the jail enforcement system, local officers can investigate the immigration status of any arrested person and independently flag an individual for detention if the officer feels they are deportable (American Immigration Council, 2012).

Despite its inception in 1996, the 287(g) mechanism was not aggressively implemented until 2009 when the Obama administration embraced the agreements to increase local enforcement and arrests, which raised concerns about racial profiling. Participating counties in Arizona, Georgia, and North Carolina have been defendants in lawsuits alleging unconstitutional profiling of Hispanics leading to significant increases in Hispanic arrests across the board. In Alamance County, North Carolina, the U.S Department of Justice found that Hispanic drivers were more likely to be pulled over than non-Hispanic drivers by a ratio of 10 to 1 (American Immigration Council, 2012). Jurisdictions with these agreements routinely receive complaints from citizen and noncitizen members alike about targeting activities such as disproportional arrests for Hispanics, checkpoints set up in Hispanic neighborhoods, and discrimination between ticketing Hispanic and non-Hispanic drivers for identical violations. In a study of the effects of immigration enforcement on immigrants in seven US counties,[5] Randy Capps and his colleagues found that many immigrants were moving from towns and counties where 287(g) agreements were being energetically enforced to municipalities where 287(g) had not been implemented (Capps, Rosenblum, Rodriguez, & Chishti, 2011). In a reflection of this internal migration, public schools in communities not implementing 287(g) saw a rise in student enrollment, whereas schools in the counties where 287(g) was in effect saw a corresponding exodus of students. "Secure Communities" is another federal immigration enforcement strategy that partners with local law enforcement. Under this program, any local jurisdiction that scans fingerprints to cross check with Federal Bureau of Investigation (FBI) databases will automatically have the prints forwarded to ICE.

DETENTION

If ICE determines that an individual detained by local law enforcement is undocumented, it will issue a "detainer" directly to the enforcement agency to request that it hold the individual for 48 hours, the maximum amount of time that an agency can detain someone without filing charges (ICE, 2014b). At that point, ICE must retrieve the detainee from the local facility or the law enforcement agency is obligated to release the individual. Although local law enforcement is not legally required to honor ICE detainer requests, many do. As of 2013, the Secure Communities strategy seems to be everywhere and continues to funnel individuals from localities to ICE for deportation. Municipalities around the country (e.g., in California, Illinois, Texas, and others) are fighting back.

Some individuals with immigration allegations may not immediately be transferred to ICE for processing. For cases in which local law enforcement files criminal charges, the immigrant must pay the criminal bond or serve the required jail time if convicted before being released to ICE custody. ICE may also become involved in cases even where the individual has proper documentation. Depending on criminal convictions, the Immigration and Nationality Act allows ICE to detain and deport individuals who are legal permanent residents if the criminal conviction is sufficiently serious. The only nondeportable individuals are US-born citizens. (Under extreme circumstances, naturalized citizens can be stripped of their citizenship and removed from the country.)

These are just some of a wide range of methods that can bring an unauthorized immigrant into ICE custody though, of course, every situation is unique. Once in ICE custody, officers generally process the immigrant at a local ICE office and run an additional background check to determine whether the individual has any criminal record or has been deported in the past. Based on the unique circumstances of the person in custody, the officer may elect to release the individual on bond or on his or her own recognizance, or may continue to detain the immigrant without bond until termination of the case (Morton, 2011). Save for circumstances that result in mandatory detention, such as the Garcia case in Chapter 1, in which the father had been stopped several times for immigration violations, ICE officers are largely given discretion in making this determination.

While waiting out these unexpected separations, children may be forced to remain with relatives or local child welfare for a span of days or months (Capps et al., 2007). In a 2007 report, the US Government Accountability Office (USGAO) observed that ICE officers can exercise the most discretion in deciding how to handle an unauthorized alien in the early processes of discovery and arrest (USGAO, 2007). At this point, an ICE officer can make the decision to release the immigrant on humanitarian grounds (e.g., caring for a young child; having a serious illness; being sole provider or guardian of a family). According to the GAO report, if the detained immigrant is the sole caretaker of children, ICE officers are required to take steps to ensure that the child or children are not left unattended. The GAO report, which was highly critical of ICE procedures, went on to state that ICE officers and attorneys have much less discretion once the process of apprehension and removal process is underway. After this initial period, when the detainee is transferred into the ICE detention system, the arresting officers can no longer exercise discretion; it's simply out of their hands.

It is at this point that concerns for the detainee's immediate well-being escalate, like those cited by the GAO report. Detainees can be subject to intentional or unintentional neglect, abuse, or even traumatization, as they are being held and processed or transferred from one detention facility to another. Moved further away from their families and lawyers, detainees lose the ability to care for their dependents as their own risk of exposure to trauma rises. Immigrants' length of time in detention depends on a number of factors, including their eligibility for relief, past criminal and/or immigration history, and familial financial resources. Most detainees facing deportation should have three options: (1) the individual can apply for asylum, withholding of removal, or relief under the United Nations Convention against Torture and Other Cruel, Inhuman or Degrading Treatment or Punishment;[6] (2) he or she can ask to see an immigration judge to request relief from deportation; or (3) the individual may agree to "premerits" voluntary departure (i.e., the individual acknowledges that he or she is in the country unlawfully and agrees to be returned or return to his or her country of origin in lieu of removal proceedings and at his or her own expense).

Asylum is a type of relief that is limited for most unauthorized immigrants. In order to apply for asylum, an immigrant must present a "credible fear of persecution or torture" and have been present in the United States for less than one year. Immigrants who meet these criteria may file an asylum claim while in detention as a defense to removal. If the immigration judge grants asylum, the individual will be released from detention. Alternatively, asylum seekers may qualify for "parole" in order to leave the detention facility while awaiting the results of an asylum hearing. ICE officers generally have discretion in determining whether an asylum-seeker may be paroled, and generally take into account whether the individual is a flight risk or a threat to society. As with other cases, the individual may be required to pay a bond before being able to leave detention (Nolo, 2014). Ultimately, as most asylum applications are unsuccessful, many immigrants who elect to apply eventually end up facing removal orders. Withholding of removal and relief under the Convention Against Torture are similar forms of relief, based on credible fears of persecution and/or torture, but available for persons who are applying outside of the one-year deadline after entry into the United States.

For immigrants without an asylum claim, there may be avenues for relief from deportation that do not require the challenge of proving a "credible fear." If the immigrant is eligible and can afford an attorney, or is detained in a facility that is served by a pro-bono service agency, he or she may apply for relief from deportation. Generally, this lengthy process involves at least two hearings in immigration court, and can span a year or even more. In this scenario, the length of detention depends on the bond determination, specifically whether the individual is a "mandatory detainee" or receives an immigration bond. In all cases, ICE has the discretion to set a bond for a detained individual. In some cases, the bond amount set by ICE may be reviewed by an immigration judge, who can raise, lower, or agree with the bond amount set. For individuals with certain convictions, including misdemeanor controlled substance offenses, aggravated felony or firearm offenses, an immigration judge has no authority to review the custody decision of ICE.[7] These "mandatory detainees" must remain in detention until the conclusion of their cases in court. For all other cases, the officer can assign a bond to the detainee paid in cash or money order. Depending on the individual's history, this bond can increase to the tens of thousands of dollars or more. Particularly at these higher prices, tight financial resources often prevent families from paying the bond of the detainee in a timely fashion, if at all. In the end, as we will see in Chapter 7, a successful application for relief from deportation requires a combination of resources that not all families enjoy. Lack of access to legal counsel, the cost of bonds, and the prolonged detention associated with a court case can make this option less desirable to parents who are anxious to return to their children.

For individuals in mandatory detention who select the voluntary departure option, and those who face removal after their pursuit of options 2 and 3, the length of detention depends, in part, on the time that deportation and repatriation will take. For instance, in regions of high immigration enforcement in the United States, the Department of Homeland Security (DHS) has buses departing for nearby countries such as Mexico, which shares a border. A Mexican national, for example, may wait just a few days before being deported. Sometimes the person is given enough time to notify a family member to bring a suitcase or duffle bag of belongings to the ICE office for the deportee. This may be possible in locations in the interior of the United States, rather than in a border state, and when individuals show they have family and other roots in the community. But it is also the case that some deportees are not told the location they will be deported to or when until the day they are loaded on a bus and brought to a point of entry on the border. The drop-off location may not be near their original point of entry or near their families. If the individual's country of origin is less common than Mexico or Central America, the amount of time in detention can be much longer. ICE may wait to physically deport the individual until there are enough other detainees who will be sent to the same country to minimize travel costs. The transportation of deportees to more distant countries usually is done by Judicial Prisoner and Alien Transportation System.[8]

For someone who has been deported before, the detention and removal process provides fewer options and the consequences are more significant. Upon apprehension, a deportation history, even one that occurred many years back, will usually trigger a "reinstatement of removal," in which ICE simply uses the existing deportation order to remove the individual once again. This approach bypasses the step of the immigrant electing to submit to deportation, apply for asylum, or see an immigration judge. In addition to reinstating the previous removal order, the government may also choose to prosecute a criminal case against the immigrant. In this scenario, the undocumented immigrant will remain in detention until the end of his or her criminal case, at which point the judge may order a sentence to be served prior to deportation. Re-entry after deportation can carry a hefty penalty depending on the person's criminal history or other aggravating factors. Federal law allows a sentence of up to 20 years in a federal prison. Only after serving this time will the individual be automatically deported to his or her home country. In 2011, the two most frequently prosecuted offenses in the federal judicial system were unauthorized entry and re-entry, exceeding such offenses as murder, robbery, or financial fraud. As a result, there has been a huge growth in the numbers of immigrants from Latin America in prison. These individuals make up more than 50 percent of all those sentenced to federal prison.[9]

ICE contracts out the operation of detention facilities for persons charged with immigration violations, including difficult-to-place groups such as unaccompanied minors. Many of these contracts are held by corporations in the private prison industry. These facilities house detainees for prolonged periods of time. Under the "detention bed mandate," a 2009 directive from Congress, ICE is required to fill approximately 34,000 beds per day in detention facilities, ramping up the pressure to provide enforcement results in the form of "body counts." Since ICE does not own the facilities, it pays the private prison companies to meet this quota, to the tune of $120 to $160 per detainee per day. The financial return encourages jail operators to have, and fill, as many beds for ICE detainees as possible, and may provide the prison companies additional incentive to keep immigrants detained. Most of the 34,000 plus detainees are noncriminal offenders and many detainees are mothers with children or pregnant women. The fact that these populations are unlikely to flee or pose a physical threat to the community makes the profit motive for private immigration jails particularly barbaric.

If an arrest or extended detention of a parent leaves a child without a caretaker, local authorities may place the child with an available relative or guardian. Depending on the length of detention and availability of relatives, the child may be placed with foster parents to wait out separation. Depending upon the state, after 15–18 months of separation, family courts may begin the process of terminating parental rights and allow for adoption of the child. Detainees with children must often decide whether their child will accompany them in deportation or remain in the United States with a guardian. However, once their sons and daughters enter the child welfare system, the parent's ability to decide between these options decreases considerably and their participation in the decision becomes a costly venture.

Detained parents who are in ICE custody while their children's dependency cases are before family court are especially vulnerable to permanently losing their parental rights. Detained parents are unable to comply with family unification plans, and ICE officers will not transport immigrants to family-court custody hearings (Wessler, 2011). Likewise, child welfare agencies typically lack training on immigration policies and procedures, and consequently will not make allowances for parents in immigration detention (Dettlaff, 2012). In most instances, immigration agencies and child protective services operate independently and without coordination. Still, both systems routinely assess incorrectly what the child's best interests are. In Chapter 10, I describe the plight of many parents and children who have been ensnared in the conundrum that characterizes the disorganized links between the child-welfare system and our immigration enforcement system. It is often the case that child protection workers subscribe to the bias that children are generally better off in the United States with a foster family than in a foreign country they may have never known even if they will be there in the care of their parent. Given some of the harsh conditions abroad that motivate individuals to emigrate, caseworkers may feel the best interest of the child is to keep them in the United States, even if his or her parent is deported, according to a report by journalist Seth Wessler (2011). Wessler estimates that in 2011 approximately 5,100 children in foster care had detained or deported immigrant parents. Indeed, Wessler notes, without changes in how the immigration, child welfare, and judicial systems coordinate their activities, the number of children of immigrants in foster care could rise to 15,000 children by 2016.

Increased immigration enforcement and detention has resulted in an increase in fragmented families. Because of the variability in how much time an immigrant will spend in detention, families may be forced to wait months or longer to be reunited with the detainee. Parents may be held *incommunicado* involuntarily because telephones are not easily available or because the parents are moved around from one detention center to another, maybe even one that's farther away from the family's home. Research demonstrates the toxic effects that arrests and long absences from parents can have on children. Psychologist Christina Jose-Kampfner (1995), for instance, reported on 30 children who had witnessed the arrests of their mothers. While the mothers in Kampfer's study were not arrested for reasons of immigration violations, the findings are illustrative. The women's children showed high levels of anxiety and depression associated with the trauma of seeing their mothers arrested and then experiencing long separations from their incarcerated mothers. Likewise, attorney and criminologist Phyllis J. Baunach (1985) studied mothers incarcerated in women's prisons in Kentucky and Washington State and their children. Baunach reports that 70 percent of the children of the incarcerated mothers exhibited a range of psychological symptoms including aggression, hostility, and withdrawal.

THE CONSEQUENCES TO MARICELA AND MAYA

Even when they sit still, behave, and keep quiet, children cannot protect their parents from being discovered and arrested. When the dreaded day comes that the undocumented parent comes into contact with the police or ICE, the emotionally charged event and the separation that ensues can be extremely painful and damaging to young children, particularly those who have a limited understanding of why their parents are suddenly no longer present. Such is the case of Maricela and Maya, two sisters who suffer the emotional and psychological aftermaths of their parents' arrests and detentions.

The e-mail asking me to conduct an evaluation of the sisters, whose parents had pending deportation orders, came in early December 2010 from Rachel Groneck, an immigration attorney practicing in St. Louis, Missouri. Rachel was in pursuit of cancellations of removal for both parents, Carlota and Jaime, and wanted me to explore the potential psychological effects that (a) Carlota's possible removal to Mexico would have on Maricela, 8 years, 10 months old, and Maya, 5 years, 5 months old, and (b) the effects on the girls if they were to relocate to Mexico with the parents if one or both of them were forced to leave the United States. Of the two cases, Carlota's was first in line for a hearing, primarily because of her complicated history of having been removed from the country once before. Thankfully, Jaime's case was not yet scheduled but would take place sometime after Carlota's hearing. This gave Rachel time to prepare a solid case for the mother that would, if successful, benefit the father's case, or so we hoped. The parents were wise to place their trust in Rachel, a deeply ethical and hardworking attorney who leaves nothing to chance in representing her clients. She is an attorney I always felt proud to work with on cases. She is representative of the many honest and dedicated immigration attorneys I have collaborated with: committed to justice for immigrants who deserve a fair chance to show how their deportation would constitute an exceptional and extremely unusual hardship for their citizen-children. After gathering some brief information from Rachel on the case and asking for copies of any educational and medical records on the girls that she might have, including a report from the child protective service of the county in which the family resided, I contacted the family. I reached Carlota on her mobile and she agreed to an appointment in my office on a Saturday morning when the girls would be out of school and Jaime off from work.

The family arrived promptly for the scheduled appointment a couple of weeks later, accompanied by an older male relative who had driven them to my office from their home in De Soto, Missouri. The meeting was an opportunity for me to get to know the family; ask lots of background questions; and to observe the family's interactions, the parents' relation-ship, each parent's behavior, and the girls' interaction with each other. It served also as a chance for them to get acquainted with me and ease into a trusting rapport. The girls were nicely dressed in festive clothes. A bit shy, as would be expected in meeting a stranger, they whispered questions or comments to their parents. Carlota and Jaime were relatively timid as well, and the interaction I saw between Carlota and Jaime, and Carlota and her daughters gave me the impression that theirs was a matriar-chal family. The elder gentleman sat in a waiting area on another floor of the building.

After exchanging some pleasantries and introductions with parents and daughters, I asked the girls to wait in a conference room next to my office and gave them paper, pencils, and crayons to keep them occupied. They agreed and I returned to be alone with the parents to learn about their biographies, marital history, the girls' developmental histories, and other things about the family's life. I had the parents sign consents permitting me to contact the girls' teachers. During the time I was with Carlota and Jaime, Maya returned at least three times in the course of the first half hour to check in on her parents, once ostensibly because she had to go to the bathroom, causing an interruption while Carlota took her to the lady's room. When I asked Maya why she came back each time, she simply smiled without answering. She seemed to need to be reassured that her parents were nearby and still there. Each time Maya came to the door, Carlota would remind her "*todavía estamos aquí*" (we are still here). It was the first hint of Maya's anxiety about being away from her parents for too long. Later that day, when I set aside the time to meet with her alone, Maya refused and became visibly distressed, but did not cry, more clues of her insecurity. I decided to speak with Maya only while her parents were present. I stressed to them that I wanted Maya to respond to my questions, and asked them not to intervene, even if they felt like they wanted to jump in to help her. Maya's hesitance to relax continued even later, though to a lesser degree, when I made two visits to their home to complete my evaluation.

Carlota, 39, is a full-time homemaker who immigrated from Michoacán, Mexico about 13 years before. She had been removed from the United States at the border when she tried to enter the first time. It was after re-entering the country unnoticed that she met Jaime in the United States through family networks and was soon pregnant with Maricela. Also from Michoacán, Jaime, 31, had immigrated a year after Carlota. He works for a barrel manufacturer and has an impeccable work record. The family lives on one income and shares a home with Carlota's brother, his wife, and their two pre-adolescent daughters. Like many Latin American immigrant couples I have met and served over the years, Jaime and Carlota are not legally married, preferring to hold off until they can have a formal church wedding, an event more important to them than a city hall marriage license. The family manages well on just Jaime's wages, allowing Carlota to remain home with the girls. She accompanies the girls to school and participates in many school activities, including plenty of time spent in the school library with the girls' after school. In time I came to recognize that Carlota is taking advantage of these opportunities to improve her own literacy while supporting her daughters' educational progress. In the family system, it is clear that Carlota is the leader of the family, the more ambitious of the two parents, and the one who makes many of the family's major decisions.

The family moved to De Soto, Missouri a few years before, initially renting a house that only they occupied, a home that they have since left for all the unhappy memories it holds. Within a month of moving into the house, Carlota shared that she and her husband began to hear comments, mostly ethnic slurs and insults, from the men at the fire station next door to the house. Weeks later, Carlota waited for Jaime to get home from work so that she could get some things from the corner grocery to complete the family's dinner. The parents made the unfortunate decision of leaving the two girls—then ages 7 and 3-and-a-half years—alone for what they told me were "two minutes," but probably more, so that Jaime could drive Carlota to the store and back as soon as possible. In the parents' brief absence, Maricela tried to toast some bread, which became lodged in the toaster and burned. Smoke started coming from the toaster. She became frightened and did not know what to do.

This is where the account I got from Maricela gets murky and her parents do not fully know what happened. Maricela told me that a woman knocked at the door of the house—a woman in a uniform of some kind but not a police officer Maricela told me, maybe a firefighter—who asked if everything was all right. In her fright about the burning toast, Maricela told the woman that the toast was burning and that her parents were out, and that her sister was scared. There was some smoke, Maricela told me, but it did not seem to be filling the house or billowing greatly. The unidentified woman took care of the toaster and stayed with the girls and soon thereafter fire trucks and police arrived. In our meeting, Carlota hypothesized that the men at the firehouse who had been jeering at them for months may have waited to act vengefully against her and Jaime. I was not able to verify the woman's identity or Carlota's theory. Eyewitness testimony about events and people in moments of crisis are notoriously poor renditions of the actual events. Fortunately, these facts were not essential to my evaluation of the girls.

Carlota and Jaime told me that upon their return from the store, they found several police cars and an emergency medical ambulance in their driveway and surrounding the home. With their limited English, the parents could not explain adequately why they had left the girls. The local police notified child protective services, and handcuffed and arrested the parents before they could even enter the house. The girls were taken out of the house in the arms of police to an ambulance and as they were being carried both girls got glimpses of Carlota and Jaime being placed in the back seats of the police cars. Maya told Maricela later that she saw the handcuffs on her parents' arms but Maricela does not recall seeing the handcuffs. Each parent was placed in a separate patrol car. It was a scene that would return as a significant and traumatic event for both girls during my interviews. Maricela and Maya were taken to the police station where a caseworker from the local child-protective service interviewed them. A maternal uncle and his wife with legal status who lived in a nearby town were called and officers released the girls into their custody within hours.

Jaime and Carlota were detained. For the days that followed, the supportive extended family called around to find out where Carlota and Jaime were being held. The better part of the rest of the time was spent consoling the sad, weeping Maricela and Maya. Four days into his detention at a local facility, Jaime was released without prior notice and sent home. When he arrived to stay with his wife's family, the girls clung to him. Carlota was transferred to a detention center near St. Louis and was kept there for approximately a month. Because it was Carlota's second immigration violation, ICE handled her differently than Jaime. For the month that she was detained, Carlota could not contact her children directly by telephone and there was no date set for her release; in fact, there was no indication of when or even if she would be released. During that long, agonizing month, the two girls slept in the same room as their father and were overwrought with whether he would come home from work every night. Their school performance declined. Jaime told me that every day the girls would ask him when their mother was returning, then cry themselves to sleep at the end of the day. The family was eventually able to hire Rachel Groneck, and at the end of the month, Carlota was released. Custody of the two children was transferred back to Jaime and Carlota from the uncle and aunt, after Carlota's release, when the Department of Social Services made its determination that there was insufficient evidence that Carlota and Jaime had put their children in danger. However, both parents received immigration charges, and since Carlota's case was considered a priority for removal, her case went forward first.

The first meeting ended after I interviewed the parents, and the interview with Maricela and Maya ended after I had gotten a good deal of information on the family and the girls to plan the next steps in my evaluation. We agreed that I would visit their home for the next meeting to chat some more with the two girls. I had gotten enough background information from the parents that it would no longer be necessary for them to be interviewed at length, except to answer some questions that might emerge in my conversations with Maricela and Maya. As they left my office that Saturday morning in December, Carlota pulled a bundle of four *tamales* from a paper bag. She had prepared them that morning and gave them to me as a token of their appreciation. I could see the heartfelt expression on her face.

Maricela's Evaluation

On two Saturdays in 2011, one in January and the other about three weeks later in February, I visited De Soto, Missouri, a small town, population 6,400, about 45 miles outside of St. Louis, and the home of Maricela and Maya. In 2010 there were about 512 Hispanics living in De Soto, a town whose population is mostly white. The Saturday in January was cold and overcast and the drive seemed long partly because of my anticipation of the meeting and partly because of my concerns about getting lost. The Saturday in February was a sunny one, feeling more like an autumn day than one in winter, and now it felt like a familiar drive. It was a beautiful day to travel to parts in rural Missouri and see the charming farmlands. My wife joined me on the trip that day to see some small towns, look at local shops, visit the nearby Missouri wine country, and to explore new places. While I met with the girls, my wife drove around De Soto and visited the local library.

The family was waiting each time, greeting me with a warm friendliness. They lived in a very modest but clean and well-tended house in De Soto. The home was comfortable and nicely heated against the cold outdoors. Around the home were many Catholic figures, pictures and symbols, and at least one shrine to the *Virgen de Guadalupe*.

Maricela was 9 years old at the time of the evaluation. She was born in Sedalia, Missouri, where her parents first settled before they arrived in De Soto. Her sister, Maya, was 5-and-a-half. Although Maricela was born three weeks prematurely and weighed 5 pounds 4 ounces at birth, she had an unremarkable developmental and medical history. The only medical complication described by her parents is that she was diagnosed as having a "weak" eye and was assigned by her optometrist to wear a patch over the right eye in order to force the use and strengthening of the left eye muscles.

Maricela is a petite, sad-looking, soft-spoken child who appears her age. Offered the selection of languages to conduct our conversations, Maricela spoke English with me. Her short- and long-term memory was fine. She had no speech or thought impediments; was generally calm; and showed good concentration and attention. In spite of all these positive signs, her general affect was that of sadness. In the first meeting, as in the other two at her home, Maricela engaged very easily with me and seemed to enjoy the time spent together talking and completing the psychological measures that I administered.

Our conversation covered how much she enjoys playing house with her Barbie and Ken dolls and told me, "We make up stories, like we're a family." Maricela said she enjoyed her teacher and liked her because "she lets us not do too much work." When asked, Maricela was able to name all of her teachers since Pre-K. One routine she had every day was walking her sister Maya to her classroom before she heads to her own. Maricela said that her family had dinner together every night. After school, she said she would take a shower, then do her homework around 4:30 every day. Maricela also helped Maya with her ABCs, and the two girls spoke English to one another and Spanish to their parents. When I asked Maricela why she and her sister spoke English when they talked and played, Maricela answered, "Because I grew [up] in Missouri." Maricela initiated the conversation about her dog, Chubs, the family pet who stays outside.

"I have lived in this town all my life," she told me. De Soto, Missouri had indeed been her home for her nine years and she attended a local elementary school from prekindergarten to the third grade. She had several friends and had no conduct problems in school. Her academic record had been very good but had deteriorated in the past year. In first and second grades she maintained grades in the A and B range but in the third-grade her grades had dropped to mostly Bs and Cs, a distinct decline from previous years due almost entirely to the traumatic circumstances of her parents' arrests and their upcoming immigration hearings. She often accompanied her mother and sister to the school or local libraries where they spent time reading and looking at books.

Maricela's teacher, Mrs. K confirmed in a phone conversation a month after the second home visit that Maricela was a normal third grader and her parents had been very responsive and cooperative with the school. She noted that Maricela's parents took advantage of the library's reading program and Mrs. K's extra tutoring schedule. Due to the bad weather, Mrs. K. said the family had been absent recently since they walked to and from the school. What struck Mrs. K was Maricela's sadness, and she became more alarmed when Maricela wrote at the top of one of her written assignments "I'm angry. I'm upset." When Mrs. K asked Maricela about why she felt that way, Maricela said that she had been feeling this way since February but could not specify why since that time. Maricela told her that someone in the family had died in Mexico in late February but it was not clear who that person was. In fact, it was Carlota's father who had died, a person Maricela had only heard about but never met. She may have been reflecting Carlota's anguish at the loss of her father and her inability to be by his side.

When I asked Maricela if she understood why she was meeting with me these few times, Maricela's face became sadder and tears quickly streamed from her eyes. Maricela said that she did not actually see when her parents were taken away since she was in the ambulance but, "My little sister saw them." Maricela recalled crying with her sister when they were placed in the ambulance. To calm the girls, ambulance personnel told them stories, showed them things, and made them laugh. At the police station, Maricela said, the people were "nice to us."

During her mother's month-long detention, Maricela's classmates would tell her that "they don't give food in jail and your mom is not eating." Jaime had commented that, after his release from detention, Maricela and

Maya did not want him to be out of their sight. After Carlota's release from detention, Maricela told her mother, "I'll be a good girl and that won't happen to you again." She was still carrying the guilt that her attempt to toast the bread had brought upon the family the troubles they were in. Since their arrest and detention, Carlota and Jaime told me that both Maricela and Maya will tell their parents to "put on your seatbelts so the police don't stop us" and the girls are often frightened when they see police cars on the road.

As part of the evaluation, I conducted a number of psychological tests. When I asked Maricela to draw pictures, she drew a woman with earrings and a necklace. Her drawing of a house provided a warm ambience, with smoke coming from a chimney, potted plants on the window, a child looking out of a bedroom window, a dog house, and a dog entrance in the front door of the house. As to what she would wish if she had only one wish, Maricela answered "that we could live in a house together and have money and play with other neighbors who have children."

On a test of perceptual-motor integration, Maricela did well and showed no problems.

However, on a test of childhood depression, her scores were in the clinical range as were her scores on an instrument that measures a child's possible posttraumatic symptoms. When I gathered all the data, the trauma seemed to be related to her parents' arrests and detention. Her answers to the psychological tests pointed to a very low self-worth and poor sense of self-efficacy: she felt ineffective as a person. In tests for behavioral adjustment, intellectual and school status, physical appearance and attributes, and freedom from anxiety, Maricela scored consistently in the low range. These scores indicated a child who perceived herself as having (a) behavioral difficulties in meeting the conduct standards set by her parents and others; (b) difficulties in school; (c) deficits in her physical appearance, body image, and physical strength; and (d) significant problems with moods, and anxiety about school and social functioning. On two other subtests—popularity, and happiness and satisfaction—Maricela scored in the average range, suggesting that by her own evaluation she had friends but not many. The positive scores on some tests were related primarily to the strength of her family bonds. However, it was the variability across measures and sometimes within the measures that raised concerns for me about her psychological functioning and her fragility.

When completing the objective measures, Maricela looked to me to encourage her or to answer questions about how she should complete the forms. Maricela's answers to some of the scales she completed with my help gave me cause for clinical concern. To the statement "I am sure that terrible things will happen to me," Maricela added that she feared "someone will come here and will take someone from my family away. That someone will die." She said she "felt like this for a long time." To the item "I do not like myself," Maricela said that she felt that "people laugh at me." Additionally, she reported she felt like crying every day and that she could never be as good as other kids. In fact, she thought of them as much smarter than her. To the item, "I am not sure if anybody loves me," Maricela added, "I see people walking around and they look at me. I feel like they don't like me."

A questionnaire completed by the parents indicated that Maricela might have been suffering from posttraumatic stress symptoms. In response to an item asking if Maricela had thoughts about things that have happened, her parents reported that Maricela often cried when they drove past the home where the parents were arrested. They said that Maricela often appeared sad and depressed, a point reinforced in my conversation with Mrs. K, Maricela's teacher. On an item about excessive worry, Carlota and Jaime reported that Maricela often said, "You don't have money to buy things, so I won't ask [for anything]." Maricela was afraid of causing her parents additional stress, costs, or discomfort, and guarded against making her feelings or needs known too often.

Altogether, the background history, clinical findings, interview impressions, and academic records reflected that Maricela was a child who was suffering a significant level of depression and trauma-related stress. As to her strengths, Maricela was a child who was well behaved and liked by her teachers. Her cognitive, perceptual, and motor abilities provided some sense of comfort, since there were no indications that Maricela was suffering from any more serious mental problems; her connection to reality was intact; there were no delusions or hallucinations, or other indications of severe mental illness. She seemed to have good interpersonal skills.

Although she had friends and got along with other children, there was a fragile sense of self-worth and her worth to others. My observation of the family's neighborhood environment was that the family had very few ties to the immediate neighbors who did not share their ethnicity, culture, or language. Their source of social connections was other family members and church friends. The parents reported that until recently there was a family across the street with children Maricela's age with whom she played and who visited each other's homes. Since the neighbor's departure, Maricela has been more isolated at home.

Maricela was in need of psychotherapy. I made a referral to Maricela's school for school-based mental health services and reiterated this in my conversation with Maricela's teacher. I determined that stability and predictability at home and in her immediate social and geographic environment, and a sound psychological intervention program would benefit her enormously. A major disruption in her life such as Carlota's or Jaime's removal to Mexico would have had untold negative effects on Maricela.

Maya's Evaluation

Maya was born in a nearby hospital that served the De Soto community and she attended kindergarten at a local elementary school. She took a school bus daily with Maricela. The sisters relied on each other and shared a room at home. The two cousins who live with them are considerably older than Maya and seem to indulge her. After her parents' arrest, Maya told her parents that she saw them in handcuffs from the ambulance. Carlota says that of the two girls, Maya had the most separation reaction while she was in detention, due to her very young age and perhaps due to having seen her mother in handcuffs. On the first night of her mother's return home after the arrest, Maya insisted on sleeping with Carlota because she was afraid that her mother would leave again. Like Maricela, Maya warns her parents to "put on your seatbelts so the police don't stop us" and is frightened to see police cars passing by. I interviewed Maya three times, once during an office visit and twice during home visits.

I observed Maya playing with her sister as two normal siblings. Maya did not speak to her mother directly in my presence but whispered to Carlota in Spanish. When I spoke with her, Maya answered in simply yes or no answers. Open-ended questions about her life, her dog, and dolls were also met with one-word answers. Throughout, she smiled and was compliant with my instructions and requests but seemed constantly wary of me, often looking to her parents for reassurance or permission. Maya identified everyone around her, spelled her name, stated her age, and counted to 40. Her behavior was appropriate, but a bit more reserved than other children her age in an examination situation, but I attributed this to her age with respect to cultural factors that teach children to be very deferential to adults, especially those in authority.

Though she couldn't pronounce my name, Maya recognized me when I visited her home and came to greet me without hesitation but always with others present. Much of our interaction was characterized by an attentive Maya with an engaging smile, but speaking very few words. Her parents noted that Maya talked much more when she was among family but was shy around new adults. Maya was reported by teachers to be well-behaved and progressing well in her academic performance with no developmental delays. Maya's drawing of a person was age appropriate with the general features of a person present and gender appropriate. Her attempt at drawing a house was more constricted. She stopped drawing the house and looked at me. When I asked if she could continue drawing the house, she shook her head indicating "no." I urged her to try anyway, but again Maya refused. When I asked why she did not want to go on, she shrugged her shoulders. Because Maya was so young, she had trouble talking about the memory of her parents' arrests and detention. Indeed, pursuing her memories and the meanings she had made of these events during an evaluation process was contraindicated by both her age and the potential for additional trauma.

For her age, Maya had an unusually high level of separation anxiety, a childhood disorder characterized by recurrent excessive distress when separated or anticipating separation from family or home, persistent worry about something bad happening to her parents or losing them, excessive worry of being alone or with others if her parents are not present, and fear that something bad will cause her to be separated from her parents. The history of the sudden separation from her parents under unusual circumstances—the appearance of numerous police, emergency medical personnel, and child protective workers; the arrest of her parents (which she witnessed) and their removal to a police station; loss of contact with father for about four days and with mother for a month—had led Maya to be hypervigilant of the world around her. She was shy around me and refused to be interviewed alone, showing some problems with attachment and separation anxiety. These behaviors are most often evident in children who have suffered a traumatic separation from parents or other significant person or place. It was not surprising considering Maya's experiences. I became concerned that additional upheavals in her young life could cause significant damage to her fragile emotional condition in which she harbored a constant fear that she would lose her parents and other important figures in her life. If Maya's emotional status had worsened, she would have needed a therapist to help her explore and work through these issues.

My assessment of Maya concluded that she suffered from a separation anxiety disorder. Although Maya did not show enough symptoms to diagnose her with a reactive attachment disorder (i.e., a marked disturbance in social relatedness characterized by a child's persistent failure to initiate or respond in a developmentally appropriate fashion to most social interactions) or even posttraumatic stress disorder, I was concerned that any other event like those she suffered when separated from her parents could cause her to suffer additional psychological strife. The fact that she only showed separation anxiety and no other major symptoms was a tribute to her parents' handling of the situation and the nurturance and stability they had provided at home and in school.

A Coda

A few months after Carlota's case was heard and decided in her favor by the judge, I visited the family again to update my clinical evaluation and review recent records to prepare for the testimony I would have to give in Jaime's hearing. Little had changed in Maya but she was doing better overall; her separation anxiety seemed to have lessened now that the family was enjoying a modicum of relief from Carlota's legal permanent resident status. But Maricela was not doing as well. Her school report showed that her school performance had continued to decline since my previous evaluation. Now in the fourth grade, her grades in subjects such as language arts, reading, math, science, and social studies were in the B, B-, and C range, lower than before. Carlota told me that there had also been several F's on homework and exams. Maricela, she said, had told her that she was worried about her father's case and that "I don't want to be without him."

Maricela was receiving additional attention after school to remediate her academic performance. Yet, despite my written request to the school in February 2011 to provide Maricela with psychological counseling services, none had been initiated. Maricela reported that she saw a "Mr. Smith" once in school and that he asked her questions, but there was no follow-up or communication with the parents about this session. In my assessment, Maricela's scores showed that she suffered less depression and trauma in comparison to girls her age, and the only measure that had gotten worse was "feeling ineffective as a person." This was indeed an improvement since my previous report and indicated that once the hurdle of Carlota's legal status was settled, Maricela's mood had improved. However, Maricela remained fearful of the "police and where she lived before." Maricela may have felt better emotionally but her rebound in school was taking more time. The next hurdle in her family's life was her father's removal hearing.

Maricela knew that I came to see her again "because of my dad's court [case]." When I inquired into her knowledge of her father's situation, Maricela contended that "they're going to check if he's going to Mexico or not." She went on to say, "If he wasn't here, he couldn't help us and it would be hard for my mother to take care of us [by herself]. We would need a babysitter while she went to work." Her hopefulness about her father was palpable though when she said with a slight tone of happiness that "I think they're going to let him stay here because they already did for my mom and it's like the same thing." As to how she was handling Jaime's legal process, Maricela said she tried not to think about it or ask her parents about it. Still, her psychological health remained fragile. While she had improved in some areas since Carlota's legal status was settled, this was counterweighted by her father's uncertain future and her perception of what would happen to her, her mother, and her sister if her father were to be returned to Mexico. I had grave concern for Maricela's future should her father be removed to Mexico. The options facing her would be to stay back with her mother and sister or join her father in Mexico, neither of which would benefit Maricela or her family.

We were all delighted when Carlota's hearing concluded in a positive ruling. We were even more delighted nearly a year later when the government attorney agreed to cancel Jaime's removal on the basis that Carlota's case had provided sufficiently compelling evidence of "exceptional and extremely unusual hardship." Carlota and her family returned to De Soto where the girls are thriving academically, socially, and psychologically.

Ultimately, leaving the only country, community, school, and situation they have ever known would have untold negative effects on both Maya and Maricela's psychological and emotional health. Maya and Maricela needed a stable home, community, and school life to protect them from further psychological harm. Removing them to a country and town and culture they had never known and for which they were ill-prepared to adapt, particularly under duress, would have caused undue stress and psychological damage to both girls, perhaps in different ways given their individual profiles, but harmful nevertheless.

Removal to Mexico would have sent Maya, Maricela, and their parents to Michoacán. Their parents' hometown has about 10,000 inhabitants and is about three hours by car from the state capital of Morelia and six hours from the national capital of Mexico City. The towns in Michoacán typically do not have adequate pediatric or psychiatric services for children such as Maricela and Maya. Even in Mexico City, with its more abundant resources, pediatric and psychiatric services for children with emotional and behavior disorders are sorely lacking (Benjet, Borges, Medina-Mora, Zambrano, & Aguilar-Gaxiola, 2009). In all respects, the family's ancestral home in Michoacán was not the environment in which Jaime and Carlota wanted to raise their daughters. The place that they would have returned to would not have provided the standard of living, education, socialization, safety, and health care that Maricela and Maya knew. The move would jeopardize the stability their parents had worked to re-establish.

While Maricela and Maya remain in the United States with their parents, each year thousands of citizen-children are not so lucky. The conditions they face abroad may be equally harsh, or worse.

NOTES

1. I use the term *arrest* in this situation rather than using DHS's euphemisms of *apprehend* and *detain* not to imply criminality but to convey the reality of the event for the immigrant. Though they may not be charged with a criminal act, they are treated comparably.
2. The public safety argument for such policies is issuing licenses regardless of proof of immigration status decreases the number of unlicensed and uninsured drivers on the road.
3. Retrieved from http://www.ice.gov/news/library/factsheets/287g.htm
4. Alabama, Arizona, Arkansas, California, Colorado, Florida, Georgia, Maryland, Massachusetts, Nevada, New Jersey, North Carolina, Ohio, Oklahoma, South Carolina, Texas, Utah, and Virginia all have law-enforcement agencies who have signed 287(g) agreements.
5. The seven counties covered by the study are Cobb County (GA), Frederick County (MD), Gwinnett County (GA), Los Angeles County (CA), Prince William County (VA), Las Vegas (NV), and the state of Colorado.
6. Convention against Torture and Other Cruel, Inhuman or Degrading Treatment or Punishment was adopted by the United Nations General Assembly on December 10, 1984.
7. See INA §236(c).
8. The Justice Prisoner and Alien Transportation System (JPATS) was created in 1995 through a merger of the air fleets of the Marshals Service and ICE. It is managed by the US Marshals Service. JPATS handles about 804 requests per day to move prisoners between judicial districts, correctional institutions and foreign countries. In fiscal year 2013, JPATS transported 106,609 prisoners and deportees by air and 189,350 by ground.
9. For details, see any of the following websites:
   http://detentionwatchnetwork.files.wordpress.com/2013/02/fact-sheet_ end-operation-streamline-car-prisons-criminalization-2-11-13.pdf
   http://www.pewhispanic.org/2014/03/18/the-rise-of-federal-immigration-crimes/
   http://articles.latimes.com/2013/may/21/local/la-me-ff-immigration-prosecutions-20130522
   http://www.hrw.org/news/2013/05/22/us-prosecuting-migrants-hurting-families;
   http://www.hrw.org/sites/default/files/reports/us0513_ForUpload_2.pdf

CHAPTER 7

Fighting to Preserve a Life

While Justice Brandeis wrote that deportation threatens the loss of "all that makes life worth living" about a hundred years ago, those words apply as aptly to the many undocumented immigrants of today who have made American lives for themselves and their children. Like waves of immigrants since the founding of this country, these individuals help strengthen our country. They aspire for their children to become fully American. Deportation after establishing their lives here means the potential loss of all the things of which they dreamed.

One damaging consequence of our current immigration laws and deportation practices is that they compel parents to make the choice between family unity and the American dream, agonizing choices about their children and spouses. Couples facing the threat of separation by deportation are forced into conversations that few intact couples have to navigate in a lifetime. Parents have to ask themselves: Do we split up our family or do we stay together? With which one of us will our children suffer the least? Will we ever be a family again under the same roof?

KING SOLOMON AND *SOPHIE'S CHOICE*

The US immigration system presents families with decisions with no happy alternatives for parents and their children. In these circumstances, parents must act with the wisdom of King Solomon. The biblical King Solomon, as the familiar story goes, is presented the case of two women who are each claiming to be the mother of a child. To end the argument and to uncover the real mother, Solomon threatens to cut the baby in half so that each woman will have a piece of the infant. One of the women accepts the decision without care. The other woman relinquishes her claim to the baby so that the child can be spared death and live a long life, even if that life will not be spent with her. With her expression of sacrifice and love, King Solomon determines that she is the true mother.

Another way to envision what it might be like to be a desperate immigrant parent making decisions about her or his children is by considering what happened to the fictional Sophie Zawistowski in the motion picture, *Sophie's Choice*. In this adaptation of a William Styron novel (1979), the Jewish Sophie tells her lover a story of being asked to translate some stolen documents for the Gestapo. For refusing, she is arrested and sent to Auschwitz with her children. Sophie is forced upon arriving at Auschwitz to decide the fates of her two children: which one will she choose to be gassed and which one will she choose to be sent to the labor camp? It is a certain and abrupt death for one child and a probable and gradual death for the other. In deciding to avoid the instant death of both, Sophie chooses her son Jan to be sent to the children's camp and her daughter Eva to be sent to her swift death.

King Solomon's decision or Sophie's choice are inexact applications of decision-making that individuals facing deportation must entertain. But the emotional upheaval can very well seem to undocumented parents like a choice between life and death, between losing their children or keeping them. In the face of deportation, parents have to choose whether they take their US citizen-children into exile or leave the children in the care of others, effectively orphaning their children. This decision is even more wrenching in cases where the citizen-children are dependent on their parents' care because of their tender age or a because of a physical or mental health need.

The estimates vary, but we know that millions of family members have been separated from one another through deportation. Many are long-term US residents whose deportation has done harm to the people who depend on them: their US-born children, their undocumented children, their spouses and partners (whether undocumented or holding legal status), their dependent parents back home who stave off poverty through the remittances they get from their children, and the businesses kept alive by the labor and skills of undocumented people in the United States and abroad. Deportees take with them children who do not know and are often ill-prepared to adapt to their parents' home countries. Sometimes, citizen-children are left in the United States in the care of family, friends, or others, occasionally in the child welfare system. Citizen-children may be torn from noncitizen siblings who, due to the fortunes of birthdates and birthplaces, are sent on different paths. This situation forces an artificial but terrible choice: is it better for children's mental health to stay with parents in another country under conditions of deprivation or remain in a place of abundant services and stability but without parents to nurture and socialize them? Or is either option even justifiable under American ideals?

Citizen-children frequently face sudden separations from a parent or primary caregiver, sometimes shrouded in uncertainty as the immigration-enforcement wheels of arrest, detention, and deportation turn. The sudden, uncertain separations that come about by detention and deportation jeopardize children's fundamental attachments to the adults they rely on for love, guidance, succor, and care (Zayas & Bradlee, 2014). As we saw in the cases of Maricela and Maya, often the child does not know if or when a parent will return, an uncertainty that complicates the grieving process of the child. Such sudden and confusing separations can lead to disruption of eating and sleeping habits, to sadness, anger, guilt, and anxiety. In the wake of enforcement, rushed separations of parents from their children have ranged from weeks to months, during which children are commonly left in the care of relatives or others to wait out their parents' detention (Capps et al., 2007).

The Women's Refugee Committee (2013) notes that ICE does not customarily screen individuals to identify whether they have children or if they are primary caretakers, and there are no policies in place that protect children in day-to-day ICE operations. In recent history, ICE has been under no requirement to give parents time to make arrangements for the care of their children, and parents do not have access to or know about custody hearings and child-welfare procedures. Seldom having the funds to retain lawyers to fight for them, undocumented parents must seek reunion with their children while abiding by the orders of removal and returning to their original countries. Even with the availability of immigration clinics in law schools or social service agencies devoted to protecting immigrant rights, the availability of low cost and pro-bono services does not begin to meet the demand. These services are usually overwhelmed with requests from unauthorized aliens to initiate cancellation of removal procedures in federal immigration court.

Given legal recourse to seek the cancellation of their removal or deportation orders, the undocumented immigrant must argue convincingly that the removal would cause his or her citizen-child(ren) exceptional and extremely unusual hardship. We saw in the previous chapter that Carlota and Jaime won their cases, saving Maricela and Maya from the effects of deportation. I now present an immigration-court decision in which a father fought to have his removal order cancelled. It is an actual public document, and it is presented here for the reader to get a glimpse into how a cancellation case occurs. It is not a transcript of the court hearing but rather the judge's decision that summarizes the case. I have retained the original formatting and content but made some minor edits to illustrate how such a document appears when it is issued. Like many court documents I have read over the years, the decision repeats many of the facts of the case and the legal precedents that inform the judge's decision. It isn't light reading but it is highly informative reading that reveals the legal process and judicial thinking. In this presentation of the case, I have changed the man's name and those of his wife, ex-wife, and their children, and deleted names of other family or friends and the ICE attorney to protect their privacy. The only names that are unchanged are those of the defending attorney and two expert witnesses who gave written consent to have their names used in this book, and the presiding judge, John R. O' Malley, whose identity is a matter of public record.

UNITED STATES DEPARTMENT OF JUSTICE
EXECUTIVE OFFICE FOR IMMIGRATION REVIEW
IMMIGRATION COURT
KANSAS CITY, MISSOURI

IN THE MATTER OF	)	October 30, 2013
	)	
Aurelio R.	)	File No. [omitted]
	)	
RESPONDENT	)	IN REMOVAL PROCEEDINGS

CHARGE: Section 212(a)(6)(A)(i) of the Immigration and Nationality Act, as Amended: Alien Present in the United States Without Being Admitted or Paroled.

APPLICATIONS: Section 240A(b) of the Immigration and Nationality Act, as Amended: Cancellation of Removal for Certain Nonpermanent Residents.

Section 240B(b) of the Immigration and Nationality Act, as Amended: Voluntary Departure.

ON BEHALF OF THE RESPONDENT

Kenneth Schmitt, Esq.

ON BEHALF OF THE GOVERNMENT

Assistant Chief Council, ICE

WRITTEN DECISION OF THE IMMIGRATION JUDGE

I. Procedural History

Aurelio R. ("Respondent"), a thirty-four-year-old divorced male, is a native and citizen of Honduras who entered the United States without inspection in August of 2000. In October of 2011, the Department of Homeland Security ("Department") personally served the Respondent with a Notice to Appear ("NTA") charging him with removability pursuant to section 212(a) (6)(A)(i) of Immigration and Nationality Act, as amended ("INA" or "Act").

At a master calendar hearing held in May 2012, Respondent acknowledged receipt of the NTA, admitted the allegations contained therein, and conceded the charge of inadmissibility. On the basis of these pleadings and there being no other issue of law or fact relating to the charge, the charge was sustained and removability is established. *See* INA § 240(c)(2); 8 C.F.R.[1] § 1240.10(c). The Respondent designated Honduras as the country of removal should removal be necessary.

The Respondent seeks relief from removal in the form of cancellation of removal under section 240A(b) of the Act. He bases his claim for relief upon his thirteen years of continuous presence in the United States, good moral character, and lack of criminal convictions under section 212(a) (2) of the Act. In addition, the Respondent contends that his United States citizen children would suffer exceptional and extremely unusual hardship if he were removed. At the start of the individual hearing, the Department stipulated that the Respondent had the requisite continuous physical presence for cancellation of removal. The Department also does not argue that the Respondent has any disqualifying convictions or lacks good moral character, but contends that he did not establish exceptional and extremely unusual hardship to his qualifying relatives.

And so begins Judge O'Malley's decision in Aurelio R.'s case. Aurelio R. did not argue that he was in the United States legally but he asked that the removal order be cancelled in order to remain and pursue the life he had built for himself and his family. His utmost concern was the welfare of his children. But like so many undocumented immigrants, the odds were stacked against Aurelio R., as he had violated immigration laws. What did the judge take into consideration in rendering his decision on the case?

II. Evidence and Testimony Presented

The record of proceedings consists of five exhibits. In addition, the Respondent, his former wife, Silvia, his daughter, Dulce and his daughter, Lucy all testified at an individual hearing on June 19, 2013. Dr. Mark A. Bonta and Ms. Nancy D. Spargo, LCSW, also provided expert witness testimony. The Court has considered all evidence and testimony contained in the record, even if not specifically discussed in this decision.

A. Documentary Evidence

Exhibit 1:   Respondent's Notice to Appear.

Group Exhibit 2:   Respondent's Form EOIR-42B, Application for Cancellation of Removal & Adjustment of Status for Certain Non-Permanent Residents, and Supplemental Documents in Support of Relief.

Group Exhibit 3:   Respondent's Supplemental Documents in Support of his Application for Cancellation of Removal.

Exhibit 4:   Respondent's Supplemental Documents in Support of his Application for Cancellation of Removal.

Group Exhibit 5:   Respondent's Supplemental Documents in Support of his Application for Cancellation of Removal.

B. Testimony of the Respondent

Aurelio R. was born in 1979 in Cortes, Honduras and entered the United States in August 2000.

In 2002 the Respondent began a relationship with Silvia and they married in January of 2004. When the Respondent met Silvia she had a three month old daughter, Dulce (age 11). The Respondent never met Dulce's natural father, and he considers himself to be Dulce's father. The Respondent and Silvia also have a biological child in common, Lucy, who was born in December of 2003. The Respondent and Silvia were divorced in June of 2009. Currently the Respondent lives with his partner Norma and their two sons, Rolando and Diego. All of the Respondent's children, including his stepdaughter Lucy, are United States citizens.

In 2009 the Respondent opened his own business. He earns approximately $40,000 a year. At any given time he has approximately five employees and hires a company that handles the payroll, taxes, and other administrative tasks. His current partner, Norma, has no legal immigration status in the United States and has never worked in this country. She did not graduate high school and has no employment skills. The house that the Respondent lives in is in his sister's name, but the Respondent is paying the mortgage. He purchased the home for $170,000 and made a $15,000 down payment. He owns five vehicles, four of which are cargo vans and trucks that he uses for work. He also has 1998 Buick. The Respondent estimated that his work assets were approximately $10,000 to $14,000, including his business bank account, vehicles, and tools. The funds in the Respondent's business account are used for his regular business expenses and are not savings.

During their marriage, both Dulce and Lucy lived with the Respondent and Silvia. Although the Respondent and Silvia both worked, the Respondent was the primary provider for the family. He worked as a carpet installer and was responsible for paying the mortgage and other bills. When the couple began divorce proceedings, Silvia offered the Respondent the home they purchased during the marriage because she could not afford the mortgage on her own. Instead the Respondent asked that she and the children remain in the home and he paid the mortgage during the divorce proceedings. The Respondent now pays $1,774 per month in total support to Silvia. This includes their child support, maintenance for Lucy, and their health and dental insurance. The Respondent has never missed a support payment or made a late support payment. He also pays for his daughters' extracurricular activities, including gymnastics for Lucy and tae kwon do for Dulce.

At the time of the individual hearing, both of the Respondent's daughters attended the local elementary school, but Dulce began middle school in the fall of 2013. Dulce excels in reading and Lucy is very good at math. The Respondent assists both of them with their classwork, and he and Silvia attend parent teacher conferences together. He has a good relationship with Silvia and considers her to be a friend, despite their divorce. The Respondent and Norma live approximately five minutes from Silvia and the family and sees each other often. During the school year Silvia has physical custody of the girls during the week and they stay with the Respondent every other weekend. During the summer the girls alternate between the two homes, living one week with the Respondent and the next with the ex-wife. The Respondent takes Dulce and Lucy to their activities when they need a ride and also attends all of their tournaments and meets.

If Rolando and Diego remain in the United States, they will also attend the same schools that Dulce and Lucy have attended. The local school district is very good and close to the Respondent's home. The children are bussed to the school, have access to books, and many other benefits. The Respondent provides health and dental insurances for his sons.

The Respondent works from six in the morning to approximately four in evening, which allows him to spend the evenings with his sons. On weekends the Respondent spends time with his daughters as well. They have a very close relationship, and both of the Respondent's daughters identify themselves as Honduran or Latina.

If the Respondent were removed to Honduras, he would return to his mother's home in San Jose de Cordoncillos, a village in the state of Cortes. Norma and their sons, Rolando and Diego, would accompany him but Dulce and Lucy would remain with their mother in the United States. Although Silvia is also from Honduras, her family lives in a one bedroom home and there would be no space for the Respondent and his family.

At this point in the written decision, the judge summarizes some details of the town and region in Honduras where Aurelio R. [the Respondent] came from and to which he would likely return. The information is based on the testimony of one of the expert witnesses, Dr. Bonta, which is presented in full detail later in the document. The judge notes that Aurelio R.'s town of San Jose de Cordoncillos is about an hour drive from San Pedro Sula, the capital of the *departamento* (state) of Cortes, and that Aurelio R.'s mother, who still resides there alone, is 56 years old. Her home is described as having electricity and plumbing but no running water because there is not enough water in the town. For Aurelio R.'s mother to get water for regular use, she must undertake an hour's walk to the river with empty buckets and return with the buckets, laden with river water, which slow her down and require frequent stops to rest. After this, she must boil the water because it is "dirty." In fact, in 1996 there was a cholera outbreak because of river water contamination, and the townspeople have since learned to boil the water before use. Apart from water-borne illness, dengue is also very common in San Jose de Cordoncillos. The nearest clinic is 30 minutes away by bus and the nearest hospital is an hour away in San Pedro Sula.

Aurelio R. argues that his children, if taken to Honduras with him, would not get an education like that which they now receive in the US We learn that his two sons, Rolando and Diego, would have to board a public bus for a half-hour ride to the other town to attend school. The school near his mother's hometown goes only to the Honduran equivalent of ninth grade. In 2006, Aurelio R. testifies, his sister was raped after armed men stopped this bus. The judge refers to the violence in and around the town. In the year preceding Aurelio R.'s hearing, three bodies were found dumped just outside the town and on Mother's Day a taxicab driver was attacked and killed. Aurelio R.'s brother went to San Jose de Cordoncillos in 2008 to be with his mother but was forced to return to the United States. During his rounds as a delivery truck driver he was the victim of an attempted robbery. He was also robbed on another occasion while off from work. The many disadvantages to Aurelio R.'s two sons, his wife and himself in returning to

Honduras are quite clear. The judge continues with Aurelio R.'s testimony and those of others.

> The Respondent does not believe that he would be able to continue making his support payments to Silvia if he were removed. Although there is little or no work in San Jose de Cordoncillos, based on the Respondent's experiences and his conversations with friends and family he believes that he could possibly work in the towns closer to San Pedro Sula at a ranch or in a sugar cane field. There are also clothing factories located approximately forty-five minutes from San Jose de Cordoncillos by bus. These jobs would offer him an income approximately $300 per month. Before leaving Honduras in 2000 the Respondent worked as a billing clerk in San Pedro Sula and earned about $100 per week, but the industry has changed and now requires computer skills that the Respondent does not have. He indicated that he would sell his business in the United States if he returned to Honduras. The Respondent and Silvia have discussed possible financial ramifications of his removal and she does not believe that she will be able to continue living in her home without the Respondent's assistance. The monthly payment on the house is $1,300 per month. Silvia's current husband works full-time but she works part-time from home.
>
> The Respondent was arrested for driving under the influence (DUI) in October of 2011. He was driving home from watching a baseball game at a friend's house and was stopped because he did not have his headlights on. He spent one night in jail, and was then transferred to Immigration and Customs Enforcement ("ICE") for another night. The Respondent pled guilty, attended a SATOP[2] program, paid a fine and was placed on two years' probation. He successfully completed the program, paid all fines and fees, and has had no problems during his probation. The Respondent's arrest "made a big impact" in his life. He learned that he had put himself and others at risk and has not driven after drinking since his arrest. The Respondent had never been a heavy drinker and now he rarely drinks at all, and only in his home.

C. Testimony of Silvia, the Respondent's former wife

Silvia is the Respondent's former wife. She and the Respondent divorced in 2009 after they had problems in their relationship. Silvia denied any abuse and indicated that she was young when she married the Respondent and had expectations of her marriage that were not feasible. She is currently remarried and lives in Missouri with her husband and her four children. Her oldest child is Dulce whose biological father has never known Dulce and considers the Respondent to be her father.

Lucy is Silvia's second daughter and the Respondent's biological daughter. Silvia also has two children with [her new husband], a daughter and an infant son. The Respondent is also in a new relationship and has two children with his partner Norma. The respondent lives approximately five minutes from Silvia's home. Dulce and Lucy consider Rolando and Diego to be their brothers and all of the siblings are very close.

The Respondent and Silvia purchased a home together during their marriage. She and the Respondent owned the home jointly, but only Siliva's name was on the mortgage. The Respondent provided the majority of the funds to purchase the home and make the monthly mortgage. When Silvia and the Respondent divorced he moved out because he wanted his family to keep the house. He also provides their health and dental insurance and pays for Lucy's gymnastics and Dulce's tae kwon do. The Respondent treats his daughters equally and has never distinguished between supporting the two daughters.

Silvia uses the check she receives from the Respondent to pay her mortgage each month. She works part-time for a supplement company and stays home with her children. She previously worked as a waitress for Applebee's, but left that position in August of 2012 because she could not continue to pay for daycare. Silvia could not remember exactly what she earned at Applebee's but indicated that after paying for daycare it came to approximately $17 each week. She is capable of working full-time, but does not currently work because daycare is cost-prohibitive with a toddler and infant. Silvia last worked full-time in 2010, but during the time she worked full-time she never earned more than $24,000 per year. [Her new husband] works full-time for a company called [omitted]. He earns approximately $2,200 in net income per month; his income is used for family expenses outside of the mortgage. The Respondent pays both maintenance ($500) and child support ($948). The child support is for Dulce but Silvia uses all of the money that the Respondent provides for both her children. Silvia indicated that she and her husband would not be able to pay the mortgage and their bills on their own or without the Respondent's assistance.

Dulce and Lucy attend elementary school and are doing well. Dulce's favorite subject is currently spelling and she also likes to read. Lucy's favorite subject is math; the Respondent helps her with her math homework. Both the Respondent and Silvia attend parent teacher conferences. If Silvia is unable to take the children to practices the Respondent takes them. He also attends all of their tournaments and meets and takes them to practice when they stay with him. The Respondent maintains a good relationship with Silvia parents and facilitates visits between the girls and their grandparents.

Silvia indicated that her daughters have been extremely emotional about the prospect of the Respondent's removal from the United States. The girls are upset that they will not be able to see their dad. They have expressed worry about his safety if he returns to Honduras. Silvia stated that she would help her daughters to speak to their father, but is unsure what the logistics would be because of the long-distance phone charges.

D. Testimony of Lucy, the Respondent's Daughter

Lucy is the Respondent's daughter. She stated that it was important that the Respondent stay in the United States because "he means everything to me and I would be really upset if he had to go." Lucy indicated that she enjoys spending time with the Respondent and that they go on vacation, visit Six Flags, and play soccer together. She stays with her father on weekends during school year and every other week during the summer.

The judge's summary of Lucy's testimony does not convey the emotional power of her presence in the court. Those who were in the courtroom that day describe it as riveting and compelling. From the moment she entered the courtroom, young Lucy was anxious and in tears. The commanding stateliness of the courtroom even if small relative to other courtrooms and the magnitude of the event in which her father's and her own future hung in the balance were overwhelming to Lucy. Then there was the presence of a judge at the bench. She could not contain her emotions. On the stand, Lucy cried throughout but was able to answer all questions that were asked. All observers were moved by Lucy's testimony. Then, Dulce took the stand.

E. Testimony of Dulce, the Respondent's Stepdaughter

Dulce identified the Respondent as her father. She indicated that she was present to testify in Court because she wanted the Respondent to remain in the United States and stated that if he left "my world would probably end." Dulce indicated that both her mom and the Respondent help her with her schoolwork. The Respondent also takes her to gymnastics and on trips. Dulce spends every other weekend with the Respondent and during the summer she spends every other week with the Respondent. She does not know her biological father.

From others, I learned about the atmosphere in the courtroom. Dulce at the age of eleven came into the courtroom appearing stern and detached, arms folded in indignation, and maybe revealing a bit of anger at what her father was undergoing. She exuded a tough demeanor, almost a willingness to take on the mighty judicial apparatus. With the first few questions from Ken Schmitt, Dulce kept her composure. But it dissolved under the solemnity of the proceedings and their importance to her father and to her and to her sister and to her two little brothers. Dulce wept and answered questions. She volunteered to the court that she wanted to change her surname to his because he was in every way her father except for biology. As happened with Lucy's testimony, during Dulce's testimony everyone was moved to tears. Judge O'Malley then summarizes the testimony of both expert witnesses.

F. Testimony of Dr. Mark A. Bonta

At the time of the individual hearing, Dr. Bonta was a Professor of Geography at Delta State University, where he taught courses on general geography and specifically on poverty and health problems in Latin America. In August of 2013 Dr. Bonta began working at Penn State University as a professor of geography. Dr. Bonta has a PhD in geography from Louisiana State University and is a Latin American expert with a focus on Honduras and the social and environmental issues in the country. He previously worked with the U.S. Peace Corps for two years focusing on sustainable development in Honduras and has researched environmental and social issues within the country in depth. Dr. Bonta traveled to Honduras on twenty-seven different trips; he has lived in the capital city and traveled to the states of Cortes many times. He was last in Honduras in February of 2013.

Dr. Bonta was contacted about the Respondent's immigration case in April of 2012. He spoke with the Respondent on the phone for approximately forty-five minutes and later conducted a short field trip to San Jose de Cordoncillos in June of 2012. Dr. Bonta had already planned to be in Honduras, and added two days to the trip to meet with the Respondent's mother and brother and conduct interviews in the village. His report and testimony are based on his research, conversation with the Respondent and eyewitness observations on his trip to San Jose de Cordoncillos. During the trip, Dr. Bonta hired a field assistant to accompany him for reasons of personal security and also to ensure that he had a local, trusted individual who could assist with interviews. He interviewed the villagers with the help of his assistant and was not assisted by any of the Respondent's family members.

The village of San Jose de Cordoncillos is located in northwestern Honduras, about forty-five minutes by car from San Pedro Sula, which is the "second city" in Honduras. It has approximately 450 houses and a population of 3,000 people. Dr. Bonta visited the local school and interviewed the principal. The local education system goes through middle school and there are eight teachers for five hundred students. Private education is available in some areas of Honduras, but it is extremely expensive and not available in the village.

Dr. Bonta also visited the Respondent's mother's home during his trip. It is typical home for the area, constructed of concrete with tile flooring, but it is not protected against mosquitoes. The house is near a busy road and has a fenced area for pigs and livestock. Dr. Bonta does not believe that the yard or street would be safe for small children. There is no regular water service and he did not see any nearby streams that could be used for water on a permanent basis. Water for consumption must be purchased because water from rivers is not safe, perhaps not even if it was boiled. The cost to purchase water is $20 to $30 a week on average and gasoline costs approximately $4 to $5 per gallon.

Honduras is consistently the most violent country in the world for a number of different and interrelated reasons. After Hurricane Mitch infrastructure was damaged and many left the region for work. Their children were left without parents. Approximately 70 to 80 percent of cocaine moves through Honduras on its way to the drug cartels in Mexico. The 2009 coup has also contributed to the violence due to a lack of faith in the government. Street kids were assassinated in droves in the 1990s and lesbian, gay, bisexual, and transgendered leaders are still regularly assassinated. Honduras is also known for the complete immunity available to powerful people and significant corruption.

The state of Cortes is one of the worst and most dangerous in Honduras. The homicide rate in the state of Cortes of is 300 per 100,000, whereas the rate in East St. Louis, Illinois is 88 per 100,000. There is a gang presence within the village of San Jose de Cordoncillos but it is relatively small and the two largest Honduran gangs are not represented. There is no police station in San Jose de Cordoncillos, and the villagers are not likely to trust the police in neighboring areas because so many officers and former police officers are involved in criminal activity. Dr. Bonta indicated that he did not travel at night during his trip because it was too dangerous. The roads in Honduras are unsafe and there are regular hold-ups even during the day.

Generally in Honduras there is a lack of affordable medical care. Healthcare is technically free, but there is very little care available. Public hospitals exist in the large cities, but most villages don't have any clinics and it takes at least twenty minutes by car to receive any treatment at all. Individuals who can afford private care are the only ones who receive adequate care. There is no medical facility in San Jose de Cordoncillos and it is necessary to travel to Rio Lindo for a clinic.

The state of Cortes actually has more developed job opportunities than most other areas of Honduras. In the state there is some steady wage labor, work in the clothing factories and in the port. Many of the jobs would be between an hour to two hours away from San Jose de Cordoncillos in the direction of San Pedro Sula. It is not atypical for individuals who live in rural areas to leave for work at three in the morning and not return until seven or eight in the evening. Given the Respondent's educational background, $400 each month would be the most that the Respondent could earn, and it is likely that he would earn less. It would be impossible for him to continue to send support to the United States with such income.

In Dr. Bonta's opinion, there would be significant hardship to the Respondent's young United States citizen children if they moved to Honduras. There is very little educational opportunity in Honduras. The school of San Jose de Cordoncillos is lacking compared to United States schools and there is no school available after the ninth grade. It is unsafe to travel and the high school must be accessed via public bus. The health situation is also a large risk; intestinal infections are common for small children, especially those who have not developed immunities.

G. Nancy D. Spargo, LCSW

Nancy Diane Spargo is a licensed clinical social worker ("LCSW") and child, marriage, and family therapist. She has a Master of Science in clinical social work from the University of Chicago and a postgraduate certificate in marriage and family therapy from the University of Illinois. Ms. Spargo began working in social services in 1980 and previously worked as the program director for a Counseling Center of Lakeview in Chicago, Illinois. She focused primarily in mental health and integrating child welfare and mental health. She worked with the Latino community and branched into other immigrant and refugee groups from African Countries.

Ms. Spargo is currently the founder and executive director of the St. Louis Center for Family Development, a social service agency that provides "trauma informed" mental health service. The method of work is guided by the impact of trauma and the goal is to provide services and counseling that avoid re-traumatization. Her position has a number of responsibilities. At the clinical level she works with primarily monolingual Spanish speaking populations to provide therapy services and assessments. Ms. Spargo also provides licensure supervision, clinical supervision, and professional development training to other organizations. She consults and collaborates on issues such as early childhood or immigrant family health. Ms. Spargo is also an adjunct faculty member at the Brown School of Social Work at Washington University. Although she had never testified in an immigration court before, Ms. Spargo has testified in family courts regarding child protection, juvenile delinquency and criminal cases in both St. Louis and Chicago. Less than five percent in her work is related to legal cases.

The Respondent and his family were referred to Ms. Spargo for a psycho-social assessment. She evaluated the children and family to determine the potential hardship to the children if the Respondent was removed. As part of the process Ms. Spargo first interviewed the Respondent. She also had two assessment sessions with the Respondent's daughters, Dulce and Lucy and his ex-wife, Silvia. Another session was held with Norma and the Respondent's sons, Rolando and Diego. Each session was approximately two hours long and she spent about eight hours with the family in total. She did not provide any mental health diagnoses because the children did not visit Ms. Spargo for treatment.

Ms. Spargo had the opportunity to observe the Respondent with his young sons while she interviewed Rolando and Diego. She was impressed with his familiarity with the children's needs and his ability to soothe and interact with them. Both children were very responsive to the Respondent. He was clearly a "hands-on" father despite the fact that he works outside of the home. His wife described the Respondent as her "rock" and indicated that he provides for the family's mental, social, and financial needs.

After observing the Respondent's interaction with Rolando and Diego, Ms. Spargo believes that they rely upon the Respondent significantly. Both of the Respondent's daughters depend on him for social outlets and opportunities, for financial support, and for cultural identity. During the sessions, both Rolando and Diego brought up how they identified themselves culturally. They placed a lot of importance on activities that are typical of the Latino community such as soccer games, extended family gatherings, etc. Lucy also speaks Spanish and indicated that she relates to Latino culture despite the fact that she is Caucasian biologically.

The Respondent and Silvia both provided information about the biological father and indicated that he was never part of Dulce's life. Dulce sees herself as having been abandoned by her biological father. During the sessions, Dulce shared, unsolicited, that she would like to have the Respondent's surname but that it is not possible because he cannot legally adopt her. Children who have issues of parental abandonment have "ambiguous loss" and they spend a lot of time speculating about the missing parent and his or her life. Both Dulce and Lucy also experienced a loss when the Respondent and Silvia divorced. They each expressed that the divorce is still troubling and that they wished that their parents were reunited. A child who has already experienced abandonment and loss is predisposed to further issues when she experiences other losses and become vulnerable with each loss incurred.

Ms. Spargo had Lucy and Rolando draw pictures of their family because children do not have the capacity to articulate their thoughts the same way than an adult does. Children communicate more effectively through expressive therapies. In one of Lucy drawings she identified her entire family, including her mother's new partner, all of her siblings, and her father's new partner. This was striking because not every child would identify her family that way. Other assessment tools and drawings indicated that Lucy is very concerned that she will be unhappy without her daddy. Lucy's drawings indicated that she is sensitive to the ethnic differences in her family. When asked about what would happen if the Respondent left, she included only picture of a plane and a suitcase. Ms. Spargo believes it was too painful for Lucy to put people in that picture. Lucy verbalized to Ms. Spargo on more than one occasion that "the world will end and she will not be able to continue without her daddy."

Based upon her observations from the sessions and her assessments of the family, Ms. Spargo believes that it would be "tragic" if this family was separated. She has worked with many children and families, and the fact that these families are interrelated and integrated in such a thorough way is highly significant. Although the family lives in two separate households, they have been careful to stay in close proximity. The Respondent is clearly the backbone of both families and relied upon by both families.

If the Respondent was removed, the girls would experience a change in their standard of living. Ms. Spargo does not know how exactly their living situation would change, but she does know that both Rolando and Diego fantasize about losing their house, changing schools, losing their friends, losing their connection to the Latino community, and not participating extracurricular activities. They also verbalize their fear of losing their father's affection and love.

After completing her evaluation, but before writing her report, Ms. Spargo also reviewed Dr. Bonta' report and referenced materials on the impact of poverty on children and the impact of trauma and violence on neurological development. Trauma is a very broad term that includes natural disasters, domestic violence or child abuse, community violence, traumatic grief, and other experiences. The impact of trauma depends on the developmental age of the child. Traumatic environments can alter processes in the brain during development and that would affect the Respondent's children if they were to move to Honduras.

Up to this point, the decision shows the crucial elements that are part of a cancellation of removal case. But before he can take into consideration all that he has heard, the judge must make a statement about his assessment of the credibility of all of the witnesses that appeared in his court. Under the standards set by the laws that rule immigration procedures, there is no presumption of credibility. Instead the immigration judge must consider all the facts and evidence, or "the totality of the circumstances in making his determination" (US Department of Justice, 2014). The factors that the judge takes into consideration are such things as witnesses' demeanor, candor, and responsiveness, and the inherent plausibility of the their accounts. The judge also takes into consideration how consistent witnesses' accounts are in both their oral statements in court as well as in the written documents that are before him. Does the information he got from different sources line up, that is, were they in general agreement? Are there any inaccuracies or falsehoods in any of the statements? On the credibility of the defense, the judge wrote the next section of his decision.

III. Credibility

The Respondent filed his application for cancelation of removal after May 11, 2005, and thus a REAL ID[3] Act credibility determination applies. INA § 240(c)(4)(C). Under this standard there is no presumption of credibility, and the immigration judge may consider the totality of the circumstances in making his determination. Relevant factors include the demeanor, candor, or responsiveness of the applicant or witness, the inherent plausibility of the applicant's or witness's account, the consistency between the applicant's or witness's written and oral statements, the internal consistency of each such statement, the consistency of such statements with other evidence of record, and any inaccuracies or falsehoods in such statement.

The Court finds the Respondent to be a credible witness. He testified in a candid and straightforward manner, and his testimony was consistent with his application and the testimony of other witnesses. This Court also finds Silvia to be credible. Each testified in a sincere and genuine manner, and their testimony was consistent with that of the Respondent as well as the documentary evidence of record.

In addition, the Court finds Dr. Bonta to be a credible and qualified expert witness. His testimony was detailed and he sufficiently developed background information and country conditions. Moreover, Dr. Bonta is well qualified to testify as an expert witness on socio-political geography of Honduras and current conditions there. His curriculum vita indicates that he has the education and experience necessary to give an opinion and he sufficiently observed the situation in San Jose de Cordoncillos to convincingly speak of the conditions there at this point in time.

Finally, the court finds Nancy D. Spargo to be a credible and qualified expert witness on the emotional and mental state of the Respondent's children, their integration as a family, and the potential impact of the Respondent's removal as based on her assessment and evaluation of the family. She is an LCSW and marriage and family therapist with extensive experience working with children and assessing trauma as well as working with immigrant communities. Although she has never testified before in immigration court, she has been accepted as a witness in family courts in both Illinois and Missouri.

We see from the judge's words that Aurelio R.'s credibility was founded on his "candid and straightforward manner" and that "his testimony was consistent with his application and the testimony of other witnesses." Silvia, Lucy, and Dulce were also very credible, each testifying in "a sincere and genuine manner, and their testimony was consistent with that of the Respondent as well as the documentary evidence of record." The two expert witnesses proved their credibility and qualifications, and it is clear that all witnesses presented their testimony with a level of confidence and veracity that were convincing to the judge.

As he goes further in his decision, Judge O'Malley provides legal and historical background for cancellation of removal cases. The applicant for cancellation of removal must prove that he or she satisfies the applicable statutory requirements and merits a favorable exercise of discretion. But to be eligible for cancellation of removal, the immigrant must establish (1) physical presence in the United States for 10 continuous years or more; (2) be a person of good moral character during such period; (3) have not been convicted of an offense; and (4) show that removal would result in exceptional and extremely unusual hardship to a spouse, parent, or child, who is a US citizen or LPR.[4]

Aurelio R. has four qualifying relatives. Dulce is a qualifying relative because stepchildren who meet the definition of "child" are qualifying relatives for purposes establishing exceptional and extremely unusual hardship for cancellation of removal. Dulce was not yet two years' old when the Aurelio and Silvia married. The Department of Justice attorney argued in this case that Dulce automatically ceased to be Aurelio R.'s stepchild when her biological Mother, Silva, divorced Aurelio R. But the judge disagreed with this argument.

Although the INA does not discuss the status of a stepchild upon dissolution of the marriage, there is longstanding, analogous case law that addresses the definition of stepchild under the section 101(b)(1)(B) of the Act. The Board of Immigration Appeals first addressed the issue of status of stepchildren upon termination of the marriage that created the status in *Matter of Simicevic* (holding that "affinity" had ceased and the stepchild relationship did not continue after divorce when there were no biological children from the marriage, sole custody was awarded to the natural parent, the stepmother moved to Norway after the separation, and she had not lived with the child in six years). The Board stressed that its decision was based on the specific evidence and facts of the case. In 1981 the Board affirmed that the correct manner for determining whether an individual continues to be a stepchild or stepparent upon the termination of a marriage by death or divorce is a factual inquiry as to the continuing family relationship.

The overwhelming evidence in this case is that Dulce and the Respondent continue to have a familial relationship. The Respondent is the only father that Dulce has ever known and she refers to him as "daddy." Although divorced, the Respondent and Silvia have a joint custody agreement in which the Respondent has physical custody of Lucy and Dulce every other weekend during the school year and alternating weeks in the summer. He provides not only child support, but continues to pay maintenance in order to provide adequate care for both of his daughters. Dulce is also a dependent on the Respondent's health insurance. He accompanies her to gymnastic practices and meets, takes her on vacation, and organizes outings with her. The Respondent continues to treat Dulce as his child and does not differentiate between his daughters. In fact, Dulce wants to have his surname instead of her biological father's surname, a remarkable request from an eleven year old child. Moreover, Ms. Spargo testified that the family is incredibly integrated and that both Dulce and Lucy include the Respondent, Norma, and their sons when describing their family. Finally, even under the older test outlined in *Matter of Simicevic*, affinity continues: Dulce's younger sister Lucy is a biological child born to her mother and the Respondent. It is clear that Dulce continues to be the Respondent's stepchild and is, therefore, a qualifying relative for cancellation of removal.

"The overwhelming evidence in this case," Judge O'Malley writes, "is that Dulce and the Respondent continue to have a familial relationship." This is an important turning point for what is to follow. Has Aurelio R. presented compelling evidence that exceptional and extremely unusual hardship would befall his family? First the judge provides a definition of what this term means in general and in this case specifically. He writes that "an applicant for cancellation of removal must establish that his removal from the United States would result in exceptional and extremely unusual hardship to his spouse, parent, or child who is a lawful permanent resident or United States citizen." Judge notes that the hardship presented must be something "substantially beyond" the hardships ordinarily associated with an alien's ordered departure from the United States. The judge notes that the Bureau of Immigration Appeals set forth factors that courts are to consider in determining whether a qualifying relative will suffer exceptional and extremely unusual hardship. Strong cases could be made if, for example, an immigrant has elderly parents in the United States who are solely dependent upon him for support or has a qualifying child with very serious health issues, or compelling special needs in school. If a lower standard of living or adverse country conditions would affect the qualifying relative (i.e., the citizen-child), it may be insufficient to support a finding of exceptional and extremely unusual hardship.

The judge now turns to the accumulated evidence of the case and reviews all of the information about the citizen-children, their mothers, and the impact that deportation might have on them. He restates that Aurelio R. asserts that "his removal would result in exceptional and extremely unusual hardship to his United States citizen children," Dulce, Lucy, Rolando, and Diego. The judge is placed in the position of having to address two situations in Aurelio R.'s request for cancellation: one is that Dulce and Lucy will remain in the United States if he is removed and the other is that Rolando and Diego will accompany Aurelio R. to Honduras. These are two distinct issues. Judge O'Malley continues:

> The Respondent avers that his removal would result in exceptional and extremely unusual hardship to his United States citizen children Dulce (age 11), Lucy (age 9), Rolando (age 4) and Diego (age 2). Rolando and Diego live with the Respondent in St. Louis, Missouri. Dulce and Lucy live five minutes from the Respondent with their mother, and spend significant time in his home.
>
> The Respondent indicated that Dulce and Lucy will remain in the United States if he is removed, but that Rolando and Diego will accompany him to Honduras. As such, the Court will address both situations.
>
> A significant hardship factor is the financial instability that all of the Respondent's children, but specifically Rolando and Diego would face

if the Respondent was removed to Honduras. In the United States, the Respondent earns $40,000 per year and uses his income to not only support Norma and his sons, but also to make support payments and provide insurance for Silvia and Lucy. Dr. Bonta estimates that, even with the more prevalent employment opportunities in the state where the Respondent would live in Honduras, he could earn $400 per month at the most. A review of the economic opportunities outlined by Dr. Bonta in his report indicates that the Respondent would be more likely to earn $250 per month and provide barely a subsistence living for his family in Honduras. With this level of poverty, it would be impossible for the Respondent to continue making support payments to Ms. Bonta, and she depends on those payments to pay her mortgage. Although her husband works, his income is used for other family expenses. If the Respondent were removed to Honduras it is likely that Dulce and Lucy would lose their home and be forced to share a much smaller apartment with a family of six. Their standard of living would also change radically with the loss of nearly $1,800 a month in family income. Although the Respondent owns some tools and equipment for his business, he has little in reserves to assist his family during the period of transition.

Both Dulce and Lucy would also suffer severe emotional hardships if the Respondent was removed to Honduras and they were to remain in the United States. Ms. Spargo testified to the close bonds in this extended and integrated family. Dulce and Lucy would not only lose their father, who they depend on, but also their siblings. As highlighted in Ms. Spargo's report, Dulce in particular is at risk for anxiety and depression because she already suffers from her biological father's abandonment of her as an infant and both girls suffered loss related to their parents' divorce. Given the previous experiences of Dulce and Lucy the fears and concerns that they have already expressed in assessment, and the extreme close relationship that they have with the Respondent, Ms. Spargo anticipates that both girls will demonstrate symptoms of anxiety and depression that will have a lasting effect on their development, social interactions, schoolwork, and emotional psyche. They will also lose part of their cultural identity that they both appear to value deeply.

In explaining the justification for his decision, the judge draws on legal precedents and statutes. He recognizes the effect that Aurelio R.'s absence would have on the children. The judge provides considerable additional context for his decision. Dulce and Lucy are at an age when the presence of their father is crucial "because of the new challenges they face in life (i.e., peer pressure, academics, etc.) and separation from the Respondent would be devastating." The judge quotes two speeches by President Obama on the importance of fathers in children's lives.

> June 21, 2010: Fathers are our first teachers and coaches . . . they're our mentors, our role models. They show us by the example they set the kind of people they want us to become. But we also know that what too many fathers being absent means—too many fathers missing from too many homes, missing from too many lives. We know that when fathers abandon their responsibilities, there's harm done to those kids. We know that children who grow up without a father are more likely to live in poverty. They're more likely to drop out of school. They're more likely to wind up in prison. They're more likely to abuse drugs and alcohol. They're more likely to run away from home. They're more likely to become teenage parents themselves.[5]
>
> February 15, 2013: In too many neighborhoods today—whether here in Chicago or in the farthest reaches of rural America—it can feel like for a lot of young people the future only extends to the next street corner or the outskirts of town; that no matter how much you work or how hard you try, your destiny was determined the moment you were born. There are entire neighborhoods where young people, they don't see an example of somebody succeeding.

"The Court," the judge writes, "strongly agrees with these sentiments, and believes the separation hardship would incur merits significant consideration." He continues.

> There would also be hardship for Rolando and Diego if they were relocated to Honduras. The schools available in San Jose de Cordoncillos do not provide education above the ninth grade, and it is difficult, dangerous, and expensive to travel to the high school. Although they are young and would be able to eventually adapt to their new way of life, the disparity between secondary education in the United States and Honduras would make it quite difficult for the children were they to return to the United States as adults, with insufficient education or training to attend university or find employment.
>
> The poor security in Honduras creates another significant hardship for the Respondent's children. Dr. Bonta's report highlights that Honduras is considered to be the most violent country in the world, and that the state of Cortes is the most violent within that country. The murder rate in the state of Cortes is 175 persons per 100,000, but jumps

to 300 per 100,000 in the areas surrounding San Pedro Sula. The rate for Honduras as a whole is between 80 and 90 per 100,000. These rates are astronomical when compared with the rates of even the most dangerous cities in the United States. This and other examples of violence indicate that it would be extremely unsafe for Rolando and Diego live in the state of Cortes. Dulce and Lucy would also suffer additional emotional trauma related to their fear that their family is unsafe. Moving to another, potentially safer, area of Honduras is unlikely given that other states have even less economic opportunities, the lack of family or resources in other states, and the high cost of procuring housing.

Health and sanitation in San Jose de Cordoncillos and the surrounding areas are also hardships to Rolando and Diego that must be considered. Dr. Bonta's report indicates that although HIV, Aids, Dengue Fever, and other serious illnesses are prevalent in the area, there is little or no medical care available to them. There is no clinic or doctor in their village and the nearest clinic is twenty minutes away by car. Even in larger cities adequate care can be difficult. This is in addition to the poor water conditions and the lack of sanitation that leads to increased disease and can be particularly dangerous to small children.

Having thoroughly considered the hardship factors in the aggregate, the Court finds the Respondent has met his burden of providing exceptional and extremely unusual hardship to his qualifying relatives. His children's ages, educational needs, emotional needs, medical conditions, and physical safety are hardship factors that, when coupled with the Respondent's apparent inability to provide for his family in Honduras, would lead to a hardship "substantially beyond that which ordinarily would be expected to result from the alien's deportation." *Matter of Monreal*, 23 I&N Dec. 56, 59 (BIA 2001).

I asked Attorneys Ken Schmitt and Gustavo Arango about their thoughts and feelings as they awaited the judge's ruling, when he used language that "the Court finds the Respondent has met his burden" and "would lead to hardship" substantially beyond the usual in cases of deportation. Ken Schmitt replied that "I was, of course, very happy to know that our client would be able to stay in the United States and continue to contribute to our community and that his family would remain intact" (e-mail communication, March 10, 2014). A triumph in having one removal order cancelled seems to Schmitt so little in view of the many deserving immigrants who are not granted a cancellation. "I am always saddened," he continues, "by the extreme efforts necessary to achieve this outcome and the much larger numbers of equally worthy individuals who are excluded from this outcome because they do not have 10 years of [physical] presence or [the perception that] their child or family members won't suffer enough by the respondent's removal. What a loss to the family, to the US citizen-child's future and our own community!"

Attorney Arango reflected on the decision (e-mail communication, February 18, 2014), applying the tried-and-true aphorism to this and other cases, "it truly takes a village to win a cancellation of removal case." Arango goes on: "Representing a client in a cancellation of removal case requires team work: social workers; psychologists; teachers; family therapists; doctors; country condition experts, religious leaders, etc., [they are all] essential." At the heart of the case is that the team's work demonstrates to the judge, and to the government attorney, with all available evidence and the persuasiveness of the litigator, in this case Ken Schmitt, that the hardship that will befall a family would indeed be tragic and the family would suffer the loss of their relative if removed to his home-country. When the judge utters the words, "the Respondent has met his burden," there is a sense of relief and of accomplishment. Arango, however, points to the group rather than any individual: "the hard communal work performed [by a team] to provide the client and his family a chance to remain and grow together in the United States, that [leaves you with] a feeling of comfort and satisfaction that surpasses [just the sense of] personal achievement." It is the group around the client, the community of family, supporters, advocates, and experts that contribute to the final outcome.

As the decision continues, Judge O'Malley addresses the issue of the discretion available to him. The term *discretion* is an important one to understand in order to place the judge's ultimate decision into context. Aurelio R., the judge found, had met the barebones legal requirements for arguing for a cancellation of his removal. These elements are that he had maintained a continuous presence in the United States, had been a lawful resident for more than five years, and had not been convicted of an aggravated felony or other high crime. Discretion goes beyond meeting the basic elements. The judge weighs all the other positive and negative factors—the totality of the case—to exercise his discretion for a decision favorable to Aurelio R.[6] As found in the *Immigration Judge Benchbook* (US Department of Justice, 2014), the key for a successful decision is "taking the information you have gathered and then clearly explaining why you reach the conclusion you do. How do the relevant facts you have gathered combine within the confines of the law to lead you to the conclusion that the respondent does or does not deserve a second chance to remain in the United States?"[7]

Judge O'Malley's decision follows these suggestions.

A. Discretion

The Respondent's primary adverse discretionary factor is his 2011 DUI[8] conviction, for which the Respondent has taken full responsibility. Against this concern, the Respondent exhibits a number of positive discretionary factors, including his long-term residence in the United States, contributions to the community, and gainful employment. In addition, the Respondent has filed his taxes dating back to 2004. Finally, the testimonial evidence and affidavits submitted indicate that Respondent is a hard worker, loving father to all four of his children, and upstanding member of the community. After weighing these factors in the cumulative, the Court finds that the Respondent warrants a favorable exercise of discretion. Therefore, as he has otherwise established his statutory eligibility for cancellation of removal, the Respondent's application for cancellation of removal will be granted.

Accordingly, after careful consideration, the following order shall be entered:

ORDER OF THE IMMIGRATION JUDGE

IT IS HEREBY ORDERED that the Respondent's request for cancellation of removal and adjustment of status under Section 240A(b)(1) of the Act is **GRANTED**

October 2013

_____
[signed]
John R. O'Malley
United States Immigration Judge.

All future hearings in this matter are CANCELLED.

JUST ONE OUTCOME

Aurelio R.'s case is only one example of how the search for the American Dream—a dream that is not just about financial stability—was validated by an immigration court. The dream that led Aurelio R. to enter the country illegally was inspired by the need for his and his family's safety, improved living conditions, and opportunities to live freely and strive for a better life. It was a hope for his children to continue the uninterrupted lives of any American child. Aurelio R.'s case resulted in a happy outcome for him and his family. Rolando and Diego are spared the possibility of leaving for Honduras with him—of becoming exiles—and Dulce and Lucy are spared the loss of a father—of becoming orphans. This mix-matched typical American family dodges the possibility of the terrible split that they would experience since, in the end, they are all Aurelio R.'s children. The possibility that the siblings would have been split from one another is averted. His children enjoyed the outcome of being able to return home holding their father's hands and secure in the knowledge that he would be there for them tomorrow and the day after that.

But they are the lucky ones, as Ken Schmitt noted in his response to my question. Not all cancellations are granted. After going to court to contest an order of removal, and following all available legal avenues, some immigrants cannot mount a convincing enough case that they deserve to remain in the United States. Every year, the Executive Office for Immigration Review which is based in Falls Church, Virgina, grants exactly 4000 cancellations of removal nationally—cases in which the respondent has met the requirements of demonstrated hardship, 10-year continued physical residence, good moral character, and so forth. These grants of cancellation are available starting every October and are generally gone by the following February, giving undocumented parents just a four month window for clemency.[9]

NOTES

1. CFR refers to the Code of Federal Regulations which codifies the general and permanent rules and regulations published in the Federal Register by the executive departments and agencies of the US government.
2. SATOP refers to the Substance Abuse Traffic Offender Program. In Missouri, the Department of Mental Health, Division of Behavioral Health certifies the agencies that provide services to individuals who have had an alcohol- or drug-related traffic offense. These individuals are referred as a result of an administrative suspension or revocation of their driver licenses, court order, condition of probation, or plea bargain. First, individuals are screened upon an arrest for DWI to establish their alcohol and substance use related to their driving behavior. The results of the screening determine the appropriate level of SATOP placement for each client. Once examined, SATOP officials assign the appropriate service for the individual. Retrieved from http://dmh.mo.gov/ada/satop/#.
3. The REAL ID Act of 2005 was passed by Congress on May 11, 2005 and modified the then-existing federal law pertaining to the security, authentication, and issuance standards for state driver's licenses and identification (ID) cards as well as various immigration issues pertaining to terrorism. The REAL ID Act established requirements for state driver's licenses and ID cards in order

to make them acceptable by the federal government for official purposes, as defined by the Secretary of Homeland Security as primarily for boarding commercially operated airline flights and entering federal buildings and nuclear power plants. See http://www.dhs.gov/xlibrary/assets/real-id-act-text.pdf for more information.

4. Another eligibility category is if the immigrant can establish that she has been battered or subjected to extreme cruelty by a spouse or parent who is or was a United States citizen or lawful permanent resident, or has a child who was subjected to such abuse.

5. My son Luis-Michael and I were present on stage with President Obama and other fathers and their children on June 21, 2010 when he launched his Responsible Fatherhood Initiative.

6. I am grateful to Matt Trevena, Esq., for providing a clear, lay explanation of discretion to this nonlawyer.

7. It is my understanding that by delegating this ultimate exercise of discretion to the Justice Department through the immigration judges, Congress is cutting off federal court review of this particular element of an immigration matter once the case clears final administrative review at the Board of Immigration Appeals. In other words, although a federal court can certainly interpret federal law, it does not have the legal authority to second guess the administrative authority delegated by Congress to the Justice Department, unless of course the department has acted irrationally or based on irrelevant or illegal grounds.

8. Driving Under the Influence refers to driving with a blood alcohol content in excess of a specific threshold level, typically 0.08 percent.

9. In an Operating Policies and Procedures Memorandum dated February 3, 2012, Chief Immigration Judge, Brian M. O'Leary, informs all immigration judges, court administrators, attorney advisors, judicial law clerks, and immigration court staff of the procedures for reserving decisions in nondetained suspension of deportation or cancellation of removal cases that are subject to the 4000 cap. When the first 3,500 suspension and cancellation cases have been granted in a fiscal year, the Office of the Chief Immigration Judge notifies the immigration courts around the country. That date becomes the "cut-off," date and immigration judges must reserve any decisions they have in cases that are subject to the cap. For more information, see http://www.justice.gov/eoir/efoia/ocij/oppm12/12-01.pdf

CHAPTER 8

Losing the Challenge

In the case of Aurelio R., the judge acknowledged his good moral character, devotion to his children and stepchild, and successful entrepreneurship. Although Aurelio had been convicted of a DUI, the judge respected that Aurelio R. took full responsibility for his actions and sought treatment. In the case of Carlota and Jaime, their meritorious behavior as evaluated by teachers and the demonstrable harm that had already befallen their two daughters prevailed in the judge's decision. These families met the criteria for eligibility for cancellation of removal and adjustment of status. Not all applications for cancellation of deportation are granted; not all families can mount cases like those described in Chapters 6 and 7. The sad reality is that some immigrants who apply for relief cannot be characterized as innocent victims who are arrested, detained, and deported. While some undocumented immigrants may act heroically or with high moral purpose and we question why a minor traffic violation would lead to their detention and removal, others make colossal mistakes or blatantly violate the law. Sometimes, mental illness, addictions, and other personal demons underlie the reasons they break the law. Such factors can be beyond the individual's control. Nonetheless, they forfeit an individual's eligibility for relief under Section 240A (b) (2), no-conviction and good moral character requirements, and make irrelevant the physical-presence requirements. They weaken any hardship argument.

In this chapter, I present two cases that were turned down for cancellation but for very different reasons—one decision clear and the other ambiguous. One case shows how an individual invalidated his chances at cancellation through a pattern of behaviors that violated laws and challenged his claims of good moral character. This case demonstrates how an immigration judge may take information into account in the aggregate. The other case illustrates how, even when all eligibility criteria appear to have been met, a judge's decision hinges not on the aggregate but on one rather small item in the immigrant's life. Both cases are lost, but the second case, which is so similar to those in Chapters 6 and 7 that were granted cancellation, shows the variability in judges' decision-making. For these reasons I have disguised all names.

IN THE CASE OF GUILLERMO V.

The case of Guillermo V., a man in North Carolina with multiple and serial violations, is an example of how a court may act when the misdemeanors and bad acts are too many to tolerate even if two citizen-children with some special needs would be victims. At the time of his immigration hearing, Guillermo V. was 32 years of age and a native of Mexico. He had entered the United States when he was 19. Born in the state of Hidalgo, he was raised in a small town with a population of about 200 inhabitants. At about the age of 21, Guillermo established a common law relationship with his partner, Eva, who also entered the United States from Mexico illegally. They have two daughters, 10-year-old Amparo and 7-year-old Doris, both born in North Carolina. The family would have to return to Mexico if Guillermo V. were deported. Both girls have some school and medical difficulties and the parents assert that they would not be able to get the kind of services in rural Mexico that they would get in the United States.

For his case, Guillermo V. submitted affidavits from friends and had a Catholic priest testify on his behalf. I testified as an expert witness on the general topic of children whose parents are deported and some of the conditions that these children might face if relocated to Mexico. The judge acknowledged in his decision that Guillermo V. had met the burden of establishing his physical presence in the United States for more than 10 years and a stable residential history.

But Guillermo V. pled guilty to driving without a license, reckless driving, and driving with an open container of alcohol in his car. These are not disqualifying crimes under the Immigration and Nationality Act (INA), but in the judge's assessment they raised the question about Guillermo V.'s moral character. The judge draws from INA bars to eligibility. Under the INA, an individual cannot establish eligibility if he is a "habitual drunkard" (INA § 101(f) (1)); derives income principally from illegal gambling; has been convicted for two or more gambling offenses; gives false testimony for the purposes of obtaining any benefit under the INA; has served time in a penal institution for a total of 180 days or more for acts in which moral character is relevant; or has been convicted of an aggravated felony and other proscribed conduct. There's also a "catch-all" category which states that "the fact that any person is not within any of the foregoing classes shall not preclude a finding that for other reasons such person is or was not of good moral character" (INA § 101(f)). With these guidelines, a judge weighs all the favorable and unfavorable factors in the case to decide if *in toto* the immigrant has met the burden for meriting a favorable exercise of discretion. The judge in Guillermo's case went on to some lengths on the question of moral character. The judge writes that

The Court recognizes Respondent presented some positive factors pertaining to his good moral character. Respondent maintained steady employment during the relevant period, working in lawn maintenance and doing mechanic work with a friend. He testified to supporting his family along with Eva's income. In 2004, Respondent purchased the mobile home he was renting. He also owns several vehicles that he fixes up and sells for a profit. Respondent's priest testified that he attends church regularly. Eva explained that he is a good family man and is always there.

While the Court finds none of the *per se* categories apply to Respondent's circumstances, in balancing the equities, his extensive criminal history and tax misrepresentations over the past ten years outweigh the positive factors. First, even though Respondent was not convicted of a crime that would make him *per se* without good moral character, the Court finds that his recidivist and undeterred pattern of disregarding the law of the United States and safety of the public-at-large warrant an adverse good moral character finding. Within a ten-year period preceding the decision, Respondent pled guilty ten times in North Carolina for failing to have a valid driver's license. Several of these convictions involved him being arrested and charged under his father's name, which he failed to correct. Two of these convictions resulted in Respondent serving jail time, and the rest gave probation. A condition of Respondent's probation mandated that he "live and remain at liberty without violating any law." The Court finds Respondent failed to respect the letter of the law and the terms of his probation, most significantly in the year 2007 when he received four no-driver's-license convictions in a one-year period. Although Respondent claims he learned his lesson, the Court notes that his actions of repeatedly violating the law lend greater credence than his words. Respondent's temporary driver's license expired in late summer of 2013 and the Court remains skeptical if Respondent would forego driving should he fail to renew it.

Guillermo V. presented several things that seemed to force the judge's hand in making a decision. First, Guillermo V. presented contradictory information about his church attendance, saying he had been a parishioner since 2005, whereas his priest said it had been since 2002. Worse still is that Guillermo V. could not remember the name of the church despite being a parishioner for so many years. Second, the court paid special attention to his driving violations—some within one month of each other—as well as his attempt to deceive the authorities. His case appeared doomed just on those issues alone.

> Respondent's cumulative criminal history includes other behavior leading the Court to question his good moral character. He was arrested for DUI in late summer of 2004, and pled down to reckless driving for which he received one year probation. In 2005, Respondent received a citation for having an open bottle container. When asked on cross-examination the circumstances surrounding this incident, Respondent explained the bottles were not his, and he allowed his friends to drink in the car because they only had one beer each. Respondent was also arrested and charged with aggravated assault with a deadly weapon in early 2010, which was eventually dropped by the State six months later. Respondent testified that he drove to a party, presumably without out a license, and tried to break up a fight between a group of people against his friend. He was then arrested after the owner of the house told police he had weapons, but the police did not find any. Respondent's repeated confrontations with law enforcement throughout the good moral character period militate an adverse finding as a matter of discretion.
>
> In addition to Respondent's chronic criminal recidivism, the Court also finds a lack of good moral character based on falsifications on many of his tax returns. First, Respondent filed his 2003, 2004, and 2005 tax returns in 2012, and all three claimed daughter Doris even though she was not born until the spring of 2006. When asked by DHS on cross-examination to explain the falsification, Respondent stated that a tax preparer told him to complete the form like that. He also explained on redirect that he does not read English and the tax preparer did not read the form to him. Second, Respondent's 2006 tax return was filed as having no dependents, despite the fact that he had two minor children at the time. Third, Respondent filed as "married filing jointly" in 2007 and 2008 even though he is not married to Eva. The Court finds Respondent's repeated failure to file accurate tax returns constitutes a negative good moral character factor in exercising its discretion.
>
> In considering Respondent's recidivist criminal history and pattern of tax return errors, the Court applies section 101(f) of the INA to find Respondent

lacks good moral character under the "catchall" provision. During the preceding ten-year period, Respondent drove without a driver's license for a majority of the time, resulting in 10 convictions for driving without a driver's license. Respondent would have the Court believe that he drove illegally for his daughters' appointments and [for] getting food, but his testimony on cross-examination contradicts this. Specifically, Respondent drove to parties, to garage sales, and "for spring break purposes." The Court finds his disregard for the laws of the United States and the safety of the traveling public of serious concern. Respondent testified that if he got his license taken away again, he would simply move back to Mexico instead of facing the possibility of not driving. Further, his carelessness with regard to his tax returns shows a continued pattern of failing to abide by the rules and regulations of the United States. Thus, Respondent lacks a good moral character and is not eligible for cancellation of removal as a nonpermanent resident.

Guillermo V.'s pattern of irresponsible behavior and violations of the law might have been sufficient it seems for the judge to determine that he did not qualify simply on the basis of proving good moral character. However, the judge also considered what the potential harm to Guillermo V.'s children would be if he were to be deported. In this regard, the judge showed a disposition to take into consideration the "best interest of the child" principle, a topic I provide more detail about in Chapter 11.

"Even if Respondent had demonstrated the requisite good moral character, he still must establish that his removal would result in exceptional and extremely unusual hardship to his United States citizen daughters," the judge wrote. Guillermo V. and Eva testified that if Guillermo V. were deported, his children Amparo and Doris would go as well. Guillermo V. pointed to three disruptions in his children's lives that he thought would demonstrate exceptional and extremely unusual hardship to his US-citizen daughters: (a) decreased access to services to help his daughters' speech and attention deficit/hyperactivity disorder (ADHD); (b) impoverished conditions and lack of opportunity in rural Mexico; and (c) increased danger and discrimination in Mexico. Indeed, the two girls were receiving health and educational services for the ADHD and other diagnosed problems. Amparo was on medication for ADHD but her medical records indicated she was not taking it every day. Her teachers had expressed concern also about her language and reading acquisition skills, and an educational assessment was scheduled for the near future. Doris had a severe speech articulation disorder and ADHD, but could not tolerate the medication she was prescribed. Both daughters were struggling in school and Amparo had already been held back a year. The judge wasn't convinced.

Respondent claimed his daughters would have trouble getting similar services in Mexico. For example, he testified that he would have to drive 36 miles to get special aid for his children if he moved to Remalato. He also stated that most U.S. citizen children in Mexico have to "fight" to obtain aid in Mexico, and he heard about this from his wife's sister who returned to Mexico with her removed spouse. The Court is sympathetic to Respondent's situation. Although Respondent's children will suffer some hardship and lost opportunities after moving to Mexico, Congress imposed a high standard of hardship that has not been met in this case. Like the Respondent in *Matter of Andazola-Rivas*, Respondent has not shown his children would be deprived of all school or opportunity to obtain any education. Instead, he has argued that the speech services and ADHD attention they received in public schools in North Carolina would be less streamlined and accessible in Mexico.

The judge found that the loss of school-based services and educational quality do not establish exceptional and extremely unusual hardship because these factors are commonly shared by US. citizen-children returning to any developing country. In other words, the loss of services is a reality that U.S citizen-children experience upon moving to Mexico. The girls' specific learning disabilities did not constitute, in the judge's mind, an exceptional and extremely unusual hardship. Guillermo V. testified that Doris' speech problem arises at school and that she has no problem communicating at home or with neighbors, and Eva testified that she speaks Spanish at home with her parents, though it is "bad." The judge was unconvinced, and to the contrary, determined that a return to Mexico "may actually improve once she begins speaking Spanish as her main language. Both children are very young and will likely learn Spanish quickly through immersion in the Mexican culture, especially with parents who are native speakers."

The fact that Amparo and Doris were not taking their medication for ADHD regularly weakened Guillermo V.'s case. Further, Guillermo V. had not presented any evidence that medical care would be unavailable in Mexico or that they would be unable to obtain prescriptions. Despite "the scant medical treatment in rural Mexico in contrast to the United States because of expense and access," the Court found that "the decreased availability is a function of any move to a less developed nation. Thus, without evidence to the contrary, medical treatment remains available to Doris and Amparo though not in the abundance and ease as in the United States." As a result, the judge determined that the "Respondent failed to establish exceptional and extremely unusual hardship to his U.S. citizen daughters."

Once again, Guillermo V. and his wife Eva provided information contradicted by others. The judge noted that the parents' testimony that the girls would go to Mexico contradicted the affidavits submitted by friends, who asserted that Guillermo V.'s deportation would cause a separation and leave his daughters devastated without a father. While this could be viewed as evidence that the parents were undecided about what they would do with their daughters, rather than intentionally misleading the court, it was among the many weaknesses in Guillermo V.'s case.

Guillermo V. also gave testimony on the small village he was raised in and the "primitive and subsistence-level conditions" there. The judge ruled that the Board of Immigration Appeals has held that poor economic conditions alone are not sufficient to establish extremely unusual hardship. On the stand, Guillermo V. said that he would not be able to buy a nicer home in a better area near his village but also agreed that he had not looked at other affordable areas or determined what made him financially unable to do so. Further, he would be returning to Mexico with enough assets to start a new life there. With the sale of his home and automobiles in North Carolina and a small savings account, the court did not agree that he would be subject to the same destitution of his childhood. When Guillermo V. said that he did not know what kind of work he would do in Mexico, the judge responded in his decision with the rejoinder that "the Court notes the Respondent's resourcefulness while in the United States," citing as evidence how he learned to be a mechanic on weekends under the tutelage of a friend and that Guillermo V. had been able to convert these skills into a full-time job. Although the judge applauded Guillermo V. for his work ethic, it was not enough, and the judge determined that the socioeconomic impact on Guillermo V.'s daughters did not qualify as exceptional or extremely unusual hardship.

Guillermo V. raised grave concerns about the violence that has overrun Mexico. The judge reasoned that the subjective belief of danger through testimony was not enough, and the record did not support a finding that Amparo and Doris would be destined to face more danger in Mexico. The judge turned to information provided by the US Department of State's Human Rights Report for Mexico that indicated that Mexico was continuing its fight against narcotraffickers and other organized criminal groups and that this battle included frequent clashes between security forces and the criminal elements. Not deterred, the judge ruled that the mere threat of a clash was not "substantially beyond the ordinary hardship that would be expected when a close family member leaves this country." Eva may have testified truthfully that the drug gangs were somewhat near their village, but she did not cite drug violence as the biggest danger. Instead, the biggest dangers in the village, Eva told the court, were loose animals that bite people and two mentally ill brothers who scared children. The judge recognized that Mexico has an increased risk of violence, but did not see any evidence that it pervades all areas. Even on the issue of the discrimination that Amparo and Doris would face in Mexico, the judge reasoned that discrimination in a new country is generalizable to anyone moving to a new country where cultural and language differences create a difficult but surmountable adjustment. Thus the judge wrote, "The Court cannot find it an exceptional and extremely unusual hardship."

Guillermo V.'s many violations of the law and his attempts at deception had already influenced the judge negatively, so very little could be said that would change his mind. It's possible that Guillermo's multiple un-redeeming qualities simply biased the judge such that the judge minimized the danger to the girls in Mexico and did not think that the discrimination the girls would face there would be any different for anyone else moving to a place of linguistic and cultural differences. The judge examined the cumulative effects of lower economic opportunity, access to educational and medical services, community safety, and possible discrimination, but determined these factors to be insufficient. Combined with the inadequate proof of good moral character, the judge ultimately wrote, "Respondent's application for cancellation of removal for a non-permanent resident . . . is hereby denied. The court further orders Respondent removed to Mexico on the charge sustained in the Notice to Appear."

With those words, the judge decided the future of Guillermo V., his wife, and his two young daughters.[1] It's possible that an immigration court could give the unauthorized alien the benefit of the doubt, but as one reads the judge's decision and traces the accumulating evidence, it becomes obvious that the judge was disinclined to act sympathetically toward Guillermo V. A minor traffic infraction may have been forgivable, especially if Guillermo V. had shown remorse and kept a clean record. Lamentably, he had not, and thus the judge saw all the other evidence as insufficient to sway him from denying Guillermo V. the cancellation. His behavior was his undoing, and the saddest part was the harm that it would bring to his two innocent daughters. Guillermo V. could not get the benefit of the doubt for his behavior from this judge and would probably not accrue much sympathy from most US citizens or even, I daresay, most undocumented immigrants.

IN THE CASE OF RAUL

Other cases that are denied cancellation are not as understandable as Guillermo V.'s. Raul, a Honduran immigrant challenged the deportation order against him, but was denied for reasons that are not entirely clear since he presented a very compelling case for a grant of cancellation. His attorneys sought not just cancellation of removal but also sought "Temporary Protected Status" (TPS) for Raul. Temporary Protected Status is available to persons from countries that the US Secretary of Homeland Security has determined have conditions that temporarily prevent the country's nationals from returning safely, or in certain circumstances, are unable to handle the return of its nationals adequately. US Citizenship and Immigration Services (USCIS) may grant TPS to eligible nationals of certain countries (or parts of countries), who are already in the United States.[2] During a designated period of time, the individual who is the beneficiary of the TPS designation is not removable from the United States, can be authorized to work in the United States, and can also be granted travel authorization. Once granted TPS, an individual also cannot be detained by DHS on the basis of his or her immigration status in the United States. However, TPS is only a temporary benefit that does not provide a pathway to citizenship or any other immigration status. At time of this case, Honduras had been placed on the list of countries eligible for TPS in January 1999 and the expiration date was set for January 2015. [3]

My involvement in the case began in January 2010 with a call from Ken Schmitt and Gustavo Arango, who requested an evaluation of Raul's three daughters, Emily, Jessica, and Brittany. I did not have the requisite training or experience evaluating children as young as Jessica and Brittany, ages 3 and 1, respectively, and thus conducted only an evaluation of Emily. At the time I met Emily, she was 7 years old. Raul, age 35, worked as a landscaper and roofer and his wife, Mabel, age 28, was a cook in a restaurant. They had been married for eight years. All three girls were born in Kansas. Emily was in second grade in the town's elementary school, where she was described by teachers as a student of average academic abilities but excellent academic effort and exceptional classroom citizenship. Teachers noted in the school records that "Emily continues to come to school with a wonderful attitude and works very hard."

On the several occasions I was with the family, I found them to be a lively, friendly group and very expressive of their affection for one another. The girls laughed and teased each other in warm ways that elicited laughter from their parents. It was impossible not to become engaged in their playfulness. The girls sat near or on their parents' laps, caressed their parents affectionately, and obeyed instructions. The girls all appeared to be healthy and happy. They played among themselves and indulged Brittany because of her age. In April 2011, Emily's paternal uncle was deported and her father opened his home to his sister-in-law and a 4-month-old infant niece. Emily understood what deportation could mean to a family; she was living it.

Emily is a bright, friendly, tall girl who appeared her stated age. She related very well with me in each of the three evaluation sessions. Emily's interviews were all conducted in English, her dominant language. In my first meeting, Emily told of making a book about her family and how she was teaching her father English. She added that because he wanted to learn from her. The sisters tried to speak English with one another in order to help Raul learn faster. Emily said that she was proud of her father when she watched him play soccer because he is a very good athlete and "he always helps his team win." She was able to name all of her extended family. Her parents reported that Emily is often fearful of what will happen to her father if deported. She will cry when her father's situation is discussed at home, and her mother told me that Emily will often wake up and ask if her father is still there.

Emily talked animatedly about her favorite books. She said her parents buy her books, and further offered, "I like to read and my favorite food is pasta." In her drawing of a house, she placed a rainbow over the house. She mouthed or whispered to herself the rainbow spectrum as a means of coloring them in correct sequence. The home was a rudimentary figure, as would be expected a child of her age. She drew a few clouds in an otherwise clear, sunny sky, and adorned the yard with flowers. Emily drew a doormat at the front of the house. The drawing suggested a happy, healthy home environment. She took a longer time to draw a tree.

The second meeting was scheduled for several weeks later. Then, on the day before that appointment, I received a call cancelling the upcoming meeting. The family's attorney told me that the previous week Raul had lost a paternal uncle in Honduras under tragic circumstances. Raul's uncle was at home in the small town of San Juan in the Honduran state of Atlántida with his wife and another female family member when a group of men burst into his home and assassinated him in the presence of the two women. He was shot multiple times and died instantly. The men fled but no arrests were ever made. It appeared to have been a contract killing sponsored by a rival in the cattle business. The hired killers were assumed to be linked to drug gangs because of the efficiency of the murder and their swift escape. This information was provided by the family but never verified by the police. We were provided with copies of the newspaper accounts of the killing and of other homicides in their small town. Educational and medical colleagues at the Universidad Nacional Autónoma de Honduras provided me with independent verification of the prevalence of criminal gangs in the area of the family's home town. They were not surprised by the senselessness of the crime, for it was too frequent an event in their country.

Although Emily did not know her uncle, the tragedy struck the father deeply and added to his worry of the deportation process that he was challenging for the sake of his children. Two months after the initial session, I saw Emily again. She told me about how she was rehearsing for an end-of-year show at school and about how much she liked to read. Emily said that she had learned of her grand-uncle's assassination and that "I feel sorry for my papá."

Because of postponement of Raul's case by the immigration court, it was another year before I saw Emily again. In that third session, Emily was just starting fourth grade and had completed third grade with very good grades. During this meeting, I administered several psychological tests and I was impressed with Emily's insightful questions and comments about the tests. For example, the depression instrument asks about sadness. Emily asked, "what if I don't feel sad?" In another test, she asked for clarification about who the persons were that were referred to in the question, "does it mean people I know or strangers?" In an instrument that measures a child's self-concept, Emily showed similar clarity of thinking. On an item stating "I am unpopular" (to which she replied 'no'), Emily added that she could not really decide if she was popular or not but, she added, "my teacher says that kids try to be popular by being mean." And to the item "In school I am a dreamer," Emily asked, "does it mean a day-dreamer or some who dreams about what they want to be when they grow up?"

With a chance to get to know Emily over a period of 18 months, I concluded that she was a normal child with intact perceptual-motor abilities and no depression (apart from being prone to tears when discussing her father's possible deportation). Her self-assurance and emotional and behavioral stability were indications of a stable home life and effective childrearing by her parents. The picture that emerged was that of a stable and intact family whose daughter had benefited from a structured, secure home environment. The interaction of siblings is often a reflection of the parents' own relationship, and Emily and her sisters' interactions show a healthy pattern, one we associate with a normal family. It is worth noting that, although parents could have tried to portray their daughter as troubled for the purposes of this evaluation and its implications for their future as a family, the parents answered honestly and did not try to garner any advantages by misrepresenting their daughter.

In my mind, there remained serious reservations about the potential effects that her father's deportation could have on Emily. At the time,

Emily woke from naps asking if her father were still there. Her anxiety about what would become of her father indicated underlying vigilance and preoccupation. My report included a developmental perspective that in the next few years, Emily would be entering middle school, puberty, and full adolescence, critical developmental periods for the emergence of disorders if major life disruptions occur. Accordingly, in my report to the court, I raised concerns of what her reaction might be in the case of father's deportation.

> Neither being left in the U.S. in the care of her mother alone or a family (or foster care) nor moving to Honduras with her parents in a deportation will resolve the challenges that Emily will face. Generally speaking, fathers play critical roles in family systems in their partnership with the other parent. Parents must establish a good balance between them in nurturing, monitoring, supervising, and disciplining. Raul's role in his family is not that different. He is an engaged father and husband. His presence provides a certain level of structure, consistency, and discipline, particularly as his children age into adolescence and begin to challenge authority more. If Emily were to move to Honduras with her family, the risks rise considerably for her and for her parents. There will be the problem of the father's employment; family economic hardship; much lower educational standards and opportunities; inadequate medical care; and the risks of living in a hamlet that is rife with violence. He may have to work at some distance from his home in Honduras and may be away for days if not weeks. It is certain that his absence will be felt in that he will not be available on a daily basis to assist his wife in raising the three girls. The emotional impact will be felt by the girls.

> Emily does not speak Spanish or know the cultural nuances of living in Honduras. She is an English-dominant, U.S. citizen. She is making very good developmental progress and maturity in the only community, school, and social-cultural environment that she has ever known. A disruption in this stability, especially under the duress of father's deportation, can have untold negative consequences on her. Rather than continuing on a strong developmental trajectory, her psychological and social advancements would be derailed, possibly irreparably damaged.

As part of the preparation for the cancellation of removal case, the attorneys retained an expert on Honduras to provide an assessment that could be included in the final hearing in immigration court. The country expert was, in fact, an international security consultant with extensive experience in diplomatic and intelligence roles. This expert put a human face to the many of the issues that Emily and her sister would face in Honduras. His detailed report substantiated that Honduras' literacy rate was among the lowest in the hemisphere; that the national average level of education attainment was only 6.5 years; that Honduras historically had the lowest percentage of university graduates of any Central American nation and the highest percentage of graduates who emigrate; that while official statistics claim nearly 100 percent enrollment in primary education, enrollment simply means that children are on a list, and the term is not related to attendance or even to school and teacher availability; that only 70 percent of children make it to the fifth grade and those who finish sixth grade take an average of 9.4 years to do so and only 30 percent go on to high school; that teacher education is poor and salaries low and strikes by teachers are frequent; and finally that there are few facilities for children with special needs and what exists is confined to major urban areas and of uncertain quality.

The expert's report stated that Honduras' gross national income per capita was barely a quarter of the average for Latin America and the Caribbean, and the rate of economic growth in recent years had at times fallen below the rate of population increase. The report cited two other developments that exacerbated Honduras' economic and social problems. One was the explosion of juvenile gang activity. "While Honduras managed to escape the worst violence of the late-20th century Central American wars," the expert wrote, "it was awash in arms and its economy suffered, leaving thousands with no real job prospects." One result was the huge proliferation of gangs that were becoming increasingly vicious. This was further complicated by an inadequate police force that was subject to corruption; some politicians estimated that 40 percent of Honduran police were actually involved in organized crime. The expert continued:

All these factors would have a special impact on the prospects for Emily's family should they be deported to Honduras. Their only family ties are in the small town of Colomoncagua located in the *departmento* of Intibuca. This is among the poorest areas of Honduras with illiteracy and malnutrition rates twice the national average. Near the border with El Salvador it was the site of a massive refugee camp in the 1980s which contributed to severe problems of deforestation and soil erosion. Jobs are scarce and unemployment and underemployment high. This would impact the health and education prospects of the three girls. The *departmento* is among the most isolated in Honduras. Roads to Colomoncagua are dirt and at times impassable during the rainy season. In the best of times in takes from two to three hours to reach the small capital of the departmento, La Esperanza, and eight or more hours to reach the nearest major city, Tegucigalpa, so commuting to work in other urban areas would be virtually impossible. Health facilities in Colomoncagua are very limited, and, according to a US Peace Corps volunteer who spent nearly two years there "local public health centers lack adequate facilities to treat patients and the patients lack the money to buy the medications required to treat their ailments."

His report was different from others I had read in previous cases in that it contained very specific descriptions of the effects that moving to Honduras under the circumstances of deportation would have on Emily and each of her sisters. Most country experts I have heard testify do not connect individual children's needs to the specific conditions they will face.

The impact would be especially severe on the eldest daughter, Emily, who is entering her fourth year in the U.S. education system. For a child who has spent several years in the U.S. school system the shock of entering the Honduran system would be overwhelming. Classes are overcrowded, teachers poorly prepared, and facilities inadequate. Very limited family resources would close the door to private and parochial schools where the well-off send their children. According to a May 21, 2011 article in the Honduran newspaper, *El Heraldo*, the situation in Colomoncagua is so bad that some families actually travel to El Salvador, whose border is five kilometers away, to obtain education for their children. Discrimination is likely and because she is fluent in English the potential for becoming a gang target would be high. Her chances of going on beyond primary education would be significantly reduced. Facilities are limited, and in this *departmento* the challenge is even worse for females, as only 20 percent receive a secondary education. This child clearly has good educational potential but in this environment it would likely remain unfulfilled, with resulting frustration and emotional distress.

The second child, Jessica, is a special needs child and the U.S. system would provide her with much needed facilities. None of this would be available in Colomoncagua. Her future prospects would be dismal under these circumstances, and would pose a heavy additional burden on the entire family. In summation, moving to Honduras would likely impose extreme hardship and significant potential physical danger to children who had previously been raised in the United States and with limited family income. Of all the children, the impact on Jessica would be the most severe.

The youngest child, Brittany, would also be adversely impacted, though the exact degree is more difficult to measure. Much would depend on how disruptive the move was to the family as a whole and on what happens to her two older sisters. At a minimum her prospects for a healthy and successful future would be greatly reduced. Her nutrition would be negatively impacted and pre-school preparation would be absent. In summation, deportation to Honduras would have a severe and potentially disastrous impact on the life and prospects of all three girls.

In spite of two independent reports from expert witnesses about the exceptional and extremely unusual hardship for Emily and her sisters, the judge was not convinced that the respondent had met this burden. The ICE attorney had raised questions about two driving while intoxicated (DWI) violations that Raul had accrued. Raul had presented evidence that he had attended Alcoholics Anonymous and no longer drank, but the issue was whether Raul's two DWIs were convictions for misdemeanor offenses or less. His attorneys, Schmitt and Arango, argued that, under state law, these were municipal offenses charged under the cities' municipal ordinances and, therefore, were infractions rather than misdemeanors. This was significant because for TPS, an immigrant cannot have two or more misdemeanors, and with only two infractions Raul would have a lesser burden to prove. The judge allowed Schmitt and Arango to supply her with the municipal offense definitions and postponed her decision accordingly. Unfortunately, a regulation of the *United States Citizenship and Immigration Services* (*USCIS*) contains its own definition of a misdemeanor regardless of how the offense is classified by state law. That regulation states that if the offense is punishable by more than 5 days in jail, it is a misdemeanor for immigration purposes.

After the immigration court received this clarification, the judge denied Raul's cancellation request. The judge found him statutorily ineligible for cancellation because she did not find that Raul's removal would cause the requisite degree of hardship to the three qualifying relatives, Emily, Jessica, and Brittany. The judge's finding seems contrary to the great weight of the evidence that was put into the record.

In their situation as in others like it, the respondent's attorneys can file a notice to appeal within 30 days after the judge denies the case. The Board of Immigration Appeals (BIA) then issues a briefing schedule and the attorneys receive the transcript of the hearing. ICE and the respondent's lawyers file written briefs to the BIA. It's not easy. The attorney's job on appeal is to identify any factual misstatements and erroneous legal conclusions that the immigration judge may have made, and find support in case law and the record for all arguments. The attorney writes a detailed statement of the facts of the case and legal argument explaining why the immigration judge's decision was wrong and should be reversed. Successfully reversing an order of the immigration judge at the BIA requires a careful review of the transcript and broad knowledge of controlling "precedent" decisions, which will help guide the BIA's analysis of the case. ICE attorneys may file a responsive brief, presenting arguments in favor of the judge's decision. The appealing party may request oral arguments, but these are rarely granted. Decisions from the BIA are generally rendered in approximately 12 months, however, this time frame can vary depending on the complexity of the issues and whether the BIA orders oral argument on the case.

As for Emily, her father's case has been pending for 20 months at the time of this writing. Raul remains in the United States and he is authorized to renew both his employment document and driver's license while the case remains pending.

COMPLEXITIES OF JUDGING CASES

Challenges to cancellation do not always end up positive for families. The denial of Guillermo V.'s case seems clearer by his multiple and flagrant violations and his misrepresentations to the court. But for Emily and her merry band of sisters and loving parents, the loss was rested largely on the question of the definition of two DWI infractions despite a strong case. It is very troubling, though, that the decision-making of judges can have such variability in the consideration of cancellation hearings. The juxtaposition of these two cases is stark: Raul deserved much more discretion by the judge to grant the cancellation of removal than Guillermo V. did. One man committed two infractions, whereas the other committed multiple misdemeanors and displayed brazen acts that annulled the good-moral-character clause. Because I was involved in both cases, it is much easier to sympathize with Raul and Emily.

It is, of course, understandable that immigration judges must look at the requisite legal standards in the INA for making determinations about challenges to removal orders. These determinations are about jurisprudence, taking into account serious legal, moral, social, humanitarian, and philosophical matters. To what extent are immigration court procedures so inviolable that municipal infractions convert into misdemeanors in immigration law? How much discretion does the immigration judge have? Would another judge have applied any latitude available to the case of Emily and grant her father a cancellation?

Worst still is the fact that courts are constrained by the numerical limits of grants of cancellation. Decisions by immigration judges are influenced by this silly and indefensible administrative issue that has little justification in demography, mathematics, or social science. On what basis is the annual cap on cancellation grants determined? It is this limitation that makes the legal process so capricious: a decision about a politically derived numerical cap on grants of cancellation trumps fundamental moral and legal principles and people's rights. Even otherwise law-abiding, contributing individuals raising citizen-children may be denied an opportunity to challenge a deportation order because the government ran out of grants. While immigration judges may work around the cap by delaying a decision until the following fiscal year, this tactic contributes to the backlog of cases. The limited availability of cancellation grants puts further pressure on judges to grant cancellation in only the direst cases instead of to all eligible individuals. Is there anywhere else in our judicial system that a number taken from thin air determines who stays and who goes?

It makes no sense. A premier judicial system like that of the United States should make its decisions on the basis of laws, morality, and humanitarianism, not some random number. Administrative rules simply do not match the legal standards. The rule on cancellations granted each year weaken the principles of fairness and justice and overlook the very human consequences that deportations have on US citizen-children.

By any measure of childhood misery, the loss or dissolution of a family—Level 6 on the pyramid of deportation burdens—has to stand as among the most adverse conditions a child can face. Dissolving a family by splitting parents from citizen-children who stay in the United States has the potential for long-term psychological damage as I have shown in previous chapters. While being forced into exile to another country is no less adverse, the only comfort one can squeeze out of these cases is that the family unit remains intact. In the next two chapters I discuss deportation's exiles and orphans. These are the families who were either not able to prove exceptional or extremely unusual hardship due to any number of obstacles I've mentioned earlier or not lucky enough to present their case before the annual cap on cancellation grants was reached.

NOTES

1. Guillermo V.'s children remained in the United States with Eva. It is likely they will continue to remain if the economic circumstances permit it. Guillermo V. indicated that he wanted Eva, Amparo, and Doris to remain in the United States. Often, when undocumented spouses like Eva do not have a criminal record and a compelling case against her removal, DHS is not likely to file a Notice to Appear for removal. Eva's conduct does not rise to a level that is a

priority for immigration enforcement officials who have many more serious cases to pursue. If Eva had a negative encounter with immigration or law enforcement officials, then she would become more vulnerable to deportation. If Eva were to receive an order of removal, she may have a strong argument to make that her removal would amount to exceptional and extremely unusual hardship to her daughters, who, at that point, would have nobody else to care for them. Of course, DHS could argue that the father is already back in Mexico, and that reunification would actually be to their benefit. Though arguing that exile benefits a child belies any understanding of the harm this process can have on children.

2. Eligible individuals without nationality who last resided in their countries of origin may also be granted temporary protected status (TPS). The Secretary of Homeland Security may designate a country for TPS when conditions such as ongoing armed conflict (e.g., civil war), an environmental disaster (e.g., an earthquake), an epidemic, or other extraordinary conditions exist in that country.

3. Retrieved from http://www.uscis.gov/humanitarian/temporary-protected-status-deferred-enforced-departure/temporary-protected-status.

CHAPTER 9

Exiles and the Limits of Citizenship

Citizenship is the "legal correlate of territorial belonging," writes lawyer and scholar Jacqueline Bhabha (2009, p. 93). It is a bond between a person and country with overwhelmingly significant implications for the individual's identity and well-being. Territorial ties are powerful—physically, psychologically, socially, economically, and politically.

> It affects children's life expectancy, their physical and psychological development, their material prospects, their general standard of living. The fact of belonging to a particular country determines the type, quality, and extent of education the child receives, as well as the expectations regarding familial obligations, employment opportunities, gender roles, and consumption patterns. It determines linguistic competence, social mores, vulnerability to discrimination, persecution, and war. It affects exposure to disease, to potentially oppressive social and cultural practices, to life-enhancing kinship, social, and occupational networks. (p. 95)

Deported parents may be forced into taking their US-born children with them if they are to avoid the fragmentation of their families. As a result, the citizen-child must frequently forfeit the fundamental citizenship right to residency in the United States in order to maintain his or her human right to parental companionship. Because minor children do not enjoy all the privileges of citizenship, their perspectives are often absent from discussion. They cannot advocate for themselves or their families and, therefore, the right to live in their country of birth without being forced to leave is effectively abrogated. The reality of such limitations, Bhabha (2009) states, has created an asymmetry in the nation's legal system that focuses on eliminating inequality between "similarly placed adults" rather than between adults and children. The citizenship privileges of the hardworking American citizen adult must be protected from the encroachment of the undocumented immigrant, yet these laws neglect to mention the protection of citizenship rights of children, demonstrating the common yet unjust assumption that "children's disabilities as citizens are self-evidently justified" (p. 99).

For children, the inability to defend their rights to residency and an intact family affects nearly every aspect of their present and future. Sociologist Joanna Dreby (2012) writes,

> U.S.-born children who move to Mexico with their parents are also deprived of the benefits of U.S. citizenship such as access to health care and quality education. U.S. citizen-children who have previously attended schools in the United States suffer when they return to school in Mexico; the transitions between school systems are not easy, and they are especially difficult in rural areas. Children who return to Mexico find adjusting to the educational system to be a challenge, both in terms of language and access issues and in discrimination against the children of returnees. Not only is the return disruptive, but it robs the United States of these children's future potential and productivity, losing out on the talent of native-born citizens. Perhaps most disturbing is the permanent loss of U.S. citizen-children's aspirations when they return to Mexico. (pp. 15–16)

Dreby is right in her description of the kinds of circumstances in which citizen-children of deported parents might be found. But it is important to clarify that the loss of country and the results that accompany it (e.g., loss of healthcare and quality education) are not necessarily specific to migration between countries but to the manner in which the migration occurred. The damage comes from the fact that the families were forced to migrate into another country and into a lowered standard of living. Children who experience cultural changes by family *choice* do not suffer the trauma of deportation and may not suffer a lowered standard of living. In such situations, moving from the United States to Mexico could be beneficial. It is the negation of choice and the unjust circumstances that make relocation by deportation an ordeal harmful to citizen-children, not necessarily that the idea of growing up in Mexico is inherently incongruent with the rights of the child.

US immigration courts frequently do not consider the exceedingly detrimental consequences to the child's well-being when they accompany their parents in the forced migration. As citizens, these children cannot be deported, and thus we cannot call them "deportees." How, then, do we look at the citizen-children of deported parents who leave the United

States? How do we define them? I propose that these children are *de facto* exiles, a term referring to both a person and a state of mind (see, also, Bhabha, 2014). In its standard definition, an *exile* is a person who has been forced to live in a foreign country, typically for political or punitive reasons. Although it is their parents who are deported, citizen-children have no voice in determining whether they may stay in the United States. They cannot influence the decision that the government makes or the decision that their parents must make of taking the children with them to the country to which they are deported or leaving them in the United States in the care of others. Then there is the definition of *exile* as a state of being, barred from one's native country. Both of these definitions are apt ones for citizen-children who leave the United States when their parents are deported for political reasons that include punishment of their parents for having entered the country illegally.[1] The protection of the child during a developmentally crucial period should take precedence in the aims of immigration enforcement, yet children often are left without any opportunity to take advantage of their citizenship privileges. Children cannot use their citizenship status to protect family unity, and, therefore, inherit the immigration status of their parents and face a shattering change in lifestyle due to no fault of their own (Bhabha, 2009).

"To be exiled is not to disappear but to shrink, to slowly or quickly get smaller and smaller," (p. 49) wrote Roberto Bolaño (2011), the Chilean novelist, poet, and essayist. When the mighty act of deportation occurs, citizen-children are banished with their parents to another country and lose connection with the country in which they were born. They may lose their sense of national identity as Americans, a poignant loss that even maintaining citizenship status cannot prevent. I am reminded of the story by Edward E. Hale (1863) titled "The Man Without a Country," in which a young American army lieutenant is tried for treason and sentenced to spend the rest of his life in exile on US Navy ships. While on board, the lieutenant is not permitted to see or hear anything about his country for the rest of his life. Exiled and *incommunicado*, in time the lieutenant loses his connection to everything he knew, including his identity as an American. And without that national identity, he becomes nothing (Wray, 2013). Without a sense of belonging, or of territorial ties, citizen-children may feel similarly lost and ultimately come to associate with another national identity.

ACOSTA V. J. GAFFNEY, 1977

When confronted with the idea of the *de facto* exile of citizen-children through the deportation of their parents, immigration (and other) courts consistently deny that temporary removal of the child would have an exceptionally detrimental effect on his or her future economic, social, and educational opportunities. "From a child's perspective," argues Bhabha (2014), "parenting should be regarded as a critical activity capable of qualifying the impact of a deportation order. But family separation is viewed primarily through the lens of its impact on the adult deportee" (p. 68). This is what appears to have happened in the case of Lina Acosta, whose Colombian parents came into the United States legally as visitors but overstayed their visas (*Acosta v. J. Gaffney* 558 F.2d 1153. (4th Cir. 1977)). The Immigration and Naturalization Service, the predecessor to Immigration and Customs Enforcement, instituted removal proceedings against the couple but then discovered that the mother was pregnant with Lina. The couple was allowed to stay till after Lina's birth. In the following months, they applied for a stay of their deportation because removal would cause 5-month-old Lina, and by definition her parents, hardship. If deported with her parents, Lina would, in effect, be deprived of her constitutional rights as a US citizen. Because of her young age, Lina could not make a decision about where she wanted to reside, instead conferring this decision to her parents. They could decide that the best thing for Lina would be to remain in the United States with foster parents or take her to Colombia with them. The circuit judge approached the issue as follows:

> The right of an American citizen to fix and change his residence is a continuing one which he enjoys throughout his life. Thus while today Lina Acosta, as an infant twenty-two months of age, doubtless desires merely to be where she can enjoy the care and affection of her parents, whether in the United States or Colombia, she will as she grows older and reaches years of discretion be entitled to decide for herself where she wants to live and as an American citizen she may then, if she so chooses, return to the United States to live. Thus, her return to Colombia with her parents, if they decide to take her with them as doubtless they will, will merely postpone, but not bar, her residence in the United States if she should ultimately choose to live here (*Acosta v. J. Gaffney* 558 F.2d 1153. (4th Cir. 1977)).

The judge hearing the case in the Third Circuit Court of Appeals in New York dismissed "as much as eighteen years of an individual's life as having 'no effect' upon the individual" (Friedler, 1995, p. 531). Despite court opinion, the potential effects of "postponement" of US residence are innumerable. Lina Acosta's childhood in Colombia was no doubt vastly different from the experience she would have had in the United States.

A child sent to Latin America with a parent is often, if entering a lower standard of living, unlikely to learn English as successfully or to receive an education of similar quality to that which he or her she would have received growing up domestically. As a result, the child is not raised to be a successful member of American society, and is likely ill-prepared for a transition to US residency later in life. He or she would face a number of employment difficulties upon return to the United States, including occupational, cultural, and language barriers. Despite the downplay of the importance of childhood location, without a comparable education "children who are already disadvantaged by racial prejudices and by an inability to speak English 'will become permanently locked into the lowest socio-economic class'" (Friedler, 1995, p. 535). For an American citizen growing up abroad, there are few opportunities to reach the same level of success in the United States as other American citizens, and the adverse effects cannot be discounted as minimal.

These child exiles face the consequences of going to unfamiliar towns and cities, assimilating to a culture they have not been a part of, and navigating dangers they have not previously experienced in the United States (Bhabha, 2009). They rest high on Level 5 on Dreby's (2012) pyramid, just under deportation-induced family dissolution. Compounding this drastic change are the often inadequate or nonexistent repatriation services provided to the returning families by either the United States or the host countries, typically poor, to which they go. Removal and repatriation (i.e., reintegration to country of origin, which begins at the point that the United States relinquishes physical custody of the individual) processes are often flawed, inconsistent in practice, and lack attention to child safety (Thompson, 2008). In Latin America, repatriation services vary in availability and efficacy, and lack structure to prevent abusive treatment or to ensure application of child-welfare standards.

Apart from these transitional difficulties, citizen-children face a myriad of detrimental conditions, including poor economic, educational, and safety standards. Severe poverty abroad, whether in Africa, Latin America, or Southeast Asia, makes food insecurity a frequent occurrence; exposure to violence becomes part of the young exiles' lives. Attorneys James Kremer, Kathleen Moccio, and Joseph Hammell (2009) describe these circumstances as follows:

> An American child of undocumented immigrant parents deported to Mexico . . . will find himself or herself living in abject poverty, experiencing substandard (if any) schooling, and witnessing (if not experiencing) gang and criminal violence of a degree and nature that is completely foreign to the

streets of . . . American communities where undocumented immigrants have been swept up in ICE raid. (p. 5–6)

Kremer, Moccio, and Hammell are not exaggerating. For instance, what would have befallen the well-adjusted teenager, Marcus, who we met in Chapter 4, if Francisco, his father, had been deported and Marcus had gone with him to Mexico? First, consider that Marcus had only known a home in a small town in the United States, a town where his father had settled and had a job. His father had established himself as a trusted employee. He was in a committed relationship with Maria and they had a stable household. Overall, Francisco had given Marcus a good life, certainly a good start and strong paternal modeling. That Marcus did as well as he did was a reflection of Francisco's devotion to his son and successful parenting. Marcus was attending high school, taking the bus every morning to school, playing lineman on the junior varsity football, and returning home after practice, either on the bus or on the occasions when Francisco could pick him up. Marcus knew a lot more about football and baseball than about soccer, and more about the United States than Mexico. He spoke English like any American teenager and spoke less Spanish than he understood. (Francisco spoke to him in Spanish mostly but some English, too, when he had to make a point, and Marcus usually replied in English).

Second, a move to Mexico would have put Marcus at a disadvantage, if not at risk, in terms of his educational needs, social status, and physical safety. These risks are hypothetical but highly likely when we contrast what he had known in Illinois to what he would encounter were he to move with his deported father. Father and son would have had to relocate to live with Francisco's parents and extended family in Tequisquiapan, a town in the southeast of the state of Querétaro in central Mexico. Tequisquiapan is a beautiful city with a 300-year-old history of colonization and a rich indigenous cultural heritage. With its cobblestone streets in the center of the town and rustic, traditional houses with ornate balconies and wrought iron fixtures, the town conveys the ancient charm of Mexico.

Nevertheless, the town's educational opportunities are sparse with only one special education school, about 16 preschools serving over two thousand children, and 36 primary schools. Marcus would probably have to complete high school through a *telesecundaria*, distance learning at a high school in another town. The quality would be measurably substandard in contrast to his schooling in Illinois. If not a *telesecundaria*, then Marcus would attend a local high school or vocational school. For a boy doing well in school, accustomed to US culture, and aspiring to attend college, such a shift would be a devastating blow to his college preparation and likely eliminate the possibility altogether. He would likely live in one of the *barrios* in town that might not have full-time running water, garbage and other services, or even street lighting. Through my collaboration with researchers and some clinicians in Mexico, I knew about the limited education, medical and psychological services that would be available to Marcus. But even if Marcus did not go to a small, remote town lacking critical educational and health services, social and employment opportunities, in a large metropolis, such as Mexico City, the health resources and particularly mental health resources would probably not be available should he need them (Benjet et al., 2009).

Exposing Marcus to the violence that has become endemic to Mexico, and particularly to the state of Queretaro, would probably be of greatest concern to a parent like Francisco. According to reports on the spread of the drug cartels (Security Weekly, 2013), the Knights Templar, one of several violent groups, have established a stronghold in Queretaro and many of the surrounding and nearby states such as Michoacán, Morelos, Guanajuato, Guerrero, and southeastern Jalisco. The Knights Templar members can be as brazen, calculating, and cold-blooded as other better-known organized gangs. Situations like this one would give every parent reason to fight a deportation. It is their children's future, maybe their very lives that are placed at risk. And there is no greater concern for parents than our children.

A COMMUNITY IN EXILE

Abject poverty, lack of adequate schools, and absence of laws requiring school attendance or protection from child labor exploitation are conditions that led to the death of a US citizen-child in the November 7, 2012 earthquake that struck Guatemala (Perez-Diaz, 2012). Aldo Dominguez Vasquez, an 11-year-old boy from Santa Clara, California, was working in a quarry owned by his aunt and uncle in Guatemala when the 7.4-magnitude earthquake occurred. Along with nine of his relatives, Aldo was buried in the rocks and rubble. Although born in California, Aldo had lived in Guatemala since he was one year old in the care of his aunt and uncle. He had been brought there by his mother who then returned to California to work. She was living in the United States at the time of her son's death. Aldo was not in Guatemala as a result of deportation. It was economic necessity that had forced his mother's decision. What happened to Aldo could happen to any citizen-child forced into exile with deported parents. The circumstances surrounding Aldo's death are comparable to the situations that exiled children can find themselves in.

Villages throughout Central American have received deportees and their children. The children and parents live in poverty, dwell in homes sometimes without water and electricity, and eke out an existence through labor that exposes them to workplace accidents and natural disasters like the one that killed Aldo. They are also placed in the midst of endemic crime and violence.

In San Jose Calderas, Guatemala alone, there are dozens of US citizen-children in exile. The presence of so many US citizens in a single rural Guatemalan town stems largely from of one of the most studied US workplace raids. That raid occurred in 2008 in Postville, Iowa. ICE agents arrested 389 undocumented workers, mostly from Guatemala, who worked in a local plant operated by Agriprocessors, one of the largest kosher meat producers in the United States. At the time, Postville was the largest workplace raid in US history. "Within weeks," Maggie Jones (2012) wrote in *The New York Times,* "roughly 1,000 Mexican and Guatemalan residents—about a third of the town—vanished. It was as if a natural disaster had swept through, leaving no physical evidence of destruction, just silence behind it."

Undocumented workers attracted by jobs at meat-processing plants had helped rebuild Postville and small towns like it in Iowa and the Midwest. Since the 1970s, the populations of these towns had been dwindling as young people went off to college and didn't return to take over the family farms. This left the strenuous work of agriculture to aging farmers who were hard pressed to do the work themselves. Then, when the Midwest farm crisis struck in the 1980s, many residents were forced to leave the small towns of Iowa and Nebraska altogether in search of new opportunities in the large cities nearby. Keeping small farms running was no longer feasible and the businesses that depended on the local residents had to shut down.

Guatemalans, fleeing both poverty and a 36-year civil war (1960–1996) that included atrocities and massacres by both government forces and rebel guerillas, found their way to Postville. The next two decades saw a resurgence of the town. Postville changed and was prospering again. Guatemalan and Mexican families lived alongside the old-timers from the town and the Orthodox Jews running the large meat plant. The work conditions weren't ideal, according to many of the workers in the meat-processing plant, but work was steady and undocumented immigrant families could thrive. Their children could attend bilingual programs from kindergarten to 12th grade, and new businesses sprouted to serve the very diverse community. A former teacher from Guatemala took ownership of a bakery that had been around since the late 1800s and "transformed it into a spot where old-time farmers lingered over doughnuts and coffee and Latinos bought *pan dulce* [sweet bread], *tostadas* [toasts] and *conchas* [a specific type of sweet bread]" (Jones, 2012, p. 4). Mexicans started businesses and mingled among the newcomers. *Rancheras* [a genre of traditional Mexican music] could be heard from their businesses. Orthodox Jews wore their *yarmulkes* [skullcaps traditionally worn by men] as they went about their daily affairs in Postville. Postville had grown through tolerance for diversity, recognizing that it was the only way to keep the town alive.

The day the raid came, with its suddenness, the town was sent into turmoil. Jones described the scene.

> Within hours of the raid—which I.C.E. had planned for months, based on evidence that large numbers of Agri's employees used suspect or false Social Security numbers and that plant managers hired minors and violated other labor laws—I.C.E. agents detained 389 undocumented workers, most of them Guatemalan. (Agri employed more than 900 workers, over three shifts.) The agents handcuffed the wrists of the men and women and loaded them into the Homeland Security buses. With one state-trooper vehicle in front of each bus and another behind, they drove 75 miles to Waterloo, Iowa. There, I.C.E. had transformed an 80-acre fairgrounds, the National Cattle Congress, into a temporary processing center for the workers. Many of the detainees . . . were then sent to prisons throughout the country, where they would spend five months before being deported to Guatemala.
>
> Back in Postville, about 400 residents poured into St. Bridget's Catholic Church, which would become the town's de facto relief center in the months to come. Women, men and children ate at the church and slept in the pews, afraid I.C.E. might be waiting for them at home.
>
> On almost any other May evening, Guatemalan families, many of whom had lived in Postville for years and were a tight-knit group from two villages in Guatemala, would have been outside, pushing strollers down Lawler Street, stopping for tacos at the Mexican restaurant, Sabor Latino, and for ice cream at the Sweet Spot. Instead, downtown was empty. At the Tidy Wave laundromat, washers and dryers were filled with clothes. No one ever came to claim them.
>
> Some families packed their cars in the middle of the night and drove to other meatpacking towns in Iowa or to another part of the United States altogether. Others turned to a van service, run by a local Guatemalan-American, that would eventually shuttle more than 100 people to O'Hare Airport in

Chicago for one-way flights to Guatemala City. Children stopped going to school. Within weeks, roughly 1,000 Mexican and Guatemalan residents—about a third of the town—vanished.

The Guatemalans dispersed to other parts of the United States, left for their home country, or were deported. Many of the Guatemalans of Postville returned to their hometown of San Jose Calderas, the place from which many had emigrated. The exact number of US citizen-children now living San Jose Calderas is hard to estimate, but a local representative of the National Council for Migrants from Guatemala knows of at least 35 (Carcamo, 2013). But the same official believes the number to be much larger, maybe three times as many. The Guatemalan government estimates that several thousand US citizen-children immigrate to Guatemala *each year* when their parents are deported (Arroyo Rodriguez & O'Dowd, 2011). Some parents who were forced to relocate to San Jose Calderas with their children reported that public clinics initially refused care to some US citizen-children because they had only US documents, not Guatemalan ones. Other parents are afraid to come forward even in the services run by the Guatemalan government or nongovernmental social service organizations under the misperception that US government officials find out and will take away their daughters and sons if they are discovered to be living in impoverished conditions. The fact is that these US-born children are living in poverty more dismal than any they may have known in the United States. One mother commented that, though they lived humbly in the cities and small towns of the Midwest, at least in the United States their children could open refrigerators at home stocked with food (Carcamo, 2013).

To have US citizens living outside its borders in conditions that are intolerable by US standards, conditions such as poor education, lack of adequate medical care, unstable governmental rule, inadequate occupational and career preparation, and little or no rule of law or protection from violence, is counterproductive. Moreover, because they are minors, these children do not have the voice that citizen adults have to advocate for themselves, and so are unlikely to seek assistance from the U.S. embassy, when they are experiencing hardships abroad. Immigration courts may defend the theory that a U.S. citizen-child can return to the United States later in life but the developmental consequences of these determining factors cannot be easily dismissed. With the birthright to come to the United States at any time (although usually after age 18, the age of majority) and possibly after years of dislocation and economic hardship, these citizens may return with low educational and vocational readiness, limited developmental skills, and untreated health and mental health disorders that can thwart their capacities to contribute to our civic life and economy.

FOUR EXILES

The following cases, drawn from the project's research on citizen-children living with deported parents in Mexico, illustrate what it is like to be a US citizen-child in exile.

Lupita

A 9-year-old girl we met in Oaxaca exhibits the feelings that some exiled citizen-children experience when they learn that their parents cannot return to the United States. Our interviewer in Mexico, Dewi Hernandez Montoya, met Lupita through the Mexican Secretaría de Educación Pública, an organization that assisted in the identification of US citizen-children to be interviewed for our study. Both Lupita and her brother were born in San Diego but now live in a town about two hours outside of the city of Oaxaca. The interview was conducted in the carport of a three-bedroom house that sleeps 10 people (Lupita's grandmother, two aunts, an uncle, three cousins, Lupita, her mother, and brother). Although the home was equipped with electricity, water, sewer, gas, telephone service, the extended family shared a kitchen and one bathroom. The family's days are often spent outdoors, in the patio and carport. The interview was interrupted frequently by a host of young cousins, chickens, turkeys, a sheep, and an old, sickly dog. Dewi and Lupita often chased the other children and animals away and swatted at the many insects that flew around them during their conversation. Dewi noticed the many insect bites on the children.

Lupita's parents had not yet really experienced a deportation, although a removal order for her father was pending. Rather than wait for the deportation order, their mother relocated to Mexico with Lupita and her brother. Her mother had become increasingly concerned with the conditions in which they lived in California under the threat of deportation. Besides the constant fear of being uncovered by immigration authorities, there was the frequent moving from one place to another as the father's employment opportunities changed—the kinds of burdens linked to Levels Three and Four of the pyramid. Most worrisome to the mother were the effects of their unstable living situation on her children's educational progress. As a result, Lupita's mother had kept the children in the same school no matter the distance created by their moves and father's employment changes. It was the one way she could provide some stability.

They were well-educated parents, both graduates of the Universidad Autónoma "Benito Juárez" of Oaxaca, where the mother had studied accounting and the father architecture. Neither could practice their professions in the United States due to their status. The mother had taken low-paying part-time jobs but was discouraged by the lack of challenge in the positions, describing one job as "work that anyone can do." Another motive for wanting to return to Mexico was that she was far from her family and missed them enormously. At the time we met Lupita, her mother expressed some chagrin that it had been at her insistence that she and her husband, emigrated in 2001 when they were young and child-free, to seek a future in the United States, only to be the one who then convinced her husband that they should return to Mexico to live a calmer life.

Lupita never wanted to move to Mexico. When she heard the plan, that she was to relocate with her mother and brother and her father would follow two years later, she rejected the idea. But she could do nothing about her parents' decision. The separation from the father had been difficult for Lupita. In fact, Lupita misses living in California and she refuses to talk on the phone with her favorite cousin back in San Diego because afterward she becomes sad. Back home, Lupita was an above average student. Now in Mexico she is struggling to keep her grades up and feels less confident about her performance at school. Her worry is pervasive; on exam or special days she gets up early, even before her mother, to study. Lupita confirmed that she is having the most problems with Mexican history and geography. Her conversational Spanish is good but her writing is far below her grade level in Mexico.

Lupita's anxiety was manifest, and on our measure of anxiety her score was in the borderline clinical level. The sadness and unhappiness we saw in the interview was confirmed by our measure of children's depression, which put her in the above-average range of intensity. During the interview, Lupita would often sob and become silent for minutes.

While she was in Mexico, her father had been arrested and detained in California but released with an order of removal. When we met Lupita, her father was negotiating with immigration to delay the date of his deportation so he could continue to work as a cook in a restaurant. As the interview continued, the conversation became more fluid and Lupita less shy.

"And so your father will join you," our interviewer stated.

"Yes, but in two years," Lupita replied, weeping softly.

"That's a long time," the interviewer said empathically, "And you want him to come sooner, huh?"

"I prefer to go there," Lupita said as her weeping turned to loud sobs. Dewi noted the sense of despair in Lupita's words, face, and the sound of her crying. Lupita felt helpless that she could not influence her parents' decision to return to Mexico and desperate that it would become permanent once her father returned to Mexico. Lupita told of wanting to return to the United States with her mother and brother to reunite with her father, and blurted out that she did not want her father to come to Mexico but to stay in California instead. Why?

> No sé. [Silencio largo] Porque . . . que como para qué. . . [Entre sollozos] para que ya no se tenga que venir mi papá. [Sollozos fuertes] Porque si se viene mi papá, ya no nos vamos a volver regresar. [Altos sollozos] (I don't know. [Long silence] Because . . . because like. . . [sobbing] that my dad doesn't have to come here. [Louder sobs] Because if my dad comes back, we will not go back again. [Loud sobs])

Her despair was evident during the interview. She is profoundly afraid that if her father returns, she will be permanently confined to the this new existence that she dislikes, in a place where she is not doing well in school, and where she is distant from her beloved cousins, the life she knows, and the schools where her self-esteem was nourished by being an outstanding student. When Dewi asked if she wanted to return to California, Lupita showed powerful conflicting emotions of confusion and guilt, wanting what she wanted but betraying her mother's wishes. Her mother is happier here and her father is set to return though unwillingly, but Lupita doesn't want to stay in Mexico or have her father arrive.

> No sé qué. [Toma aire, un suspiro y sigue llorando] Quiero que ya esté con mi papá, con mi mamá y con mi hermano ¡pero allá no acá! (I don't know what. [She takes a deep breath, sighs, and continues crying] I want to be with my dad, with my mom, and with my brother, but there not here!)

Lupita is like many other citizen-children of deported parents that we interviewed, as well as other children that I met, read about, or heard speak in documentaries. She envisions that she could have more power to help her parents. Most kids have a variant of the determination to get their parents the right papers as soon as they are adults and able to take independent action. At nine, Lupita wishes for the power to help her parents. In California, she knew that her parents "no tenían papeles" [did not have papers] to be in the United States and she had always known it; there was never a time she did not know it. Her parents' legal status adds to her unhappiness:

Pues me siento muy infeliz porque como ellos no pueden estar allá y yo si quiero estar allá. . . . Siempre he pensado que cuando sea grande se los voy arreglar para que puedan regresar allá. [Well, I am very unhappy because they cannot stay there and I want to be there. . . . I always thought that when I grew up I'll fix it so they could go back.]

Irma

Irma, a 14-year-old girl, echoed Lupita's sentiments about fixing her parents' situation, a common sentiment among both exiled and nonexiled citizen-children. We met Irma in Sinaloa, a Mexican state on the Gulf of California. Her mother had been deported and Irma's transition to Mexico had not been easy. She suffered from a pervasive anxiety that was confirmed by three of our clinical measures. Irma was doing well in school and had made friends. She worried, though, about her future and the crime and the abductions of young girls by drug dealers and other outlaws. Her anxiety affected her self-image, leaving her feeling that she was ineffective and not functioning well with other people despite all outer appearances.

Hope keeps Irma focused on school. At her age, she knows that in just three or four years she will be returning to the United States to attend college. College represents empowerment; even if it is a fantasy, it is one within the realm of possibilities. She imagines herself armed with a college education and a good job, fixing her mother's and grandmother's deportation orders and legal status. Unlike Lupita, for whom it is a vague future possibility that she can arrange for her parents to have *papeles*, Irma can see her return to the United States and feel the tangible possibilities of college and helping her family. Irma expressly does not want to attend college in Mexico.

Pues como le quiero arreglar sus papeles a mi mamá, tengo que estudiar allá y tener un trabajo allá, para que la ley de ahí . . . la ley vea que soy parte de Estados Unidos y puedo arreglarle sus papeles a mi mamá y que puedo pues que tengo un trabajo y puedo cuidar de mi mamá y puedo arreglar sus papeles. [Well, since I want to fix my mom's papers for her, I have to study there and have a job there, so that the law there . . . the law sees that I am part of the United States and can fix the papers for my Mom and that I can because I have a job and I can take care of my mom and I can fix her papers.]

And Irma recognizes that it might take some effort and time to change the papers. She looks at the future as including the possibility that *"mi mamá pudiera ir a visitarme allá y tal vez en un futuro comprarme una casa aquí y venir de vacaciones"* [my mom could go to visit me there and maybe in the future buy a house here and come for vacations].

During the interview, Irma spoke about her grandmother's deportation and what she would change or what she wished would be different. She wishes for a change in policy whereby citizen children can help their parents and grandparents who are undocumented.

> *Pues que también, no sé . . . qué les dieran también papeles a mayores de edad que están allá, que todavía no tienen papeles o que fuera más fácil de que los hijos les pudieran dar también papeles a sus padres. Especialmente la gente mayor como mi abuela que pudieran quedarse allá donde vivieron muchos anos y tienen hijos allá.*
> [Well, also that I do not know . . . that they should give papers to adults who are there, who still do not have papers or that it could be easier for their children to get papers for their parents. Especially older people like my grandmother who could stay there where they lived many years and have children there.]

Marta

Marta is a 12-year-old girl living with her father, mother, and younger brother in Tláhuac, a borough about 60 kilometers southeast of Mexico City. The neighborhood is made up of small and very modest homes of brick and cement without many finishes or colors. Some of the houses are simply one-room structures. Pedi-cabs transport people around town although there is a metro station and public buses have stops in the community. Across the street from Marta's home is a community health center and around the block a sports center.

Marta started the interview by saying, "There [the United States] is better than living here." Her mother was deported a few months earlier and the family is getting accustomed to a new routine. Marta's parents are unemployed and making ends meet by selling *quesadillas*. Marta has not attended classes since entering Mexico because she arrived in the summer when the children were on holiday. The family faced many difficulties enrolling Marta in school because of the procedures they had to go through to obtain Mexican citizenship for Marta.

Marta's father had migrated to the United States first in 1989, and had initially obtained permission to remain for some time. Her mother then migrated in 2000, and they married in the United States with the intention of becoming naturalized citizens, a dream that never materialized. After a year of marriage, Marta was born. A few years later, her younger brother was born. The infant boy suffered some unspecified developmental disabilities and would require special education services when he entered school. The father worked as a chef in a restaurant and the mother remained at home to take care of the two children. Life in the United States was rather typical but happy: the mother took Marta to school early every day and returned in the afternoon to pick her up with Marta's little brother in tow. Marta did well in school in Nebraska, where she was also played basketball.

Marta experienced two deportations in her family. The first process was when her father was arrested, taken to prison for three days, then ultimately deported. After his deportation, the family joined him in Mexico, but Marta found school difficult because teachers were intolerant of her difficulties writing in Spanish and her relative ignorance of Mexico. There was violence in school among her peers. After a few months, Marta's mother decided that Marta and her brother should return to the United States to live with an aunt. However, after some time, the aunt contacted Marta's mother in Mexico and told her that both children were having emotional problems. She said that Marta cried a lot, slept and ate more than usual, and missed her parents very much. Upon hearing this, the mother set out to cross the border to be with her children and care for them herself. She was very worried about re-entering illegally, but decided that America was a better place for their children to live, worth the risk. As she crossed the border, the mother was detained by police and taken to court. She was jailed for three months for possession of false identity documents. While the mother was incarcerated, the local child protective services visited the aunt and said they would take custody of the children. The aunt notified the father, who immediately set out to enter the United States to protect his children. He made it there safely and took the children back to Mexico. Marta felt, in her words, "ugly" because she thought it was her fault that her mother was in jail, because of her crying and homesickness.

The legal process continued while the children were back in Mexico. One day, Marta opened a letter that arrived at their home, a letter from her mother. Her mother wrote that she was going to plead guilty and would receive a sentence of five years. She didn't tell her father or brother about the content of the letter, yet a few days later, an aunt who lived nearby came to their house to tell the father that his wife would be deported the next day.

Martha was prone to pervasive worry, both about her safety and that of her family. She told us about kidnappings, that "there have been other girls" who have been abducted, and that she didn't want the same thing to happen to her. The family appeared markedly sad to Dewi, the interviewer. The mother wept when she recounted the events of her time in prison. Marta didn't not cry during the interview but kept her head down the entire time and spoke in soft tones, almost whispers. The parents and children sought counseling and are receiving care at a clinic of the National Institute of Psychiatry.

Marta is fortunate to have been interviewed for our study because we were able to provide access to care. Even living in Mexico City would not have guaranteed the availability of services. Research by Benjet et al. (2009) indicates that mental health services for citizen-children are not abundant in the capital city, Mexico City, *Distrito Federal*. In the survey by Benjet and colleagues, 9 percent or 1 in every 11 teenagers in Mexico City between the ages of 12 and 17 were found to have a noticeable serious mental disorder. Twenty percent of the youth had a disorder diagnosable as moderately severe and 10 percent of youth with a diagnosable mild disorder. Compounding this picture is that most adolescents in Mexico City in need of psychiatric services were not receiving or likely to receive them. Girls in Mexico City were at high risk for mental disorders, dropping out of school, and other negative outcomes (e.g., rape, pregnancy, early marriage). And the survey found that mental health services were scarce. There was also a shortage of general physicians, especially pediatricians, who are customarily the first line of mental health service. From these findings I surmise that even if citizen-children relocate with their parents to Mexico City, their health and mental health needs will not be adequately served. What happens to those who return to small villages where access to medical facilities is limited and where parents have even fewer options for the professional medical care their children need?

Brandon

Brandon is one of those children who worry. He is a 10-year-old boy who had arrived in Oaxaca just four months before we met him. Brandon and his mother, though agreeing to participate in the interview, seemed circumspect in speaking of his father's deportation. Brandon is the elder of two children born to parents who had never married and first lived together in the United States. At their previous home in the United States, and now in Mexico, Brandon and his younger sister see their father only sporadically. Before their move to Mexico, the family lived in a small town in the state of Washington, where the mother picked apples. In Mexico, Brandon and his sister live in an apartment they share with other families, like other citizen-children we met through our study. The mother spoke longingly of the free education in the United States and access to free school lunches and school supplies. Mother and son told of the great differences between living in the United States and Mexico in the wake of deportation.

Brandon spoke with nostalgia about watching television back in the United States, and the good grades he got in school there, and how he practiced American football with his friends, and played baseball. He related stories of how he would go to the library with friends. When he contrasted his past life with the present, Brandon described life in Mexico as, in his words, "ugly" and with "a sad people, almost without money." Indeed, his parents cannot find work and the family is slipping deeper into poverty. His new life feels small and limited.

Brandon narrated that when he received the news that his father was arrested and being deported, he told his mother that they should not go Mexico. Leaving Washington state, he said, "*iba a hacer un error*" ("would be a mistake") because they would never be able to return to the United States without papers. In speaking of this major event in his life, Brandon became nervous and evasive. His voice dropped to a whisper and some of words were unclear as he tried valiantly not to cry until he ultimately became silent. When he spoke of his friends and playing football, his voice wavered and cracked. After some coaxing from Dewi, our interviewer, Brandon relaxed and the conversation continued. Brandon said that when his father was deported, he thought his father could "come back" to the town in Washington. But then he heard about a lady whose husband was brought to Mexico by the police. "*Pero que luego el vino y luego ella vino por él y ahora está . . . ya no puede venir pa' atrás. Ahora está en México no más por eso [y no puede volver a Estados Unidos]*" But then he came and then she came and now he is . . . now he can't come back. Now he is in Mexico, that's it [and cannot return to the U.S.]"

Dewi asked what Brandon thought about this and whether he was worried.

"Yes," he answered.

"If my father tried to return [to the United States]," Brandon said, his anxiety rising, "he would have to walk but *el desierto está muy duro para cruzar* (the desert is too hard to cross). I thought that if he tries to pass there, he might stay in the desert."

Brandon knows painfully what re-entering the United States might mean to his father. During the conversation, he seemed not to be able to use the words "lost" or "dead" in his answer. The euphemism "stay" was probably more calming for Brandon. Still, our research team heard in his voice and his words the hopelessness of ever returning to his former life.

Unlike the adolescents we met in Mexico who maintained hope of returning to the U.S. despite their exile, at 10, Brandon does not see any possibility of his life going back to what it was.

CITIZEN-CHILDREN IN EXILE

It is hard on these young exiles. They have tried to adapt to the circumstances, to play as best they could the hand that fate had dealt them. Some children were enjoying their lives in Mexico but they seemed to see these more as extended vacations than as permanent situations. Some remained hopeful that they would return soon to the United States. Others were not as happy or as hopeful. The sadness and sense of displacement was plainly evident on their faces and in their words. No amount of love and embrace from the extended families that received them in Mexico (often meeting them for the first time) could alleviate the sense of loss and displacement. Some children were forced into taking perspectives on life well beyond their years, and worried about things most children in the United States would not have to consider.

Another way to look at the young exiles in Mexico or exiles in any other country is to think of them the way people in the receiving country might look at them: as immigrants. The displaced US citizen-children are not there as economic migrants or refugees who escaped a natural disaster or a famine. Rather, our young exiles are more like the immigrants who are forced by government action to flee their countries for reasons that are not their own fault. They are not running away from an openly announced government-supported action on a tribe, sect, cult, or insurgency in some underdeveloped country ruled by a dictatorship. These children are victims of a war on immigrants in the United States.

As I have written before, the United States is not a country that has in its history used exile or banishment from its land as a punishment of its own citizens. Arguably, writes Bhabha (2014), "the most significant citizen-specific entitlement today is the guarantee of nondeportability, irrespective of criminal offending. Even treason cannot lead to the deportation of a citizen" (pp. 67–68). Our history has other painful scars that history has not let us forget, such as the enslavement of Africans, the exclusion of Chinese, and the internment of Japanese. Fortuitously, we have been spared the scar of banishment of citizens in our history because of the forward thinking and the vision of our Founding Fathers. But when the history is written about our country's treatment of illegal immigrants in the dawn of the 21st century, how will we be judged?

NOTE

1. This reality stands in contrast to the uniquely existential recognition by the United States of citizenship. As former colonists, the founding fathers were fast supporters of self-determined citizenship. By design, it is essentially impossible for adults to lose US citizenship status against their will. Unlike other countries, the United States is not in the practice of expatriating citizens for punitive reasons and cannot strip citizens of their status against their will (with the rare exceptions of denaturalization cases—applicable only to naturalized citizens, and instances of a citizen's participation as an enemy combatant—when the participation is significant enough to be interpreted as intent to renounce citizenship). A US citizen is arguably more likely to be killed for treason than expatriated (i.e., stripped of citizenship status). Consistent with this existential approach, the United States defends the individual's right to expatriate themselves (as per Expatriate act of 1868).

    This right to self-determined citizenship is a refutation of the British common law system of perpetual allegiance. By contrast, US adherence to birth-right citizenship can be seen as a pillar of perpetual allegiance, as discussed in Chapter 2 in the case of Puerto Rico. The juxtaposition of these "rights"—birth-right citizenship and the right to expatriate oneself—illustrates that most-American approach to policy: the balance of competing ideals. The current reality for citizen-children is that the punitive ideology that dominates immigration policy implementation effectively denies their rights as citizens (e.g., privileges such as self-determination) and their rights as children (e.g., protections such as right to counsel in matters affecting their welfare and protection from unnecessary family separation), ideals that are otherwise enshrined and defended in the Bill of Rights, child welfare standards, and international norms. These competing ideologies must be brought into balance in order to prevent the establishment of a second class citizenship for citizen-children.

CHAPTER 10

Human Loss and Becoming Deportation Orphans

We typically think of orphans as children whose parents have died. A more inclusive definition of orphan is that of children deprived of their parents' care. Even if left in the care of one parent, for citizen-children with a deported parent it means the absence of the affection, attention, and physical presence of the other. In the absence of both parents, the child or children may be placed in the care of loving relatives and friends, or those who provide care and support but are no real substitute for the affection of parents. In the worst of all possible cases, parental deportation may cause the child to fall into the child welfare system. These decisions and outcomes are seldom morally just.

In 2013, Oregon Public Radio aired a story of three US-citizen siblings—orphans of deportation—whose mother, Liliana Ramos, had been deported more than two years before (Gustafson, 2013). From the time of her arrest by immigration officers, Liliana Ramos, a single mother, was given nine months by ICE to prepare her children for her deportation from the United States. On the day of her "voluntary departure," she packed her belongings in her car and drove more than 1000 to her new home in Mexico. At the time she left, her son Brian was 19 and his sisters, Ashley and Karleen, were 15 and 11, respectively.

Before the enforced separation from her three children, Liliana made arrangements to turn over custody of her two minor daughters to her mother. Liliana taught Brian to pay bills and how to take care of his sisters and himself. It was a maturational and developmental process, a mother's teachings, in hyperspeed. She had nine months or less to teach her children what most parents do gradually, over the course of years and decades.

When the deportation occurred, Brian was just beginning a job-training program to get a career started.

For months after their mother's departure, the children were sad and anxious. The signs of depression are still evident from the children's description of what it was like after their mother left. Brian quit the job training to return home. Ashley took to sleeping and Karleen missed many days of school, losing nearly half the academic year. The two girls cried constantly and sought therapy at school. The siblings began to suffer financially. The parents had divorced and their father had been deported several years before. He was no longer available to provide the support the children needed. Liliana was now struggling to make ends meet in Mexico.

Even with two older siblings to take care of her, a young child like Karleen needs her mother. At the tender age of 11 and at the point where puberty, menarche, and a major transition to high school are looming, she needs and misses her mother's guidance and supervision. Gustafson (2013) reports that Liliana tried to prepare Brian and Ashley to take care of Karleen, but it is a difficult thing to parent a sibling. Gustafson quotes Brian as saying "I feel like she needs that role model, and that's my mom, and we can't really do much. It's not the same. It's not the same."

He is right: it's not the same.

ORPHANS BY CHOICE OR DURESS

Deportation of parents naturally raises the specter that someone will adopt the children, very possibly a stranger. Parents fear losing their rights and their children to adoption probably more than they fear deportation itself. Adult deportees suffer the emotional and psychological hardships of having to leave their children behind. In my study, we met fathers who had been deported and returned, always vowing to be with their children and wives. No matter a parent's efforts, to stay or return, better to violate the law, risk death in re-entering the country than to miss their children's first words or first steps; or not to be there to teach them how to ride a bicycle, or see them graduate from high school. Deportation orphans and the parents who remain with them in the United States experience the traumatic effects of the loss of a parent and rupture of family unity (Capps et al., 2007; Mendoza & Olivas 2009). The citizen-children and their undocumented siblings who are left behind are left as orphans, children with the emotional scars of losing a parent.

Parents agonize over the decision. They mull over, discuss, decide, rethink, reconsider, and discuss it again whether the entire family will have to relocate to Mexico or to whatever their country of origin is, effectively exiling their children. From others back home, they hear stories about the kinds of adversity and adjustments that exiled American citizen-children there have had to face. Do they want the same for their children? Maybe, they reason, it's better for the children to stay put, to preserve their stability. The decision-making process is arduous, wrought with attempts to predict their children's welfare in both scenarios. Looking at the long-term needs of their children, some parents opt to leave their citizen-children in the United States to ensure their education and futures, as Liliana did with Brian, Ashley, and Karleen. These parents bet on their children's future.

In our research, many citizen-children whose parents had never been detained or deported worried about what would happen to them if they stayed back in the United States. Most were assured by parents that they would be taken in by aunts and uncles. But an 11-year-old girl in Chico, California spoke for many of them when she said that she tried not to think about her parents' lack of papers or the possibility that they might be deported to Mexico.

"You know, I think about it and then stop because I don't like to think about it. I feel scared because I think that maybe one day they can just take them away, *like that*, in a second," she said, snapping her fingers in the air. "Then me and my little brother would have to go to foster homes and I really don't want that." This girl had given thought to this possibility, about this problem, and considered the many different consequences for her and her brother if they were to fall into the hands of the child welfare system. They could not select the foster parents, so it would be a toss of the dice about whether the foster parents would be loving and caring or not. Throughout her narrative, the young girl gave the impression that at some point there may have been direct discussions in the family about this issue. Her parents had supposed, she said, "that we could have foster parents but that means that we can't live the life that we used to live. Because I wouldn't have my regular parents and I might have different parents and you never know how they might treat me."

Going into foster care as a potentiality is a frightening scenario since there is very little coordination between ICE, the immigration courts, and the child welfare system. Several well-documented cases drive home the complexity and the tragedy of the citizen-child's transition into being an orphan. One such case is that of *State of Nebraska v. Maria L.* (277 Neb. 984, 767 N.W.2d 74 (2009)) which began when a Guatemalan mother, Maria L., was visited by police officers and a child-protective-services (CPS) worker after failing to take her daughter to a doctor's appointment for a follow up after the child's diagnosis of a respiratory infection.

Although Maria L. was instructed in Spanish on how to care for her daughter and given a return appointment, she spoke primary Quiché, a Mayan language spoken by the K'iche' people of the central highlands of Guatemala. The language barrier prevented Maria L. from fully understanding the instructions and she failed to return to the clinic with her daughter. As a result, the caseworker had to make the mandatory report to the state children's authority. When the police and CPS worker came to her home, Maria introduced herself as the child's babysitter out of fear of her illegal status. Pressed by the official visitors, Maria identified herself as the mother. No one understood, or perhaps cared to understand, why she might be so fearful that she needed to lie.

Maria was arrested for obstructing a government operation and put into deportation proceedings. In turn, the state placed her children Daniel and Angelica in temporary emergency custody with the state department of health and human services. The state conducted child custody hearings, resulting in the determination that the children would best be served by a foster home placement. While CPS developed a case plan to reunify Maria and her children, by then Maria had already been deported to Guatemala. She could not, therefore, comply with the plan of supervised visits with children, and was stuck between two jurisdictions that did not coordinate or communicate. On one hand, the federal government would not let her enter the United States, and on the other, local CPS authorities in Nebraska required her to be present in order to comply with their reunification plan. CPS apparently did not pursue communication with immigration authorities, and neither side knew what was happening with the other. The caseworker could not by definition confirm that Maria had complied with the plan, and after the requisite 15 months lapsed for Maria to respond to the reunification plan, the state initiated termination of parental rights (277 Neb. 984, 767 N.W.2d 74 (2009)).

Maria L.'s case shows how disconnected the state child welfare agencies and federal immigration authorities can be. Because federal immigration agencies and state CPS agencies operate independently and at different levels of government, they have little to no understanding of each other's respective procedures and fail to coordinate their practices in ways that protect the child's best interest, the standard by which CPS cases are decided. As with the case of State of Nebraska v. Maria L, detained or deported parents are unable to visit their children and thus cannot adhere to family unification plans (Wessler, 2011). This lack of communication and coordination was cited by the Nebraska Supreme Court when it heard

Maria L.'s appeal. In their decision, the justices explained these unfortunate circumstances as follows:

> From the beginning, the State was less than helpful in providing Maria with a compliable case plan. Although Hannah [Lisa Hannah, a protection and safety employee for the local Department of Health and Human Services (DHHS)] acknowledged that case plans are provided to Spanish speakers in their native language, Maria never received a copy of the case plan in her native language. There is no evidence in the record to suggest that Maria ever received a written copy of the case plan in any language—despite the fact that Hannah had access to Maria's address. Although the case plan was prepared in September 2005, Maria was never directly informed of the contents of the case plan until sometime in February 2006. At that time, Hannah simply read the plan over the telephone to Maria and then told her that she would have to take the initiative herself to comply with the case plan, because Hannah was having a hard time setting up a parenting class or counseling. The record does not contain any evidence showing what efforts Hannah actually made.
>
> Despite this notable lack of guidance on the part of DHHS, Maria progressed and generally complied with the case plan. Maria remained in contact with her children, by telephone, as required by the case plan. [A person by the name of] Martha testified that she initiated telephone calls between Maria and the children approximately once a month. Additionally, the record shows that Maria has established and maintained a home for herself and her other children in Guatemala. Maria testified, and other evidence confirms, that she has everything her family needs, including running water, a bathroom, pots and pans, dishes, a kitchen table, and beds. Maria is employed, and there is no evidence in the record indicating that Maria associates with individuals involved in criminal activity.

The Nebraska Supreme Court justices concluded that state officials had not done everything they could to protect Maria L.'s parental rights.

> As such, we conclude that the court erred in finding that the State established, by clear and convincing evidence, that termination of Maria's parental rights was in Angelica's and Daniel's best interests. First and foremost, a child's best interests are presumed to lie in the care and custody of a fit parent. The State failed to sustain its burden to prove by clear and convincing evidence that Maria is unfit. This evidentiary failure is related to the State's initial failure to make greater efforts to involve the Guatemalan consulate and keep the family unified. Because the State did not make this effort, it had scant evidence to support its claims that Maria was unable to care for her children.

In conclusion, we are mindful that the children will be uprooted. But we are not free to ignore Maria's constitutional right to raise her children in her own culture and with the children's siblings. That the foster parents in this country might provide a higher standard of living does not defeat that right. Having so concluded, we do not address Maria's remaining assignments of error. An appellate court is not obligated to engage in an analysis which is not needed to adjudicate the controversy before it.

We conclude that the State properly exercised jurisdiction over Angelica and Daniel. However, the State did not present clear and convincing evidence that termination of Maria's parental rights was in Angelica's and Daniel's best interests. We, therefore, reverse the judgment of the juvenile court terminating Maria's parental rights.

Maria L.'s case points directly to the deficits in inter-governmental communication in deportation cases that involve citizen-children. Historically, ICE has not transported parents to juvenile court hearings for their children, although recently there have been some attempts at exploring how federal immigration officials and local child welfare authorities can better communicate and coordinate their practices. If parents cannot make the hearings, even if due to no fault of their own, their parental rights are at the mercy of others. Child welfare agencies are unfamiliar with the nuances of immigration law and deportation procedures, and consequently do not make exceptions for such circumstances (Dettlaff, 2012). In cases of deportation, consulates should assist reunification of the parents and children. But few child welfare departments in the United States will notify a foreign consulate routinely when a citizen-child's parent has been removed (Wessler, 2011). Furthermore, ICE's design and implementation of repatriation processes do not reflect sensitivity to deportees' family obligations and dependents. The federal operations of removal and repatriation are not designed to investigate family circumstances and to properly prevent abuse or to apply adequate standards of child welfare. And, it appears that federal officials do not investigate beyond surface level information about detainees' family circumstances.

Another publicized case that aroused the ire of many advocates and activists was that of Felipe Montes, a Mexican national who was deported after accruing several traffic violations, all for driving without a valid North Carolina license. In being deported, Mr. Montes was forced to leave behind his two toddlers and pregnant wife, a woman who struggled with drug abuse (Wessler, 2011). After she gave birth, the local child welfare authority removed all three children from the home and placed them in foster care. From Mexico, Mr. Montes requested custody of his children but was refused by the county's department of social services, which cited poor conditions in Mexico. With the help of national advocacy groups, petitions, and immigration attorneys, 18 months later Mr. Montes was finally granted permission to return to North Carolina to fight for the three children, a unique permission rarely granted to parents in similar circumstances (Wessler, 2012). Mr. Montes prevailed in his quest and was given custody of his children contingent upon a "trial placement."

It was a bittersweet ending to a sad odyssey for Felipe Montes. But it was not so for Encarnación Bail Romero, an undocumented Guatemalan immigrant in Missouri. Ms. Bail had entered the United States in 2005 and gave birth to her son Carlos in 2006. In 2007, she was working in a poultry plant in Butterfield, Missouri when immigration officers raided the site. Their search for unauthorized immigrants netted Ms. Bail and about 135 others. *The New York Times* reported that some workers with small children were released but not Ms. Bail, who had been charged with using false identification (Thompson, 2009). Then 6-month-old Carlos was placed in the custody of two aunts. But the women, also undocumented immigrants, had children of their own and were living under severe economic hardship. They could not give Carlos the care he needed and, when the aunts had an opportunity, they gave Carlos to a foster family with the participation of child protective workers.

While in detention, Ms. Bail was told that Carlos' American foster parents, Seth and Melinda Moser of Carthage, Missouri, now wished to adopt her son. It was September 2007 and Ms. Bail refused to give up her son, insisting that her own parents had lived a wholly impoverished life in Guatemala and had never surrendered her or her siblings to anyone else. They made due, but they kept their children together, and she would do the same. When an adoption petition was sent to her in jail, Ms. Bail wrote a letter to the court in October 2007 stating "I do not want my son to be adopted by anyone. I would prefer that he be placed in foster care until I am not in jail any longer. I would like to have visitation with my son." From October 2007 to August 2008, there was no communication between Ms. Bail and the child welfare court (Thompson, 2009). As with the case of Maria L., the court appointed a lawyer but then, for unknown reasons, the court removed him from the case, leaving Ms. Bail without legal counsel. The prospective adoptive parents wrote to Ms. Bail while she was in prison but the letters were returned unopened.

In 2008, Judge David C. Dally of Circuit Court in Jasper County, Missouri ruled that the adoptive couple, the Mosers, could keep custody of Ms. Bail's son, Carlos. Ms. Bail's detention and deportation was ruled as "abandonment" of her child (Cambria, 2012). The adoptive parents argued that Carlos had been with them since infancy, and that it was not in his best interest to tear him away from the home he had known for so long. In some respects, the couple had a point: Carlos had grown up in their home. Because he was so young when placed in foster care, he had spent more time with them than with his own mother and his early development occurred in their care, probably with much love and attention. But the couple and the judge overlooked the fact that Ms. Bail was Carlos' rightful mother. Whether one invokes the law of the land or a higher moral law, Ms. Bail *is* the mother of Carlos and deserves the right to continue to be his mother.

Judge David C. Dally's decree contains some of the most despicable language and rationalization for allowing the foster parents to keep Carlos. Because the couple made a good living and had adjusted their lives to give Carlos a stable home with the support of extended family, Judge Dally reasoned the Ms. Bail had little to offer. Furthermore, the judge grossly misrepresented and impugned the child's biological mother with the arrogance of a small-minded country judge.

"Her lifestyle, that of smuggling herself into the country illegally and committing crimes in this country, is not a lifestyle that can provide stability for a child," he wrote in his decision. Her "crimes" had been to work under a false identity to provide for Carlos and her—a decision she made that corresponds to Stage Five of Kohlberg's moral decision hierarchy, hardly a wrongdoing that merited a sentence of termination of her parental rights. "A child cannot be educated in this way, always in hiding or on the run." But there was no evidence whatsoever that Ms. Bail was on the run. The judge further justified his decision by reasoning that there were no certainties in Ms. Bail's life except "that she will remain incarcerated until next year, and that she will be deported thereafter." Through a private petition to Judge Dally's court, the couple was awarded custody and the judge terminated Ms. Bail's rights to Carlos, whose name was changed by his adoptive parents to Jamison Moser.

In 2009, Ms. Bail's deportation order was lifted by immigration authorities so that she could sue to recover custody. By the time Ms. Bail found a Spanish-speaking attorney, too much time had elapsed to pursue her child's case. Furthermore, it took two months for the attorney to find her since she had been transferred to a detention facility in West Virginia. The adoptive parents' lawyer said that his clients had waited patiently for a year to hear from Ms. Bail and for her to show her commitment to the child but that she had failed to do so. The judge agreed that she had not contacted the baby or provided financial support for Carlos during her incarceration. The case was appealed to the Missouri Supreme Court, which sent it back to the lower court for retrial. Missouri's highest court stated that Judge Dally had "plainly erred by entering judgment on the adoption petition and terminating Mother's parental rights without complying with the investigation and reporting requirements . . ." and reversed the decision of allowing the adoption to proceed without Ms. Bail's consent (CNN, 2011). The case went back to the lower court where the outcome was the same: Carlos remained with his adoptive parents.[1] Sadly, it seems neither the Missouri high-court jurists nor the lower court shared the wisdom of their colleagues on the Nebraska Supreme Court. Instead, they followed Judge Dally's jaundiced view of Ms. Bail's rights as a parent.

Both the case of Maria L. in Nebraska and the case of Encarnación Bail Romero in Missouri demonstrate the biases held by many administrators, judges, attorneys, caseworkers, and others: equating immigration violations with criminal intent or activity, and being prejudicial against the conditions in other countries. The assumption is that the child's best interest is to be taken away from what are deemed unsuitable parents and that it is always best for a child to remain the United States, even if in the child welfare or foster care system (Wessler, 2011). With bias like this, we can see how officials might be discouraged from trying very hard to reunite families in situations in which the parents have been removed, or will be removed, to a foreign country. Wessler notes that child welfare departments are unlikely to put children with undocumented relatives under the same risk of deportation, and thus place the children in so-called stranger foster care with people the child has never met. Child welfare departments and immigration officials continue, at best, to fail to communicate or, at worst, to be in conflict with each other when children's lives are at stake.

ATTACHMENT, LOSS, AND TRAUMA

In life there are few more devastating experiences with lifelong reverberation than childhood trauma. And, arguably, the two most destructive childhood traumas are abuse, physical or sexual, and the sudden, perhaps inexplicable, loss of a parent. In a long career in the field of community mental health, the most damaged adult and child patients I have met have been those who sustained one or both of these traumas. Consider, for example, how the boy whose father went out for cigarettes one evening and never returned was left deeply doubtful that anyone could be trusted; he feared others would abandon him, too. He could not understand why his father had left. As his therapist for over 18 months, I became closely acquainted with his poor emotional self-regulation, his tone-deafness to social cues, and to the feelings of others, and his near total incapacity to see how others saw him—traits all related to this initial abandonment. His insecurities and provocative social behaviors made him the object of derision and rejection by classmates.

Another boy of divorced parents who I treated at the same clinic was deprived of paternal validation. He lived with his mother who had custody. Visitation plans had been agreed upon by both parents, as much for her son as for her to pursue a social life of her own. His father, sadly, was a man who constantly disappointed his son with promises made and seldom kept (e.g., "I'll take you to a baseball game;" "On Saturday when I come to pick you up, we'll go for pizza"). Well-liked by other children at school, this boy remained incessant in ingratiating himself to them. He probably did not need to do that; they liked him all the same. He desperately wanted me, his therapist, to come to his little league games or see him in a school play even "if you sit in the back and leave before I can even see you." He longed for a replacement dad, reliable and caring. Each of these boys had suffered of the loss of an important relationship in life early in life that colored the relationships they formed, or didn't, with others.

The two boys reflected disturbances in *attachment*, the affectionate bond that a child establishes with his or her parents and that later influence other relationships. Attachment is understood to be a biologically driven need for closeness to caregivers who provide consistency, predictability, and security, and who soothe physical and emotional needs (Bowlby, 1982). The biological aim of the human bond is survival and the psychological aim is safety: we need our parents when we face danger. Due to the vital importance of attachment, infants and young children seek proximity to and resist separation from attachment figures such as mothers or other key caregivers. Infants and toddlers are "thought to be preprogrammed to emit a sequence of behaviors upon separation" (Shear & Shair, 2005, p. 254), reactions that include crying, protest, searching, and pining. Parents as the object of the attachment become the base that provides a consistent, available, and responsive presence for the child's development of a sense of security. According to attachment theory, the child's closeness to the parent instills in the child's mind a sense or model of the self. This theoretical model is depicted as an unconscious process or dynamic structure that holds emotionally charged cognitions about one's worth and lovability, the core elements of a child's self-image (Moss, Rousseau, Parent, St.-Laurent, & Saintong, 1998; Shear & Shair, 2005). From the earliest age, the child behaves in ways that correspond with this model of the self.

With close personal relationships, like that with a mother, young children quickly develop an attachment based on the quality of the interaction between them. If across time, the child is frustrated in reuniting with the attachment figure, he or she may lapse into despair and withdrawal, until finally experiencing detachment from others, a point at which it becomes difficult to make new, modulated connections with others. In essence, the presence *and* the quality of the relationship determine how secure or insecure the attachment bond will be.

The child's relationship with the parent is predicated on the strength of the attachment that they form, and the relationship is fundamental to a person's sense of security. The parent's own emotion regulation serves as both a model and a calming comfort that the child internalizes. Good parenting and a secure, enduring attachment provide the child with self-regulation abilities. And the child's emotional regulation aids in the development of social and cognitive skills necessary to enjoy a successful interpersonal life. Strong attachments with parental figures in particular tend to result in feelings of self-worth and value, whereas poor relationships and insecure attachment may lead the child to feel susceptible to betrayal, rejection, and abandonment. Secure attachment influences children's social and emotional growth. Children with sound models of self are usually more cognitively, socially, and physically competent. They handle stress better than other children. Insecure attachment to the source of the affectional bond is linked to feelings of low self-worth; and the child will reflect this poor self-image. Along with it come emotional problems.

In the lives of the two boys described earlier, I recognized that the losses of their fathers denied them another secure base besides their mothers with which to connect. This led to deficits in their attachments, people they would otherwise rely on to soothe them when they were anxious. In loss, it is the rupture from the secure base of the affectionate parent that does the damage. Depending on how the loss of a parent occurs, it could also feel like betrayal. The loss of a parent, according to attachment theories, has the capacity to disrupt the person's development of a sense of a secure self and jeopardizes the ability to manage the natural separations and stresses of life. The consequences of disruptions in attachment are more often seen in unhealthy interpersonal relations that stay with the person across the life span.

Traumatic loss of parents that suddenly ruptures the child's attachment is associated with mental health and vulnerability to mental disorders (Bendall, Jackson, Hulbert, & McGorry, 2008; Grubaugh, Zinzow, Paul, Egede, & Frueh, 2011). This loss is made worse when the child is young and cannot process it emotionally or cognitively, or when problems that had occurred in the attachment process had not been resolved. Therapeutic intervention to process the loss, grief, and mourning can reduce the chances of a mental disorder. In abuse, it is the trauma of betrayal (see Kaehler & Freyd, 2012). Research shows that the traumatic loss of a parent, particularly by sudden death or disappearance, has pervasive and long-term effects on the person's mental health (Clarkin, Lenzenweger, Yeomans, Levy, & Kernberg, 2007; Nickerson Bryant, Aderka, Hinton, & Hofmann, 2013). These kinds of childhood traumatic loss, if untreated, can leave people with sometimes crippling emotional dysregulation and anguish, blunted personality development, and relational problems of trust, intimacy, dependency, and insecurity. And often part of many mental disorders is emotional dysregulation (i.e., the inability to control or regulate emotional responses to provocative stimuli, an emotional hyperreactivity to events, such as fits of anger, crying, accusations, and other behaviors that seem greater in intensity or magnitude than is warranted by the situation). In fact, attachment and emotional dysregulation in childhood often predicts the emergence of psychopathology during childhood. Separation from a caregiver particularly in early childhood fundamentally affects the child's developmental processes. The loss of an important figure of attachment produces a state of traumatic loss and symptoms of acute grief. Bereavement in most cases disrupts children's lives during an acute period but, in general, the child processes the loss and adapts by incorporating the reality of the loss. The bereaved child may go on to exhibit a protracted, pathological complicated grief that is well beyond the common human grief-response (Shear & Shair, 2005).

Nearly all forms of loss are imbued with ambiguity. Even in the cases of the anticipated death of a loved one from a terminal illness, we are always left with some questions. But in the case of more sudden, tragic, traumatic losses—especially at a younger age—the principal problem is that there is no closure, no finality or resolution. We are left unable to understand our situation, we can't cope well, and moving forward with our lives is slowed. This specific type of loss falls into the category of "ambiguous loss," a concept derived and explored by child development and family specialist Pauline Boss (1999, 2007). Ambiguous loss is inherently unclear, usually resulting when a person is not known to be dead or alive. As Boss explains, the individual may be physically missing but is kept psychologically present because there is simply no proof of their death. Thus, it is unknown whether the loss is temporary or permanent.

The symptoms of ambiguous loss are not isolated to a particular group, but widespread among family and particularly children of loved ones who suddenly disappear—whether through wartime separation or arrest and detention—and are unknown to be gone temporarily or forever. The effects cover a large spectrum and can persist much later in an individual's life. Let's look, for instance, at the experiences had by families of the *desaparecidos* in Argentina during the 1970s and early 1980s. In many Argentine families with a *desaparecido* family member, their ambiguous disappearance led to the psychological defense of denial; there were often decreases in family communication, and it was not unusual to see confusion in familial roles and responsibilities (Boss, 2002).

Consider, also, another famous example, the Lost Boys of Sudan who had been suddenly separated from their families while fleeing conflict in 2000 and 2001. They fled alone and in groups to Ethiopia and Kenya before many were resettled in the United States. A study of a small group of Lost Boys (Luster, Qin, Bates, Johnson, & Rana, 2009) showed that these Sudanese refugees, ranging in age from 3 to 12 at the time of separation, reported a number of symptoms associated with their losses, including persistent feelings of loneliness, sadness, distress, and frustration. Immigrant families who experience sudden loss accompanied by an informational deficit may experience the same array of long-term consequences as the Argentine families and Sudanese boys: persistent anxiety, guilt, depression, and repressed expression of emotion. In immigration and refugee resettlement, note Luster and his colleagues (2009), parent-child separation occurs at very high rates and has pervasive negative impact on such things as emotional detachment of parents and children from each other, communication problems in parent-child relations, and different psychological problems including depression in children.

ORPHANS OF FRAGMENTED FAMILIES

Most findings on childhood loss come from research on the loss of parents through illness, accident, and incarceration. By extrapolation, the research can reasonably be applied to suffering the loss of a parent through deportation. In situations such as the sudden arrest or deportation of a parent, loss and the disruption of attachment and bonding is common. For example, Chaudry et al. (2010) identified what appear to be several indicators of a breach in attachment in children following the arrest of undocumented parents, beginning with withdrawal and despair. Parental arrest and detention destabilized multiple important sources of structure in their lives, which in turn unsettled children's daily behaviors. More than one-third of the children that were studied were angry, clingy, and anxious, behaviors that continued more than six months after the parent's initial arrest. Almost half the children showed the signs of withdrawal. Parents observed new behaviors in their children that are consistent with a fear of losing a key attachment figures. Children's withdrawal and clinginess, rooted in the child's fear of a repeated disappearance, persisted for months after the parents' return from detention. Excessive crying and problems with eating and sleeping, and other daily habits and practices, were not uncommon among the children whose parents were arrested and detained. Some children experienced a persistent loss of appetite or otherwise irregular eating patterns, two possible signs of childhood depression. As may be expected, the overall effects were exacerbated among children who experienced longer periods of separation from attachment figures. Households that had a parent in detention for over a month reported much more frequent symptoms of loss, especially for cases in which the child had to adjust to a new primary caregiver. Over nine months after the initial arrest, families of children aged 6 to 11 continued to report disruption of their child's daily habits. It would not be surprising if children continued to manifest these fears in other behaviors later in childhood.

Parental separation caused by arrest and detention is difficult for children to cope with as the split-ups are not only sudden, but also, in some cases, permanent (Baum et al., 2010). Permanency, though, is never really established in the minds of children of detained and deported parents, not the way permanency is understood when death occurs or a life sentence is imposed on a parent for a felony. In cases of immigration detention, "anticipatory" ambiguous loss is particularly applicable, whereby children ruminate on the impending loss and that they will not know where their parents are or will be. Many times, the remaining family members are unsure of the detainee's situation and unable to determine when or if he or she will return. The child may have a remote understanding of detention, but may be unsure about when or if he or she will ever see the parent again or if anyone will take the parent's place as a caretaker. In detention cases that end in deportation, separation may be a permanent change; in other cases, the family member may return home under supervision in just a few days. For the relatives and friends, this ambiguity is a tremendous source of stress, and "immobilizing [to] individuals and relational systems" (Boss 1991, p. 238). The prevailing lack of knowledge about the family member's situation creates ongoing anxiety and conflict, often a detriment to the child's home environment.

Despite children's often limited understanding of immigration enforcement, their feelings of frustration and anger are frequently directed at immigration authorities. They lump any law-enforcement groups into one overall nemesis, viewing local police with the same type of fear and anxiety they have about ICE and CBP. Even upon parents' return to their children, the kids continue to be afraid of almost anything associated with immigration and remain anxious that law enforcement is coming back sooner or later to arrest someone in their family (Chaudry et al., 2010).

Orphans of deportation told us of very painful, upsetting stories. On Dreby's (2012) pyramid of deportation burdens, this group of citizen-children had reached the point in which their families were effectively dissolved, splintered into binational families. The citizen-children are eligible to cross the border into Mexico (or other countries) to visit deported parents, but as minor children left living in poverty or financially limited situations in the United States, they can neither afford to travel nor travel alone without special arrangements. It is not easy for the children or their parents. Parents may leave the country when they are deported but hope for reunification someday. Some deported parents are undeterred from preventing the effective dissolution or fragmentation of their families and they will re-enter the country at the risk of all the dangers migrants face, the least of which may be re-arrest, detention, and deportation. They would not be separated from their children. Two cases illustrate how some fractured families cope and how their citizen-children are affected.

Cesar

In Texas, we met Cesar, whose father had been deported three times and each time had found his way back to be with his wife and children. It can be said that Cesar had been orphaned, reunited, and orphaned again. And he still didn't know what the future held.

Cesar's interview took place about six months after his father had been deported and had found his way back from Mexico in defiance of the removal. In fact, Cesar's mother told Miguel Gutierrez who interviewed the parents that her husband was to have gone to his hometown in the interior of Mexico after his deportation but that he never made it there. He called her and was already "half-way back to our town in Texas" within days of his repatriation by government authorities. The father's determination to be with his children is no less courageous than immigrants of earlier times who faced monumental odds in migrating great distances in search of better futures for their children, born and yet unborn.

His father's year-long incarceration in a detention facility before deportation and the stresses of the previous two deportations and reunifications weighed heavy on Cesar and exacerbated his constant watchfulness. Like other citizen-children described in this book, he was always apprehensive of what could happen to one or both of his undocumented parents. Would his father be arrested and detained again? Would it be his mother this time? Or could it be both of his parents at once? What would become of him? Approaching his 11th birthday, Cesar looked sad. He was soft spoken and would glance up shyly with his head tilted down. The interview had to be interrupted several times when Cesar cried or became distressed by the conversation.

Marina Islas who interviewed Cesar wrote in her notes on the interview that

> During the questionnaire he was very antsy and toyed with his shirt. Midway through the questionnaire, Cesar asked if we could stop. I asked if he wanted to quit or if he wished to take a break. He clarified and asked if we could break. We went outside together. On our way out towards the playground we raced. He wandered around the play set for a while then recruited a smaller child to play baseball with him. The smaller child tossed the ball at Cesar and Cesar did his best to hit the wild throws with a plastic bat. After ten or fifteen minutes Cesar walked towards me. I asked if he was ready to go back. He said yes and we raced each other back to the building. During the interview there were some questions that Cesar could not answer; he could not remember the details. He would start to squirm when asked certain questions and if he started to do this I would not press him.

Cesar told Marina that his relationships with his friends had changed when his father was "locked away" for a year.

"I became like . . . Um. . . Meaner. Yeah, meaner. But when my dad came back I was back to like normal."

But it was Cesar's depression that was most prominent in the interview. He could remember very little of the times when his father was arrested, events that most people would recall easily Cesar was suppressing or avoiding. He said he could not remember what happened exactly the day that his father was taken. Even in the face of evidence given to Cesar and Marina by his mother about what happened to his father, Cesar could not remember what she told him. When asked if he ever visited his father while he was locked away, Cesar said he had and spoke of his happiness in seeing his father. But he could not describe the detention center well. He described bleakness all around him when his father was deported and absent from the home.

"How did things change at home when he went away?" Marina asked.

"It was kind of like . . . being more like, everyone was sad and not. . . . Like to me it look like gray or something. Gray. Like everything was, um. . . bad feelings were around. Like sadness or pain . . . anger."

"Anger? Sadness?" Marina restated. "Who were you angry with?"

"I don't know. It was not like, not anger but sadness." Cesar told Marina that when his father was sent away he felt like he couldn't move and couldn't do anything.

With his father's first deportation, the only way Cesar's mother could survive was by going back to work and taking in her sister, brother-in-law, and their son into their small three-bedroom house. With Cesar, his mother, and two siblings this made for a crowded household.

Cesar and his younger cousin fought constantly. Until the additional relatives joined them, Cesar preferred the warmth of playing board games with his siblings and parents, going out to restaurants, and playing video games. Previously, his mother did not have to work. The family activities and his mother's consistent presence reinforced his security of attachment. But even now with his father back and both parents working, they could not live alone as a family; they had to share their home with others. Life was too precarious for them and, as much as Cesar detested it, by living together the two families could help each other financially and be there to support the other in the event of a detention. Together they achieved a modest amount of stability.

The somatic experience associated with depression was present in Cesar's narrative, too. Anhedonia, or the inability to experience pleasure from activities that are usually enjoyable, was accompanied by at least one vegetative sign of depression, excessive sleep. Cesar hypothesized that he slept a lot because he was tired from feeling overwhelmed by school. There's reason to accept his explanation at face value, but sleep impairments, or in Cesar's description feeling so fatigued that he had to sleep a lot, is a common indication of the dysphoria of depression. And though he did not voice it, managing the rage he carried with him constantly was also exhausting. His allostatic load was very high. As a clinician and as a father, I worry about what will happen to Cesar in his adolescent years and beyond if this depression continues.[2]

Cesar's words gave meaning to what the clinical measures were revealing about him. In each measure, Cesar showed that he was suffering clinical problems that appeared to be the cumulative effects of loss, wariness, deportations, anticipations, disruptions, and reunifications. On the measure of childhood depression, Cesar scored in the upper range of elevated symptoms with exceptionally negative self-esteem and high emotional problems. His scores on the instruments measuring mood, somatic symptoms, and conduct problems were all in the clinical range. There were signs of attention deficit and possible hyperactivity symptoms. His anxiety symptom scores were borderline clinical on one instrument and nearly twice the threshold level needed to indicate clinical concern. Scores on measures of oppositional-defiant disorder and conduct problems were in the high clinical range, and there was also clinical evidence of posttraumatic stress. His recent school history evinced some problems, mostly fidgeting in class and fights with others. His self-image and self-worth were low by our measures and as reflected in his own words and behavior. His anger was palpable and a factor in his defiance at home and school, his fights, and the ongoing bickering with his younger cousin. His psychological profile was among the worst of the more than 80 children we interviewed for our study and one of the most troubling I had seen, even including the children I had known in removal cases. Cesar was suffering a major depression.

This is a boy who needs his father, the important figure who provides a model of behavior. His father is his confidant and advisor, a fishing buddy, and a fellow video-gamer who likes the same type of "shoot 'em up" and competitive sports games. "My mom," he told us, "is more like into friendly games, like *Mario*." [3] The importance of his father to Cesar cannot be underestimated. He always relied on his father to "talk to him about stuff and going fishing. Sometimes he takes me to some places like an arcade or something." These kinds of activities are vital for a father and son to engage in. But when his father left, Cesar felt restless and bereft.

"I felt like, kind of like, like something bothering me. I always went to my dad to talk about stuff. But when he, um, when he went, I couldn't do anything."

Agustina

"If I could change anything," Agustina said with a long sigh, "it would be my dad leaving, being undocumented. I would change things so he could be documented and back here. But really? I know the chances of him coming back in less than a year are slim."

Agustina was 14-and-a-half when we met her. At that time she was living with her mother and younger brother, and attending a local charter school where she is known as a good student with solid grades. Agustina is an insulin-dependent diabetic. Her father had been deported to Mexico three months prior to the interview following a lengthy legal challenge. The path to deportation began as the result of a minor car accident that occurred about five years before and that was complicated by a 12-year-old domestic-violence report that his wife had filed against him. As described by Agustina's mother, after the domestic-violence episode, the couple went to counseling through a church and rebuilt their marriage. They eventually became counselors to other couples in church groups. The couple had grown up in Rio Verde in San Luis Potosi and knew each other since childhood. At about the same time as her husband's deportation, she became a Legal Permanent Resident, a status received too late to help her with her husband's case.

Agustina said she always knew her parents were undocumented. She always knew they were from Mexico but it was never a topic they dwelt on at the personal level. They tried to live a life unfettered by the parents' tenuous legal status. Like the many citizen-children I have described in this book, Agustina had to "make sure you don't do anything bad because then your parents are gonna pay the price. You are under their control so whatever you do illegally is going to affect your parents. That's kind of the thing that always made me behave, follow the rules." Both of her parents were well-educated people who strove to keep a strong family life and instill in their children a sense of social justice. Her mother, in particular, became very active in local immigration movements and organizations when her husband's immigration troubles began.

"They were always into immigrant stuff," Agustina said. "So I think I always grew up with this. I probably figured it out when I was very young. I kind of always knew they were illegal. Since I was very little I was always scared that they were going to be taken away from me because I knew they were illegal. They could be taken away at any moment. My friends and me—some of our parents are illegal—so there were times when we would talk about it. We talked about the pain of being worried about them. We would always have these discussions."

When the car accident occurred, her husband called his wife to get the insurance papers, but the other driver had already called the police. They arrested him on the old domestic-violence call, driving without a license, and being undocumented. One unfortunate aspect was that he was driving in a town whose police force is notorious for arresting the undocumented no matter the issue. He was jailed for several days and the couple challenged the removal order issued by ICE. It was a 4-year ordeal, according to Agustina's mother, one she calls a time of "torture" owing to the uncertainty of what was going to happen. They depleted their savings and the mother had to clean more houses than she already did to pay the family's bills. Agustina made a suicide attempt in the closing days of her father's immigration case.

Agustina told our interviewer, M. Andrea Campetella, that it was very difficult for her, not knowing when her dad was going to be taken away. Like most removal proceedings there were many court-appearance dates scheduled, only to be postponed. "We never knew when a court date was real," she said.

"They wanted me to go to court but I could not 'cause I had school, and back then I was really focusing on not missing school. My dad was still in jail I think when they wanted me to go to the immigration things. Mainly, I just didn't want to see my dad because they were going to show him on the screen, or something like that, and I was like that I'm not going to even see my dad, I'm not even talk to him, so what's the point of having him right there and seeing him, and not being able to be with him. I thought it was pointless to even go. It would hurt me even more to see him there."

Just a few weeks after his deportation, Agustina, her mother, and her brother flew to Mexico on spring break from school to visit her father, who was still unemployed. Agustina's mother is struggling, taking on more houses to clean, sending her husband some money, taking care of her children, driving Agustina to her doctors' appointments, and having to work more. The family has planned to meet with the father in a town in Mexico closer to the border, although it still means a 12-hour car ride for him. Her life has changed drastically.

We don't do a lot together anymore because we have kind of our separate things. And lately my mom has been busier so we don't really do anything as a family anymore. Since my dad left she has to work more, and then she has to take care of me and my little brother, so she has to drop me off somewhere, and then she has to drop off him, and then she has to pick me up and she has to get people to pick up my little brother, or she has to pick him up and then get me. And it's all crazy for her so she never really has time to spend with both of us at the same time.

That's very different from before. You see, now I feel like I have more responsibilities than before: making sure like that my mom does not break down; making sure that my little brother has a big sister. I used to never be with my brother because my dad used to be with him and I could be off doing my own things, like homework and stuff like that. But now I have to make sure that my little brother is all right, and then whenever I go out, my little brother forces me back inside, or he starts crying until I get home. If he is separated from me or my mom he starts crying. He does not want us to leave. I think it's because I had already been away from him for over a week when I was in the hospital and then my dad was deported. But since my dad left he does not want me to go anywhere. Like when I want to go off with my friends, he grabs my leg and say, 'no 'mana no.'" [Mana, or sis, is a contraction of hermana or sister.]

And this really hurts me 'cause like I wanna go out but I feel like I'm hurting him, so I feel really horrible.

Her mother tries to create a normal life for her two children, according to Agustina. She encourages Agustina to go out with her friends, to follow as normal a life pattern as possible, and urges her daughter to "not worry about my dad not being here, kind of let myself be normal for a while, like a normal teen." Still, Agustina misses the family activities, such as their

[Play] fights where me and my dad would like box and my mom would laugh and my little brother would get involved, and he would try to like play fight too but he was too little. We would all—my dad, my mom, me and my brother—have tickle fights. We would tickle one and then the others, and stuff like that; and we used to joke around with each other, and just have conversations as a whole family about something stupid or something new, and there was times when we went out to dinner or breakfast, or stuff like that, and we would just be a family eating, laughing, and there was times were we could just sit down and have a normal dinner and just talked about what happened during the day. But weekends aren't the same anymore. It's just me and my mom and my brother. It's not that normalness, that normal feeling of waking up in the morning and seeing your dad, waiting for your dad to go to buy food and fix breakfast or a barbacoa. It's not that feeling anymore.

Agustina's father was missing out on so many important milestones in her life. Like when she entered middle school. She was admitted to a local charter school with her strong academic performance. "I was really excited," she said. "But my dad was not there; he wasn't able to share experiences with me. I only saw him a few times in the detention center through a glass. It was just a really horrible thing to be able to see your dad but not be able to touch him." She would also miss an important milestone in the life of a Hispanic girl: her quinceañera (a Latin American tradition of celebrating a girl's 15th birthday when she transitions from childhood to womanhood).

"I was supposed to have my quinceañera this December and I was really excited about it. But my parents can't afford a quinceañera anymore 'cause my mom is sending money to my dad. And my dad probably won't be here for my graduation from high school because it will probably take him years to be able to come back. It's kind of like he is missing everything in my life, in the years of being a teenager that everyone says is so special. I wish I could change that, make him be part of my life again." She had not been able to celebrate her 14th birthday, either, as the family was devoting time to getting the two children their passports in order to be able to travel to Mexico to visit the father once he was deported.

Her interview confirmed that she is an intelligent, insightful teenager but the results of the psychological tests showed her to be experiencing many difficulties. Agustina's scores on our psychological measures were in the clinical range and very troubling. In the two measures that tap for depressive symptoms, her scores were in the clinical range, at the 98th percentile of teenagers with depression. Her anxiety was nearly three times the level for generalized, social, and separation anxiety, panic disorder, and somatic symptoms. Her scores on measures of posttraumatic stress and anger were also in the clinically significant range. Following this pattern of results on measures of problematic behaviors and emotions, Agustina's test results also showed that her self-concept was compromised. The only area in which Agustina felt positive was in assessing her intellect and school status.

Her suicide attempt was a culmination of the many painful experiences in her life. And it resembles those of the many Hispanic girls who attempt suicide, a phenomenon I documented in *Latinas Attempting Suicide: When Cultures, Families, and Daughters Collide* (Zayas, 2011). At the center of her anguish was the sense of loss: Agustina's therapist had to terminate her therapy because of a job change; her father was being deported; and her boyfriend had betrayed her by asking out her best friend. Neither her father nor the therapist could buffer the natural developmental tension between a pubescent girl and her mother.

"I was feeling betrayed," Agustina said. "Like I already had issues with my parents and I was already hurt because my dad was leaving. Then my counselor left and she was the one person I could talk to. And then my ex-boyfriend started dating my best friend. It was like everything happening at the same time. It was just like nobody cared about me anymore, nobody. Because, everything with the legal issues I just felt like my parents were not paying as much attention to me, as much as to the legal issues with my dad. I felt like nobody really cared about me. It was like the last straw when I attempted suicide."

The hospitalization served as a buffer for her, a place where she was able to retreat from the maelstrom in her life. But she learned a lot about herself, too, and saw things very differently after the 10 days in the hospital.

One memory is the two half-hour visits with her father during her hospital stay.

"I had an hour with my family while I was in the hospital. An hour, period. I couldn't see my little brother 'cause he was too young to come upstairs and I only had 30 minutes with each parent once a week. The 30 minutes I spent with my dad was one of the nicest times. I knew that he was going to get deported the day after I would get home. But at the time we were talking about how he was going to get me a chinchilla, and how I liked chinchillas. It was really bittersweet, like one of the most amazing times."

Agustina's encounters with other patients also had an impact on her. She remembers a girl her age who suffered from depression

> She had so many cuts on her arm, like it was self-injury. When I was talking to her I just realized some of the things I had were not as bad as other people had. That kind of stabilized me, and me being able to talk to someone, to people who knew my situation or that understood how I felt, that I was depressed and not a drama queen. I was there because I have something wrong with me. I have family issues. I have emotional issues. I have school issues. But I had a lot to live for. It hits a nerve now when everybody talks about their dad, when kids complain about how their dads are this way and that way. And I'm like 'You just shut up. At least you have him; at least he is there with you. He might not support you and stuff, but at least he is there for you. My dad is all the way in Mexico. I can't see him every day. I can't tell him I love him every day. It just irritates me whenever anybody talks bad about their dad. It's like 'You don't know how it is to lose a parent, knowing that they are in another country.'"

WHAT WILL HAPPEN?

The US immigration enforcement strategy in the first two decades of the millennium has been extremely successful in generating an atmosphere of fear among undocumented immigrants and mixed-status families. Arrest and detention practices have created a generation of citizen-children thoroughly traumatized by law enforcement authorities. These children are essentially the collateral damage of enforcement activities. As American citizens, they pose no threat to security and are not the targets of immigration enforcement, yet ultimately it is these children who suffer the most. Their citizenship affords them personal safety, security, and the right to family, yet home raids and parental separation fundamentally undermine these childhood necessities. Despite the well-substantiated importance of stability and early relationships to human development, parental deportation continues to disrupt any attempt to provide the citizen-child with a strong and healthy environment. Without an examination and reform of such strategies and practices, the effects of deportation policy will continue to misguidedly fall hardest on this most vulnerable population and our nature's future.

NOTES

1. On March 25, 2014, the *Joplin Globe* (Missouri) reported that attorneys for Ms. Encarnación Bail Romero filed a request to the US Supreme Court to hear an appeal to overturn the adoption of her son on the basis of due process, arguing that a different standard had been used to terminate the biological mother's rights. In the story by Susan Redden, the *Globe* reported that the appeal also asserts that Ms. Bail Romero lacked adequate legal representation at the hearing that transferred the custody of her son, and that the Missouri court's ruling relied on the mother's immigration status in determining if the adoption should be allowed. See http://www.joplinglobe.com/topstories/x542465440/U-S-Supreme-Court-asked-to-hear-challenge-from-Guatemalan-mother

2. After concluding the study, we provided Cesar's mother a packet of information on behavioral health clinics in her local area that could offer Cesar help. His mother stated that she was in dire need of someone to speak to for herself as the threat of her husband being deported again was taking its toll on her and the relationship with her husband.

3. *Mario* is a media franchise of video games published and produced by Nintendo starring the fictional character, Mario.

CHAPTER 11

Our Common Future

Perhaps soon after this book is published, the United States will have reformed its immigration system. It might even have developed ways of handling the complex family situations of undocumented immigrants, their undocumented children, their citizen-children, and conceivably, the children who enter the United States as undocumented unaccompanied minors.[1] We might see a much-improved definition of "extreme and exceptionally unusual hardship" that includes the mental health effects of deportation on citizen-children. Maybe our country will consider an enlightened approach that considers fully the human needs and vulnerabilities of both the US-born children of undocumented immigrant and their parents. But even if we arrive at a reformed immigration system, the practices of the last two decades—of aggressive detention and deportation policies—will have already affected hundreds of thousands of citizen-children and mixed-status families. Our national policies have preyed on the lives of citizen-children whose parents have avoided detection. Deportability—that menacing weight that follows citizen-children's parents everywhere—is frightening and ultimately damaging for the family as a whole. Parents are faced with a "choiceless choice" (Thronson, 2005–2006): take their children to another country or leave them in the United States. The current generation of citizen-children, surely the largest in US history, includes more *de facto* exiles and more *de facto* orphans than any before. These children have been deprived of either a childhood in the United States or the stable support of their parents. None have had access to the full range of protections and opportunities associated with being American. The sense of belonging that comes with citizenship and attachment to a land, a nation, to an ideal will have been denied them.

In looking at the long history of immigration in the United States and our country's historic reactions to the many waves of people arriving here, we have seen our citizenry and leaders in their most admirable moments but also their most disgraceful ones. In the past two decades, we have witnessed very little to be proud of at the federal and local levels. Instead we have gotten more, mean-spirited laws to punish the undocumented people within our borders. These shameful attacks primarily target those from Mexico and Central America, but they impact immigrants from all over the world. Despite evidence of the positive impact immigrant labor has had on our economy since the nation's infancy, counterproductive laws, statutes, ordinances, and regulations have been deliberately promulgated when xenophobia and hatred grab hold.

In the recent war on immigrants, citizen-children are forgotten— *American children*: born, raised, schooled, and socialized as members of the United States. As demonstrated by the profiles in this book, these children are typical Americans with typical dreams and aspirations for their future lives. The United States is not only their birthplace but, for most of them, the only home they have ever known. They are American citizens fundamentally and fully entitled to all related rights and privileges. These children are the future contributors to our nation's prosperity.

Citizen-children, even their foreign-born siblings who were brought into the United States as infants, do not bear responsibility for the circumstances of their birth. Yet, demagogues, responding to base fears, have painted the undocumented immigrants as "them" and their children as the "other." Many of the resultant policies and strategies described in this book, such as raiding workplaces, draining employment opportunities, restricting housing, forbidding drivers' licenses, narrowing access to medical care, and frightening immigrants away from a host of other services and opportunities, are intended to hurt the undocumented immigrant. But their citizen-children suffer these attacks as defenseless collateral damage. And as these citizen-children mature into adult citizens, how these negative experiences affect their perceptions and attitudes toward our laws and our society will in turn influence the formation of our common future.

THROUGH NO FAULT OF THEIRS

In authoring the Supreme Court's *Plyer v. Doe* decision, discussed in Chapter 3, Justice William J. Brennan wrote that the Court was "disturbed" by the fact that the law in question was directed against the children of undocumented immigrants. The Supreme Court saw the Texas law as directed against children and, therefore, imposing "its discriminatory burden on the basis of a legal characteristic over which children can have little control. It is thus difficult to conceive of a rational justification for penalizing these children for their presence within the United States." Justice Brennan went on.

> Sheer incapability or lax enforcement of the laws barring entry into this country, coupled with the failure to establish an effective bar to the employment of undocumented aliens, has resulted in the creation of a substantial "shadow population" of illegal migrants—numbering in the millions—within our borders. This situation raises the specter of a permanent caste of undocumented resident aliens, encouraged by some to remain here as a source of cheap labor, but nevertheless denied the benefits that our society makes available to citizens and lawful residents. The existence of such an underclass presents most difficult problems for a Nation that prides itself on adherence to principles of equality under law.
>
> The children who are plaintiffs in these cases are special members of this underclass. Persuasive arguments support the view that a State may withhold its beneficence from those whose very presence within the United States is the product of their own unlawful conduct. These arguments do not apply with the same force to classifications imposing disabilities on the minor children of such illegal entrants. At the least, those who elect to enter our territory by stealth and in violation of our law should be prepared to bear the consequences, including, but not limited to, deportation. But the children of those illegal entrants are not comparably situated. Their "parents have the ability to conform their conduct to societal norms," and presumably the ability to remove themselves from the State's jurisdiction; but the children who are plaintiffs in these cases "can affect neither their parents' conduct nor their own status." Even if the State found it expedient to control the conduct of adults by acting against their children, legislation directing the onus of a parent's misconduct against his children does not comport with fundamental conceptions of justice. (*Plyer v. Doe* (457 US 252 (1982))

To drive home his point, Justice Brennan quoted a decision issued a decade earlier by the Supreme Court in *Weber v. Aetna Cas. & Sur. Co., 406 US 164 (1972)*, a case that considered whether acknowledged (i.e., legal paternity) and unacknowledged dependents (i.e., "illegitimate children") had equal rights to their deceased father's workmen's compensation benefits. It is an oft-cited quotation for the power of its logic and empathy.

> Visiting . . . condemnation on the head of an infant is illogical and unjust. Moreover, imposing disabilities on the . . . child is contrary to the basic concept

of our system that legal burdens should bear some relationship to individual responsibility or wrongdoing. Obviously, no child is responsible for his birth, and penalizing the . . . child is an ineffectual—as well as unjust—way of deterring the parent (457 US 252 (1982)).

The words of Justice Brennan and the District Court, and of many uncelebrated cases where jurists have protected citizen-children, can be used to guide the development of sensitive, humane, and effective immigration laws. In the pursuit of social order, economic stability, and political convenience, our immigration policies and laws, and the legislators who pass the laws as well as the agents that implement the laws, should not dismiss the most defenseless, citizen-children. It will take political will, a lot of compassion for citizen-children, and a pragmatic view of the future of our country to make these changes. If there is not enough political will to affirmatively develop humane policies for the protection of citizen-children in the immediacy, there are at least legal precedents for challenging the harmful aspects of current deportation policies. If immigration reform fails to include citizen children's needs, we must then pursue change through litigation as has been done in the past (e.g., the class action suit of *Plyer v. Doe* that overturned the Texas law on unfair exclusion of children from schools). But litigation is only a stop gap solution and perpetuates the patchwork approach to immigration policy development that has been used in recent decades. It will take a paradigm shift.

In her ethnography of migrant youth and families in America, anthropologist Lauren Heidbrink (2014) observes that practitioners in the field are often put in the position of fighting to maintain and improve services within the very systems that directly harm their clients. In such circumstances, professionals who would on principle advocate for systemic reforms and paradigm shifts to ensure their clients' rights and needs are compelled by negative political realities to defend and improve the current system. These negative political realities often include an adversarial political climate, such as anti-immigrant legislative and attacks on current systems. They may also include resource limitations, funding-source restraints, and/or ethical restraints on, for example, professionals employed or contracted by the very agencies that apply the unfair laws and regulations. The inherent contradiction and danger of this pragmatic approach is that their support of maintaining and improving the current systems can be viewed as validation of the systems. While it is my hope that this book's case studies present lessons learned that are of immediate use to practitioners in the field, any suggestions I offer for ameliorating the suffering of citizen-children under the current system should not be taken as either an endorsement of that system or as criticism of the many dedicated people working within it. In this chapter, I propose some ideas looking forward to how we might change our future approaches to the conditions of citizen-children of mixed status families. I offer suggestions for those assisting citizen-child clients under the current system as well as my thoughts on the type of larger paradigm shift required to truly address the needs of this uniquely vulnerable population. I argue that in our approach to true reform we must not only avoid the continued creation of exiles and orphans but also provide some measure of redress for those citizen-children who have already been harmed.

IN THE BEST INTEREST OF THE CHILD

How can we reconcile the Department of Homeland Security's charge to secure our nation's borders with our societal need to defend the better humanitarian principals that define us as a nation? This is a question that has engaged the time and effort of many keen observers and thinkers in universities, independent research centers, advocacy groups, religious and social justice groups, and even businesses. We don't lack for sound, compassionate policy ideas about immigration reform. On any given Sunday, the Op-Ed pages of our nation's newspapers offer thoughtful commentaries and proposals. While the national dialogue on immigration reform continues to build, there is much that we can do through policy and practice, to begin to reconcile immigration enforcement practices with our nation's higher ideals. Since my expertise is in behavioral health—enhancing human development and preventing and treating disorders—I adhere to the child's best interest as a guiding principle in approaches to both holistic reform and rehabilitation of the current system.

The "best interests of the child doctrine" is a legal staple in American family and juvenile law for over a century.[2] It is a principle that recognizes that the child's relationships with parents, siblings, and other persons who play a significant role in the child's life at home, school, and in the community deserve careful consideration in any making decisions about the child. Depending upon the child's age and capacity, the child has some say on what's best for her or him, and the child's autonomy must be recognized and fostered. Best-interest even includes the physical and mental health of the people responsible for the child's care. None of us doubt that immigration enforcement is necessary. What we cannot afford to lose in undertaking immigration enforcement are justice and the values that define us as a nation—life, liberty, and the pursuit of happiness. The best interest lens can and should be applied to any attempted level of immigration reform: from a macro-level reimagining of the structure and balance of powers in the system to procedural amendments to the micro-level agency policies and programs and practices of its professional staff. The case studies presented in this book illustrate the immediate need and opportunity for best-interest based interventions throughout the current apprehension and removal processes.[3]

As we saw in the cases of Felipe Montes, Maria L., and Encarnación Bail Romero, communication between ICE and child welfare authorities is nearly nonexistent or simply distorted. Child welfare caseworkers and family attorneys lack knowledge of immigration enforcement (Wessler, 2011). DHS must take responsibility for working with other federal agencies, such as the US Department of Health and Human Services, and local child welfare and mental health authorities to develop child-protection practices that minimize the potential disruption to children's attachment and avoid traumatizing children when parents are arrested, detained, deported, and repatriated (Chaudry et al., 2010). ICE procedural policy should require notification of state and local social-service agencies prior to planned enforcement operations to insure that children are protected. ICE should screen those undocumented immigrants apprehended to identify detainees who are parents or primary caretakers of citizen-children and their brothers and sisters. Children must have access to their parents during detention, and arrested parents must be engaged in the development of plans to shelter and educate their children. Given that most detained immigrants pose little to no threat to public safety, it is preferable to offer noncriminal parents supervised release over a costly and sometimes lengthy detention. Leaving citizen-children in their parents' care during these releases costs less than storing their parents in detention centers and reduces the psychological and financial costs of placing children in foster care. More importantly, it is much better for children's development.

Pending federal reforms, there are opportunities for external systems to defend the best interest of citizen-children with parents in the deportation process. At the state level, legislatures can create and grant extensions of child-dependency cases, in order to avoid terminating the parental rights of detained or deported parents who are unable to participate in their child's case. Caseworkers can enlist nongovernmental organizations, such as social-service agencies and legal-rights groups, in the development of service plans for citizen-children whose parents face deportation. The combination of child-focused policy adjustments at the federal level, state agency coordination, and facilitation of related family court cases, and local community planning and preparation for children prior to parental deportation, provides the groundwork for an enforcement system that is proactive in ensuring the well-being of children.

IMMIGRATION COURT

Fundamental to reconciling the disconnection between child welfare standards and immigration court practices is the replacement of the exceptional and extremely unusual hardship principle as the exclusive guide for determining an immigrant's eligibility for a cancellation grant (Zayas & Bradlee, 2014). Presently, immigration courts are not obligated to take into account what happens to the citizen-children who will be affected by the court's decision. Instead, parents under deportation proceedings must, through their attorneys, bring to the court's attention the impact on their children when challenging removal orders. As demonstrated in the preceding chapters, this isn't a trivial matter, since the burden falls on the parent to prove the hardship without a set definition or standards for exceptional and extremely unusual hardship that includes children's mental health.

In application, the exceptional and extremely unusual hardship standard has failed to protect citizen-children from just that—the exceptional and extremely unusual privation of becoming *de facto* exiles and orphans after forced family separation. In fact, immigration law and family law as they are presently composed and applied are not only inconsistent but incompatible: immigration law compromises family integrity, a foundational principle of family law. When these two areas of law "collide, children routinely are caught in the middle" (Thronson, 2005–2006, p. 1165). Indeed, Thronson notes, the contradictions of immigration and family laws place parents in extremely difficult positions. Parents are forced by immigration law, on one hand, to put their children in harm's way by taking them to another country and then, on the other hand, parents who decide that it is in their children's best interest to leave them behind are then faced with family law values that are "highly skeptical of any parental decision to separate from children" (p. 1171). It is clear to those of us working in this area that more needs to be done in immigration court to encourage judicial discretion in cases involving citizen-children to take evidence of the physical, emotional, psychological, intellectual, spiritual, and basic needs of citizen-children and of the psychological harm that the citizen-child will face if the parents are removed from the United States and the child is left behind. Under the current system, in cases likely to result in the US citizen-child leaving the United States with their parents, immigration courts should be required to examine how the best interests of the citizen-child will be met.

The best interest of the child doctrine seems a distant notion in today's immigration courts. "There is no best-interests standard in immigration law," notes attorney and children's rights advocate Maria Woltjen (2014), "no requirement that judges consider what's best for the child before them even though the decisions can carry life-and-death consequences." Even if an immigration court attempts to recognize the best-interest doctrine, it does so within the limitations of the exceptional and extremely unusual hardship standard and in isolation from child welfare system, subject matter experts, or independent advocates. This is due to the fact that the court's mandate is to determine the parent's eligibility for cancellation and whether it will be granted or not. Immigration courts are not charged, as state courts are, with the decision of how parents or guardians will approach the custody of the child. This directive restricts the scope of what courts and practitioners must focus on and does not include the application of standards and assumptions that are common in family law. This, in turn, limits the outcomes that judges have to choose from in issuing a decision.

Considering the consequences of immigration court decision on citizen-children—whose lives are wholly affected by decisions to deport parents—the US Department of Justice which oversees immigration courts, must broaden its directives to courts to include consideration of the impact on citizen-children. Directives should replace, or at the very least expand, the existing standard of extreme hardship with consideration of the child's best interest in deliberating the removal of any citizen-child's parent. As currently defined by law, deportation is not considered a punishment but rather a status correction. Therefore, a citizen-child's best interest should take precedence over a status violation by their parents. Even parents convicted of the most heinous of crimes in our society don't necessarily lose parental rights, if they are US citizens. But the rights of immigrants whose worst offense is to be in the country illegally (i.e., a status violation because they are in the country without authority regardless of motive for entering) and the rights of their US citizen-children do not receive equal protection. Incorporating the best interest principal in immigration proceedings would recognize the child's rights as a citizen and shift the focus of the proceedings from a *de facto* punishment of the family to preservation of the family system.

The Justice Department should devote effort to establishing criteria and guidelines for ensuring that citizen-children's best interests are protected in immigration courts. One approach is for immigration courts to emulate the many state statutes that preserve the importance of the family in juvenile and family court hearings (Child Welfare Information Gateway, 2012). A comprehensive consideration of the best interests of the child in immigration court would include an assessment of the love, affection, and other emotional ties that exist between the parent(s) and child, and the capacity of the parent(s) and other family members to facilitate a close and continuing parent-child relationship. Any assessment would also include sensitivity to the length of time the child has lived in a stable, satisfactory environment, and the desirability of maintaining continuity in that location. Most states take into account that children's core attachments are to people and place; recognizing the importance of family unity they avoid splitting families. If removing children from families is necessary, the state is usually obligated to assure that the child will receive good care and treatment in a home in which the child can grow into a self-sufficient adult.

Pursuit of the best interest standard would not require the development of a federal child welfare court within the immigration system. The best interest of the child when considered in immigration court can be determined through the combined input of court-appointed special advocates, guardians *ad litem*, and social workers, psychologists, physicians, and other health professionals. Judges hearing cases in which there are dependent citizen or undocumented children should request a determination of the child's best interest from experts, counselors, and clinicians who can assist the court and the immigrant family. Examinations and testimony by social workers and other mental health experts should support these determinations. These additional members of the court can reduce the subjective bias that influences some judges. Immigration courts can define determination of the best interests of the child as the aggregate or sum total of a number of important factors that can be professionally and scientifically considered, evaluated, and decided. (In Appendix B, I offer suggestions for mental health professionals evaluating children in removal cases and testifying in immigration courts.)

As illustrated in Chapter 8, a judge's own prejudice or limited understanding regarding the home country of the parents or the fitness of the parent may encourage a decision that results in either exiling or orphaning a citizen-child. With nebulous guidelines to base their decisions on and essentially no oversight, immigration judges are left at liberty to decide these cases based on their personal perception. Although there is no data readily available to quantify the impact of judicial prejudice on cases involving the parents of citizen-children, the effect of judicial prejudice is readily apparent in data sets on other vulnerable populations. For instance, in its judge-by-judge assessment of asylum application decisions, Syracuse University's Transactional Records Access Clearinghouse (TRAC, 2013) program found that the asylum denial rate by individual judges ranges from 10 to 100 percent. In one instance, a judge who had heard over 200 asylum cases over a five-year period denied all of them, with impunity. Until immigration judges are subject to some level of oversight, stronger guidelines and additional parties to the court are necessary to guard against the prejudice of individuals and the danger this prejudice represents to vulnerable populations.

In some immigration courts there are already successful approaches in place that allow nongovernmental organizations to provide guardian *ad litems* to represent the best interests of unaccompanied minors. Why can we not do the same for US citizen-children whose parents stand before an immigration court requesting a cancellation of removal? Take, for example, the work of the Young Center for Immigrant Children's Rights (2013), based in Chicago, Illinois and Harlingen, Texas, which promotes the best interests and the expressed wishes of unaccompanied immigrant children in accordance with the Convention on the Rights of the Child. The guardians *ad litem* provided by the Young Center are "trusted allies for these children by accompanying them through court proceedings, advocating for their best interests, and standing for the creation of a dedicated juvenile immigrant justice system that ensures the safety and well-being of every child" (2013). Surely, similar approaches can be introduced in immigration court when citizen-children's best interests and expressed wishes need consideration as their parents face deportation hearings.

Of course, all the subject matter expertise and guardian ad litem support that the community can muster will not help an immigration judge to reach a decision that supports the child's best interest if there is no case. In Chapter 6, we learned that access to counsel is the gateway to applying for any form of relief, and that parents face many impediments to securing an attorney. As we've seen, even when families manage to remain intact despite deportation, the effects of parental removal on the child are extremely detrimental. In more extreme scenarios, removal may constitute a death sentence. Parents of citizen-children must be appointed counsel in the instance of a removal order to ensure equal protection and due process for all citizen-children under the law. After all, the impact of these removal decisions on citizen-children's lives is at least as significant as the impact of decisions made in child-welfare courts (where children are appointed representation to ensure the child's best interest, in recognition of the child's need for protection). And the potential consequences to the life and liberty of both the child and parent are analogous to the consequences faced by criminal defendants (who are appointed counsel to ensure due process). Given the necessity of legal representation to establish the opportunity for a judge to hear a parent's case and consider the order of removal in light of the citizen-child's best interest, that representation must be ensured.

Finally, in order for the court's consideration of the child's best interest or even extreme hardship to have any meaning, courts must have the latitude to grant relief. For this to happen, Congress must immediately revoke the ridiculously low and arbitrary cap on grants of cancellations. Allotment of the 4000 grants, as described in Chapter 7, is based on luck. Justice isn't served when persons who apply for cancellation are found by an immigration judge to have met the requirements only to be turned down because they were not among the lucky ones to be first in line that year. In this situation, the determining factor is not qualification but *when* they applied and *when* their cases were heard—the age-old wrong-place, wrong-time situation. How can the best interests of children be protected when only 4000 grants of cancellation are awarded annually? How do we distinguish the worthy from the nonworthy? We cannot assume that only 4000 individuals are eligible nationally for grants each year. Citizen-children should not have their futures determined by random chance. In no other area of law that I know of are decisions based on the number of people who have already met criteria for acquittals or convictions. We don't, for example, decide that in a given year only so many white-collar criminals can be acquitted or convicted, or that only a number of murder defendants will be found guilty and all others innocent in a given fiscal cycle. We do not cap the number of bankruptcy applications that will be allowed. Our system of justice is better than that; it's a system based on who qualifies for leniency or penalty, not a numerical cap. Merit, not quotas, should be applied to grants of cancellation.

FOR THE GENERATION ALREADY EXILED AND ORPHANED

Many of these ideas are prospective, future-oriented, what we can do going forward. Yet, there is already a generation of citizen-children living either in exile in other countries with their parents or in the United States without their parents. They have already been hurt by our nation's policies and practices. We will have to think about how we repair their loss of trust in our government, how we re-engage them as fellow citizens, and how we right the wrongs and prepare them for productive futures. With lifetime

US citizenship bestowed on them by their birth on US soil, the exiles may return later in life to pursue their lives. They may make it their personal missions to fix the system that drastically changed their lives, like the two girls we met in Chapter 9—Irma who plans on returning to the United States to study and work so that "the law sees that I am part of the United States. . . that I can because I have a job and I can take care of my mom and I can fix her papers" and Lupita who said that when she grows up "I'll fix it so [my parents] could go back [to the United States]" Some deportation exiles may choose not to return and perhaps drop their US citizenship or hold dual citizenship. Nevertheless, they deserve the offer of redress from the United States.

We can start by reaching out to them, both the orphans in the United States and the exiles abroad. We must send word that they are not forgotten and that help is available to them. Immigration and Customs Enforcement, the Executive Office of Immigration Review, Enforcement and Removal Operations (2013), other DHS agencies, and the numerous detention facilities in the United States must be required to create a database of people who have been deported that clearly identifies parents of US citizens. Reaching these individuals to identify their citizen-children (if they will trust us enough to do so) can be done through last-known addresses and public announcements on television, radio, and newspapers.

US embassies and consulates can publish the rights and services that exiled US citizen-children are entitled to and provide information on how kids can access assistance through the local offices. US offices with the sole mission of identifying, registering, and offering services to citizen-children can be opened in countries with the largest aggregation of our young exiles. Where US government offices are not within proximity of the exiles, contracts with recognized, trusted international nongovernmental organizations (NGOs) on the ground locally can serve as point of contact where citizen-children and their parents or guardians can receive information or access to register and apply for services and other relief. Electronic technology and social media can be employed to trace the locations of and reach out to our exiled compatriots.

Citizen-children exiled abroad need to know that in the event of emergencies, from acute medical needs to government upheavals or natural disaster, they can turn to US embassies and consulates protection and care. These same US agencies should facilitate access to medical services and healthcare for US exiles. Contracting with international NGOs to provide health, education, and social services in the most common host countries would ensure that the children we have exiled do not fall behind in these important areas.

I am not talking about extending entitlement services to families who elected to live in another country independently of a removal order or who have means of accessing education, healthcare, and other quality of life services. Rather, these benefits target those US citizens whose reasons for living in another country stem from familial deportations. Needs tests and means tests are a staple of American benefits programs that examine individuals' needs and means to determine eligibility for particular welfare benefits or services. In the extension of entitlement services to exiled citizen-children, we have plenty of experience from which to draw for developing these new benefits.

This is one means of providing citizen-children in exile with what they need at least until they complete high school (and into adulthood for those with disabilities). We must be prepared to provide opportunities for these children to return as young adults, if they wish to return or if parents want to repatriate them with family and friends living in the United States. Because these children were forced into exile, the United States should bear the cost of their return. Health, education, and social services must be organized to ensure that those who need them can have them as part of their reintegration into our society. We must be prepared to help those who return and encourage them to seek educational and vocational opportunities. We need them to become productive and self-sufficient workers and neighbors. With such opportunities as the Affordable Care Act, despite its many gaps, these citizens can locate health and mental health services upon their return.

By definition, deportation orphans in the United States have access to all that our great country can provide. This is a far less daunting task than finding deportation exiles abroad. Still they suffer familial separation and need support. Creative ways to enhance their connections to deported parents can be developed. Let's begin in with identifying them. Most school-teachers know which children in their classes have had parents deported and are living in the custody of another caregiver. Therefore, to identify them is not that difficult. Special outreach should be made to ensure that these children are receiving all the benefits they are entitled to as citizens. The federal government through the Administration for Children and Families of US Department of Health and Humans Services can provide funding to social service agencies as well as schools to develop and implement programs for the needs of the orphans.

While mental health services are important, other services such as youth development and mentoring programs should be created to provide for the unique needs of this population of children. Schools and local social service agencies can help the child keep in touch with parents through use of computers at schools and agencies. Helping children celebrate their parents' birthdays, to be in touch during important holiday periods, and other programs that will keep the ties to their parents alive can be very helpful. Indeed, there are thousands of creative programs around the country that help children. Those very same organizations can craft unique programs for deportation orphans that parallel existing programs for other populations of vulnerable children.

The stories in this book illustrate the harm and damage that citizen-children living as orphans or in exile have suffered already. As a nation, we must undo many of the problems that were created by impersonal and insensitive laws. The sooner we stop making exiles and orphans the more manageable the process of redress and the more stable our future.

IN THE BEST INTERESTS OF THE NATION

The United States relies on a strong and healthy labor force. From the very foundation of the nation, it was immigrant labor that built our country and its economy. The descendants of these laborers and the waves of immigrants that followed them replenished the work force, sustained strength of the economy, and ensured that enough babies were born to replace those leaving the labor force.

It is more than a large workforce and the strength of the economic environment that predicts the developmental health of our nation. The physical, social, mental, cultural, moral, and spiritual well-being of our nation's people and the quality of the general social environment—a dynamic made up of laws, institutions, and the physical environment (e.g., buildings, parks, roads) defines a nation's developmental health (Keating & Hertzman,1999).

To maintain our strength, productivity and economic growth, our offspring must be healthy, educated, encouraged, and inspired. The greatest danger to this national developmental health is when measurable inequities between groups of people persist. Research on poverty and inequality support the link between the quality of the social and economic environment and human development. Social and economic disparities among people in a nation are the best indicators of the developmental health of a country. Thus, citizens must feel engaged and efficacious in their local communities and civic process to apply their competencies for the greater good. As the disparities between groups grow wider, the lower the overall health and well-being of the populace. Ultimately, it is the quality of the person-environment interaction that determines our national well-being.

When some people, in our times immigrants and their citizen-children, are seen and maintained as outsiders, attacked and besieged by insensitive laws and deportation practices, we are only weakening ourselves. When communities have a collective sense of low efficacy, the quality of the relationships among its people are affected and their connection to others and to our social institutions is damaged.

The effects of detention and deportation are so extensive that they not only reach those directly affected by them, but also those who witness them up close (Brabeck & Xu, 2010). Children living with hypervigilance, suspicion, wariness, and fear are contending with a surfeit of stressors that strain and eventually damage their biological and psychological systems. Children of immigrants who grow up in marginalized communities, often in poverty, are more likely to be witnesses to or victims of the chronic violence of unstable neighborhoods, and they may learn to be violent themselves (Farrell & Sullivan, 2004). Other impairments accrue under these circumstances, such as delays in education, physical health, and behavioral disorders—the kinds of malignancies seen in violent communities. Psychologist Hirokazu Yoshikawa (2011) warns of what can happen to our country without better attention and more just policies for undocumented parents raising young US citizen-children.

> The undocumented are viewed in current policy debates as lawbreakers, laborers, or victims—seldom as parents raising citizen children. Policy-makers generally ignore the development of children of the undocumented. . . . ignoring these children has costs for society. . . . The consequences of parental undocumented status, reflected in the outcomes as intimate as a toddler's vocabulary at age three, are societal in their importance, because the early cognitive skills of our youngest citizens predicts the future productivity and success of the nation. (pp. 2–3)

The effects of deportation as the end-game of immigration policy bar the undocumented parents of citizen-children from full participation in our society. This, in turn, has consequences not just for their children but for all of us. In fact, the oppressive pursuit of undocumented immigrants and the manner in which immigration enforcement has been implemented is harmful to our national developmental health. Social and legal policies that impede the chance for personal development will cost our country economically, socially, politically, and morally in the long run (Zayas, 2010).

What will be the long-term psychological effects on the citizen-children living under deportability? What will be the long-term effects for those who are exiled or orphaned? How will the experiences of citizen-children affect their sense of belonging and civic engagement once they are old enough to work, vote, and serve on juries? How might citizen-children of deported parents conceptualize civic duty if and when they choose to return to the United States as children or adults? What will be their capacity and tolerance for understanding and participating in US civic processes? What skills will they bring in order to fully realize their potentials and contribute to US society? What tolerance will they have for social inequities? As for those I call the orphans, what will be their reactions and long-term attitudes? To what extent will their government's disbanding of their families affect their obligations as citizens and workers?

As the psychologist Daniel P. Keating (1999) states, we must examine

> our social structures and practices with the understanding that this link [between environment and people's developmental health] is well-grounded . . . . The urgency of this examination is heightened when we recognize that the investments we make now—or fail to make—will have large and persistent downstream effects on the developmental health of human populations and on the quality of the social environment they will be capable of sustaining. (p. 337)

SAFEGUARDING OUR FUTURE

Just as children have no say in where or to whom they are born, children have no say in determining their fate when their parents are put in removal proceedings. Whether citizen-children are in the "shadow population," to which Justice Brennan referred, or exiles or orphans they are collateral damage of the war on immigrants. Minor citizen-children cannot exercise their rights fully or advocate for themselves. Insensitivities in our immigration and deportation policies and the indifferent manner in which we implement them do harm to the developmental and psychological outcomes of citizen-children. The plight of citizen-children must be brought to the forefront in public discussion about immigration enforcement. Although the removal of their parents is done in the name of "securing the borders" and benefiting the overall well-being of the nation, the damaging consequences that citizen-children face in the wake of this immigration enforcement will carom throughout the population as a whole.

Our present immigration, detention, and deportation policies deny US citizen-children the childhood and future that is their birthright—life, liberty, and the pursuit of happiness. This status quo must change if we are to ensure that each child can acquire the necessary tools to be effective citizens later in life. We need to think about the long-term rather than be blinded by the short-term. Eliminating policies that exile citizen-children or create orphans is essential to fulfilling the American promise of a just society.

NOTES

1. As I write in the summer of 2014, there are 60,000 unaccompanied children entering the United States through Texas and Arizona. Americans are not accustomed to seeing humanitarian crises of this scale on our soil. Refugee camps are forming even if we are using detention centers to house them. The American public saw refugee camps form in faraway places like Somalis in Kenya, Syrians in Jordan, Cambodians and Burmese in Thailand in the late 1970s and in the mid-1980s, respectively. And we saw the orderly arrival and dispersal of Vietnamese "boat people" across many states in the 1980s.

2. The best interests of the child doctrine derived some of its history from Britain's Custody of Children Act of 1839, which gave rights primarily to the mother and brought about the tender-years doctrine to common-law tradition (Kohm, 2008). In the United States, the tender-years approach held that the custody of all children under the age of four should be automatically given to mothers in the belief that they were more capable of providing the nurturance of children, severely limiting fathers' rights in preference for mothers in divorce cases (Kelly, 1994). The concern for children's welfare in the United States in the late 1800s led to the development of the best interests of the child doctrine and its evolution occurred mostly in US family and juvenile courts (Kohm, 2008). The transition to the child's best interest was well-received because it took into account the child's wishes as well as those of the parents in divorce and custody matters. The best-interest standard eclipsed the tender-years doctrine.

3. Another value that comes to mind in this discussion is that of the separate-but-equal principle that existed for many years in the United States. A twist on the term, "equal (perhaps) but separate," seems applicable to citizen-children who are made orphans or exiles. The original separate but equal argument justified segregation while trying not to violate the 14th Amendment equal protection under the law guarantee. In 1896 the US Supreme Court upheld this doctrine in the case of *Plessy v. Ferguson*. Fortunately, that decision and the separate but equal notion were overturned in the historic *Brown v. Board of Education* (1954) in which the Court determined that black individuals were not receiving equal treatment. It took another 10 years for the separate but equal doctrine to be eradicated the 1964 Civil Rights Act. When I see how the lack of rights accorded to minor citizen-children is abrogated, it appears that an "equal but separate" principle is at play. Although citizen-children may have equal rights under the law, they can be forced into separation from their parents or their home country through the removal of parents. Being equal as citizen-children but separated from their rights and from others deprives children of the tangible and intangible resources and experiences that are fundamental to equal opportunity. Being unequal and separate leads to second- or third-class citizenship, not belonging, and not being able to benefit from participation in civic life.

ACKNOWLEDGMENTS

I was asked many times how it was possible to write a book, be dean of a professional school at a major research university, lead a research team, and travel to professional conferences and meetings. Each time I had only one answer: my wife Stephanie. It is she who makes possible all of the many projects that I get wrapped up in. Stephanie has been supportive and encouraging throughout our life together and always made the daily demands of home and family life seem invisible while I worked. For Stephanie I reserve my eternal love and gratitude. My children, Marissa, Amanda, and Luis-Michael, have my unconditional love and thanks; they patiently put up with the distractions of my academic career. Thanks go to Stephanie's brother, Michael Putiak, for help with some key historical data on emigration from Ukraine.

A talented and dedicated group of people at the University of Texas at Austin helped in the writing of this book, each in their own way. I'm thankful for my colleague and friend M. Andrea Campetella who led the study on citizen-children with her usual thoroughness and composure. Thanks also to members of my research team for their hard work: Lauren Gulbas, Miguel Gutierrez, Marina Islas, Eden Robles Hernandez, Jen Scott, and Hyunwoo Yoon. In St. Louis, Missouri, I thank Gabriela Camberos for her support and assistance.

My executive assistant, Julie Cunniff, and office staff Suzanne Ewing and Kelly McCoy smoothed the process of writing the book by typing revisions and printing drafts of the manuscript, and by keeping people away from my door while I worked. Community activists, Maria del Carmen Rodriguez and Miguel Cabrera, gave generously of their time to discuss apprehension, arrest, and deportation—extraordinarily valuable first-person background accounts.

I was also the beneficiary of the talents of two excellent graduate research assistants. Mollie Bradlee put her considerable skills to finding and summarizing background literature, and editing my writing. Amy Thompson applied her vast and nuanced knowledge of immigration to the final drafts and brought superb writing skills to improve the final drafts. To Mollie and Amy, I give my sincere thanks. At Oxford University Press, Dana Bliss provided support during the writing and helped smooth out the final stages. The final version is entirely my responsibility.

Several research collaborators deserve recognition: Sergio Aguilar-Gaxiola and his team, Marbella Salas, Mariana Ruiz del Rio, and Karina Martinez Juarez at the University of California, Davis; Guillermina Natera Rey and her team of Dewi Hernandez Montoya and Georgina Miguel Esponda at the *Instituto Nacional de Psiquiatría* in Mexico City.

Several very dedicated immigration attorneys deserve recognition and thanks for lending their time and expertise to my pursuit of this topic. In St. Louis, Ken Schmitt, Gustavo Arango, and Rachel Groneck opened their doors for me to learn about the legal situations facing mixed-status families and citizen-children and the legal means to contest removal orders. In Austin, Matt Trevena gave generously of his time to answer my many— mostly naïve—questions on the law. In Orlando, Florida, I am thankful to the collaboration with attorney Silvia Manzanero on cancellation cases.

No words can express my admiration for the many immigrant parents and children I have met over the years. I am grateful to those who talked about their lives for my research and to those who let me into their lives as we fought the deportation orders they faced. I will forever be indebted to them.

Research Project: Exploring the Effects of Parental Deportation on US Citizen-Children

In Chapter 1, I alluded to a research project in the discussion of the Garcia family of California, whose daughter was a participant. The study, "Exploring the Effects of Parental Deportation on US Citizen-Children," was sponsored by a grant from the National Institute of Child Health and Human Development, part of the National Institutes of Health (Grant R21 HD068874-01). I served as the principal investigator and my co-investigator (and project manager) at the University of Texas at Austin School of Social Work was M. Andrea Campetella, PhD. Lauren Gulbas, PhD, was also a co-investigator, first at Dartmouth College and then at the University of Texas at Austin School of Social Work. The study was conducted with the collaboration of several senior researchers at world-class institutions. At the University of California, Davis, School of Medicine, my co-investigator was Sergio Aguilar-Gaxiola, MD, PhD, director of the UC Davis Center for Reducing Health Disparities and Professor of Clinical Internal Medicine. At the *Instituto Nacional de Psiquiatria* (National Institute of Psychiatry) *Ramón de la Fuente* of México, our co-investigators were Maria Elena Medina-Mora, PhD, General Director of the Institute, and Guillermina Natera Rey, MA.

The purpose of the project was to examine the psychosocial adjustment of citizen-children whose parents had been deported, along with some children whose parents had not been deported. The research had two key research questions, three groups of children, and two methods for gathering information.[1]

RESEARCH QUESTIONS

Planning for the project began with the overarching research question, "What happens to the psychological functioning of citizen-children who leave the United States or remain behind after their parents are deported?" Then, as with any research project, we refined the question to take into consideration the many variables that would have to be controlled in order to make the best scientific comparisons. The first variable to control in this study was that of the parents' home country. We selected mixed-status families of Mexican origin since they are the largest population of citizen-children of undocumented parents. Deportation occurs more frequently for undocumented Mexican immigrants than other immigrants, and repatriation is relatively easy since Mexico shares a southern border with the United States. The inclusion of families from other national origins—countries that do not share a border with the United States, such as Guatemala and Honduras—would introduce other issues that would complicate our comparisons. Levels and nature of apprehensions, detention, and deportations as well as differences in the immigration experiences, cultures, indigenous languages, and country conditions make comparisons difficult unless we control as many variables as possible or locate a large number of children. Consequently, the research question was refined to be "What is the psychosocial and mental health functioning profile of US citizen-children of unauthorized Mexican immigrants who have been deported?"

Any answers to this kind of question naturally raise other questions, such as, "How would we know that parents' deportation influence the psychosocial functioning of their citizen-children?" This meant that we would need to control for the variable of deportation. A baseline comparison group of kids whose parents had not been deported would reveal differences, if any existed. Would we find differences between groups that are comparable (i.e., that they share many characteristics in common). A comparison group also yields information about what it means to be a citizen-child of undocumented immigrants without the complications of deportation. Therefore, we added a second research question: "How do citizen-children of Mexican heritage whose parents are unauthorized immigrants and have been deported compare to citizen-children of Mexican heritage whose parents are unauthorized immigrants but have not been deported and are not under any deportation process?" The citizen-children we recruited and the methods we employed were based on our scientific questions.

PARTICIPANTS

With the aim of understanding what children on both sides of the border experienced as a result of their parents' deportation, the design of the study would have to include three groups of children: two with deported parents and the comparison group of kids whose parents had not been deported. The first group of citizen-children was located in Mexico, youngsters who had accompanied their parents there after deportation. This would be the most difficult group to find since immigrants who are repatriated are dispersed in towns all over Mexico, not just one state or city. Even when found, they and their parents would have to give permission to participate in the study. It was through the collaboration with research colleagues at the *Instituto Nacional de Psiquiatría* of Mexico that we were able to find this group. Ultimately, we recruited 31 citizen-children into this group from Mexico.

The second group was made up of children affected by deportation who had (a) one or both parents deported to Mexico but who had remained in the United States in the care of the remaining parent or some other caregiver, and (b) children whose parents were in the process of deportation and would be remaining in the United States with a parent or other caregiver. We recruited 18 children who met criteria for this group.

The third group of citizen-children was made up of those whose parents had never been deported and were not under any deportation orders; this was the comparison group into which we recruited 34 children primarily from the Austin, Texas metropolitan region and the Sacramento, California region. The children in California were interviewed by our research collaborators at the University of California, Davis. By having this group, we could judge the comparative functioning of the two groups with deported parents and learn about the daily life of the citizen-child. It's important to note that we understood entering into the study that no group would be easy to identify. Unauthorized immigrants are forced to live on the margins of our society and are wary of researchers and anyone who appears to represent large, official institutions like universities.

Another variable for which we controlled was age. We decided on including only those between 10 and 14 years of age. This age group— from the preadolescent and early adolescent years, corresponding to the late elementary, middle school, and early high school period—represents children at a stage in life that is marked by major developmental achievements in cognition, emotional processing, and behavior, and also the ascendance in the influence of peer groups, extra-familial systems, and social roles. This stage of development also foreshadows adolescence, when psychiatric problems typically have their onset. This age range assures that children participating in the study had sufficient language skills to respond to written and oral questions and had a minimum of four years of education in US schools. We excluded children outside this age range; children with a severe mental illness, autism, developmental disability; and children whose parents or guardian refused to give consent. We also excluded citizen-children whose parents were deported due to a felony conviction or the citizen-children of legal permanent residents (green card holders) as they represent a distinct category of families. Finally, we excluded any citizen-child in foster care or child welfare. In families with two eligible children, we interviewed both. While we tried to include eligible children after the first three months of their parents' deportation, the vagaries of the deportation process and the difficulties of finding these children required that we admit into the study as many eligible children as possible regardless of when their parents had been deported. Thus, we could not control for the variable of time since deportation.

When a prospective participant was identified, a representative from a participating community partner approached parents of eligible citizen-children and told them of the study. If parents and child declined to participate, no further action was taken. If the parents and child expressed interest in participating, more information was provided. They could choose to contact us themselves and were provided with our contact information. Or they could give consent for us to contact them. Then the parents and children were provided the details of the study, what their participation entailed, and any risks in participation as well as protections against risks. When parents consented and the child assented, the child was interviewed and the parent or guardian completed some measures on the child. The institutional review boards for the protection of human subjects of the three participating institutions—the University of Texas at Austin; University of California, Davis; and the Mexican *Instituto Nacional de Psiquiatría*—approved the research protocol of the project. In addition, we obtained a federal certificate of confidentiality for additional protection of the children and their parents. In light of the very tenuous legal status of the undocumented immigrant parents whose children entered the study, our review boards permitted parents and children to participate in the study by giving oral consent and assent, respectively. Children and parents were compensated with gifts in the form of gift cards that they could redeem at stores of their choice.

METHODS

With the focus on citizen-children, we collected data directly from the kids (i.e., self-report) and gained some information about them from their parents or guardians (i.e., demographics, dates, immigration history). We used a mixed-methods approach to gathering the information we needed to answer our research questions. Our objective or quantitative method involved collecting data from the children using standardized clinical instruments to measure several psychological characteristics.

To measure the children's sense of competence, adaptive functioning, and emotional and behavioral problems, we administered two versions of the same instrument: the *Child Behavior Checklist* (CBCL) completed by parents for children in the 6–18 age group and the *Youth Self-Report* (YSR) for youth in the 11–18-year-old range (Achenbach & Rescorla, 2001).

To measure the possible presence of depressive symptoms in children, we used the *Child Depression Inventory-II* (CDI-II; Kovacs, 2003), a test of children's depression that includes negative mood, interpersonal problems, anhedonia (i.e., lack of enjoyment of activities), ineffectiveness, and negative self-esteem.

To measure the children's anxiety, we used The *Screen for Childhood Anxiety and Related Emotional Disorders* (SCARED; Birmaher et al., 1997, 1999; Muris et al., 1999), which included diagnostics of childhood anxiety, fears, hypervigilance, worries, nightmares, and night terrors.

To determine if citizen-children evidenced posttraumatic reactions, we used the *Trauma Symptom Checklist for Children* (TSCC; Briere, 1996) a self-report inventory that assesses posttraumatic stress in 8- to 16-year-olds who have experienced traumatic events (e.g., physical, sexual abuse, loss, natural disaster, violence). The TSCC contains six clinical scales: anxiety, depression, anger, posttraumatic stress, dissociation, and sexual concerns.

For a measure of the children's self-concept—that is, how they perceive and feel about themselves—we administered the *Piers-Harris Children's Self-Concept Scale, Second Edition* (Piers, Harris, & Herzberg, 2002). The Piers-Harris measures the self-concept of children ages 7 to 18 across several domains, but for brevity we selected items that reflected intellectual and school status, freedom from anxiety, behavioral adjustment, and happiness and satisfaction.

The second part of our data-collection process used a qualitative approach. We conducted in-depth interviews with the children to get their personal removal stories. The design of the study used a stratified purposive sample in which the researcher intentionally selects cases of citizen-children of unauthorized Mexican immigrants for in-depth scrutiny (Kemper, Stringfield, & Teddlie, 2003; Patton, 1990). In-depth interviews add supplemental information, filling in gaps that objective measures cannot (Creswell et al., 2003). Using this qualitative approach helps us get an "insider's view" (i.e., the experiences and perceptions of citizen-children in situations of deportation), and the two methods in tandem yield insights on the effects of deportation and offer different explanations or ideas about their meanings—ideas that are subsequently reexamined and verified (Morse, 2003). This approach promises information that answers scientific questions and illuminates unanticipated phenomenon, adding "trustworthiness" (i.e., validity) to learning about citizen-children (Lincoln & Guba, 1985).

Through these subjective narratives, our goal was to elicit the experiences and perceptions of citizen-children in Mexico with their deported parents, those who had been left in the United States in the care of someone else, and those residing in the United States with parents who are not under imminent removal proceedings. The clinical measures would give us additional information that we could then integrate with the narrative interview data. The interviews were not intended to arrive at absolutely accurate or chronologically ordered recitations of the deportation, but rather to explore how the children gave structure and meaning to their experiences and perceptions. Our interviewers asked the children in Mexico and the ones still in the United States but with deported parents about the feelings, sensations, emotions, and thoughts they had before, during, and after the deportation. Given that a consequence of deportation is the relocation of the child, either to Mexico or under the care of guardian in the United States, we wanted to understand the impact of the new home environment and neighborhood on the psychosocial well-being of the child. For the third group of children—the control group of citizen-children—the interviews were altered sufficiently to examine their unique experiences and perceptions *being* citizen-children of undocumented immigrant parents. Thus, questions probed for issues such as whether parents talk about their legal status; whether children think of their parents as different from their friends' parents; what they worry about most days; and whether they avoid saying or doing things that will get their parents in trouble. These were guiding questions and the interviews were sufficiently open to allow children to speak about what it was that was on their minds.

The interviews with citizen-children in both the United States and Mexico were completed in the winter of 2014. As part of the data analysis, we asked child and adolescent mental health specialists to review children's clinical scores and their interviews and provide their perspectives on the psychological profiles of the children. The clinicians provided their input via focus groups conducted in June 2014.

Findings will be published in professional journals in the behavioral and social sciences. These future publications can be accessed from psychology and social science databases as they appear by searching under my name or keywords (e.g., citizen-children; deportation; immigration enforcement).

NOTE

1. We had two other aims that were more logistical in nature since it was a developmental and exploratory project. One aim was to test the feasibility of conducting a bi-national research with citizen-children dispersed throughout Mexico, whereas the US group would be located in the metropolitan areas of Austin, Texas and Sacramento, California. The other aim was to test the utility of the measurements we were using and determine if they are suitable for studying citizen-children of Mexican derivation in distinct geographic and cultural contexts.

Cancellation of Removal Cases: Practical Information for Mental Health Clinicians

LUIS H. ZAYAS AND MOLLIE BRADLEE

Fighting an order of removal in immigration court can be very costly and the outcomes are never certain, yet many families will assume enormous financial burdens to fight for the rights of their US citizen-children and seek relief from deportation. At the point that a cancellation of removal hearing takes place, many steps will have been taken. Initially, there is the arrest of the undocumented immigrant which can be the result of any number of minor or major incidents. After processing in the early stages and perhaps after holding the immigrant in detention for some time, the US Department of Homeland Security initiates the removal proceedings by filing a Notice to Appear (NOA) in one of the many immigration courts operated by Executive Office for Immigration Review (EOIR) part of the U.S Department of Justice.[1] The NOA orders the immigrant to come before an immigration judge and contains details about removal proceedings, the alleged immigration law violations, and the consequences of failing to appear at scheduled hearings. It includes a statement that the immigrant has the right to be represented by an attorney at the person's expense, not at the cost of the government. A removal hearing is scheduled (and may require more than one hearing). In the NOA and other court documents, the immigrant is referred to as the "respondent." The first step in removal proceedings is a "master calendar" hearing, where the immigration judge ensures the individual understands the alleged immigration law violations. Following the master calendar hearing, the immigration judge schedules the individual hearing in which each side—the respondent's attorney and the government's attorney—presents the merits of the case.

The outcome of removal proceedings depends on whether the immigrant is eligible for relief from removal. Relief is available to individuals who can prove they meet certain criteria. Thus, the person may admit that they are removable but request relief through a cancellation of removal, adjustment of status, asylum, or other remedies provided by immigration law.

Immigration hearings are different from criminal and civil trials. In criminal and civil cases, the prosecution representing the state lays out the motive and evidence for the crime and the defense responds to each allegation, nullifies the evidence, and casts reasonable doubt on the prosecution's account. In immigration court, the individual acknowledges that he or she committed a status violation by being in the country illegally. That is not in question. What the individual is asking in an immigration hearing is to request consideration for cancelling the removal order. In cancellation of removal cases, the immigrant's attorney presents evidence and articulates in detail how "exceptional and extremely unusual hardship" will cause to a dependent spouse or citizen-children if the respondent is deported. The attorney for the immigrant provides evidence that deportation would cause the spouse or children a level of hardship above and beyond the suffering in a typical deportation. The attorney prepares a strategy to show the untoward impact of deportation if citizen-children are taken to another country or if they remain in the United States after the parents' deportation.

Essential to building a convincing case for cancellation is to demonstrate the clients' good standing in the community, stable patterns of residence and integration into their communities, and consistent employment patterns. The government attorney can stipulate, that is, agree with the immigrant's attorney that certain facts and issues are not in debate. For example, the attorneys might agree on any discrepancies in the immigrant's continuous-presence in the United States; evidence that the individual has shown a pattern of stable employment; evidence that the individual has a history of being integrated within his or her community (e.g., church membership, participation in children's schools), and has shown good moral character. The attorneys may even stipulated that the individual has shown that a hardship would be befall the immigrant and his or her family, thereby simplifying or expediting the hearing. The government attorney needs only to refute the immigrant's claims and cast serious doubt on all the information presented in court, including the testimony of expert witnesses and others.

Often, supportive documents from employers, clergy, teachers, and other community members are collected to support the claims of continuous presence, employment, integration in the community, and good moral character. When there are extenuating circumstances related to the children's health or education that would exacerbate the hardship of deportation, the attorney may introduce medical or school records as additional evidence. Attorneys may call on professionals to help prove hardship, such as country experts who know the educational, political, and economic conditions of the country, town, and region to which the family would return, including access to medical care in that country. Physicians may testify that a deportation would negatively affect a citizen-child's medical condition and offer their impressions of what the effects would be on the child if moved to another country or remains in the United States. Teachers, speech and hearing specialists, and special-education specialists, among others, may also be asked to contribute their assessment of the children's educational needs and developmental progress. Mental health professionals can be called on to provide expertise in the case—either as experts on a topic (e.g., infant attachment; psychiatric disorder; parenting) or as examiners of the citizen-children who would be most affected by a deportation. Cumulatively, this information not only strengthens the consideration but pre-empts questions and challenges from the government attorney.

REQUESTS FROM THE ATTORNEY

Mental health clinicians are increasingly being called on in cancellation cases to provide unique and powerful perspectives on the emotional and developmental impact of parents' deportation on citizen-children. When first approached by the attorney, mental health clinicians must recognize the high-level of responsibility they are accepting and recognized the legal standards that must be met in immigration court. Before committing to participate in a cancellation case, the clinician must ask as many questions as possible to avoid working with attorneys or clients with whom a dual relationship might exist or with whom the clinician may have differences on moral or ethical or political grounds. It is extremely important for the clinician to understand the request. What is it that the attorney would like to achieve through the evaluation? The codes of ethics of the mental health professions call for our dispassionate, objective evaluations of children and adults, rather than seeking to find a problem when one does not exist, or obscuring one when it does exist. The clinician's first step is to ensure that the request made by the attorney is clear and ethical. The clinician should consider collecting as many of the facts of the case as possible both to save time and to gauge what an evaluation would entail, if one can or should be conducted at all. After developing a better picture of the child and his or her functioning, clinicians can then determine whether they can help in the case.

Most often, attorneys will ask for an evaluation of the child-citizen to establish the child's psychological, educational, and social functioning, as well as how these might be affected by separation from the parents or a move to another country. The mental health evaluation will become part of a battery of documents and other information that will be entered into the court record. From the onset, it is important to determine whether the child has any diagnosed medical condition or learning disability. Any diagnosis that indicates that the child needs specialized care or attention will form the basis for meeting the requisite hardship standard. While at times mental health professionals can learn about any diagnoses from the child's parents, clients may not be forthcoming or may not mention a particular factor (e.g., special education plan or controlled medical condition), possibly because they think these are not pertinent to the case. In addition to interviewing the parents, clinicians should review children's school and medical records to spot any other concerns that the parents may not mention or that are not apparent in evaluation.

To avoid any iatrogenic effects on child or adult clients, the mental health professional must be ready to protect the mental health of the clients. Psychiatrists and attorneys Susan M. Meffert, Karen Musalo, Dale E. McNiel, and Reneé L. Binder (2010) recommend that the mental health expert be prepared to help immigration attorneys and other members of their team to learn effective methods of obtaining the trauma-related details. According to Meffert et al., when the client has or is suspected to have suffered trauma, techniques such as titration of exposure to recollection of events, recognition of when clients are shutting down their memories, and understanding how to start and end sessions to maximize the emotional capacity of clients to tell their stories are things that mental health experts can teach attorneys. When interviewing child and adolescent clients, the mental health professional as well as the attorney should approach the child calmly and elicit information very cautiously to ensure that the child and the clinician are safe. Meffert et al. note that the main danger is the emotional destabilization of the child that can lead to decompensation. These techniques can include adequate emotional preparation for the client, frequent checks on the child's emotional state, knowledge of the warning signs of mental health decompensation, and the ability to recognize mental health emergencies. The mental health professional can also help attorneys balance safety against the time limits of the legal process and the need for compelling details on the child's life in the family and outside the family.

In most instances, the evaluation is not a tool to gauge the child's intelligence, although testing a child's sensorimotor systems may help establish a baseline of children's functioning. Most often, clinicians will be asked to assess the child's socio-emotional functioning to determine what the effects might be if parents are removed and the child is left behind in the care of someone else or if the parents are removed and the child accompanies them. What is the child's overall emotional profile? What are the child's coping strengths and deficits? How has the child coped or adjusted in the past to other major and minor upheavals in her or his life? What life experiences have influenced the child's psychosocial functioning? The selection of the clinical measures for the evaluation is, of course, a case-by-case decision-making process. It is possible that an issue arises during the course of the evaluation, warranting further examination.

In considering the potentialities of a parent's deportation, clinicians must address a variety of questions regarding children's psychological and cultural circumstances. What does the child know about his or her parent's home country? Has the child visited or lived in that country and to what extent does the child understand the language and cultural nuances for assimilation into that society? The mental health professional can explore these and many other questions about the child's emotional status during the clinical interview as well as through conversations with teachers, school counselors, or physicians. Clinicians can further inform the court about the child's abilities by using objective measures of cognitive and behavioral functioning. These types of scales may help predict the child's functioning if left in the care of others or moved to another country with a different culture, environment, and services.

Although mental health clinicians cannot testify about the conditions of countries to which children might have to move, attorneys may ask clinicians to discuss implications of conditions already introduced into the record. Frequently, immigration attorneys will retain a separate regional expert to provide information on the specific region to which the family would return, including safety, infrastructure, educational opportunities, parental employment opportunities, access to medical care, and political climate. Given children's particular circumstances, mental health clinicians may state how these factors will impact the specific child's development and emotional stability. For example, if a parent must commute long hours for employment, how would this impact the parent's ability to maintain an active role in childrearing? How would the child's educational development suffer with the schooling available in that location in contrast to the education currently enjoyed in the United States? What type of behavioral and emotional effects may the child experience as a result of community violence and insecurity? Viewing conditions abroad through a developmental and emotional lens constitutes a crucial part of meeting the "extreme and exceptionally unusual" standard.

To gather information, the clinician may choose to meet with the child and family in a single session, or over multiple sessions, depending on the family's availability and necessity of follow-up evaluations. The immigrant will frequently choose to communicate in his or her native language, yet her or his US citizen-children will often prefer English, the dominant language in school. For cases in which the clinician is unable to speak the preferred language of the child or parent, an impartial interpreter may be used. Meffert et al. (2010) stress the importance of this impartiality, stating that using family members to interpret can cause the person to obscure certain facts, misrepresent symptoms, or otherwise provide incomplete or false information in an attempt to avoid shame or embarrassment. Similarly, the interpreting family member may be reluctant to translate certain information that the child or parent divulges, or may interject his or her own bias into the information provided. Using an impartial translator reduces this risk, although any time an interpreter is used, there is a risk for loss of nuance or sentiment that may otherwise be important to the evaluation.

There are two additional points for mental health clinicians to consider. First, visits to the clients' home to conduct interviews and meetings enhance the evaluation in ways that no number of meetings in the clinician's office cannot. How the family lives adds immeasurable information and nuances to any impressions that come from a clinical interview in the office. Moreover, it provides detailed information that the clinician can write into the evaluation report or raise in testimony to confirm the clinical findings. Impressions gathered in home visits may also come in handy to avert challenges or distortions on which the government attorney may want to seize. Second, parents in immigration cases are typically honest and candid about their children for they know that their immigration hearing hinges on truthfulness. Nevertheless, clinicians should always consider the extent to which parents are presenting a balanced picture of the citizen-children that will be affected by the deportation. In most instances, parents provide an honest appraisal and description of their children; some may even understate problems the child has for fear that is unimportant, irrelevant, or something shameful. These parents need to be encouraged to provide all the information. However, there are cases in which parents will overstate or even fabricate problems their children have in order to persuade the court to grant the cancellation. Both attorneys and clinicians must be aware of such situations and be prepared to discuss them openly before the court hearing occurs.

THE EVALUATION REPORT

In advance of the client's individual merit hearing (i.e., the trial setting to prove the immigrant meets requirements for cancellation of removal), attorneys often request a detailed report of the clinician's finding to submit to the immigration court and trial attorneys as evidence. Not unlike any other evaluation of a client, the report contains the child's name and date of birth, dates of the evaluations, clinician's names, date of the report, sources of data (e.g., school and health records, measures, interviews with parents, collateral contacts with teachers, clinical interview), and reason for the referral (cf. Gregory, 2011). When the clinician presents results of objective measures, he or she must provide brief descriptions of the instruments and present the findings with indications about whether the child's scores are in the clinical or nonclinical range. Any unique findings or responses by the child are worth mentioning, especially if they reveal special insightfulness or abilities.

Evaluations for immigration court are distinct in that the clinician must derive a profile of the child that constantly ties back to the potential effects of moving to another country with deported parents or being left behind. Prior to writing the report, the mental health professionals, attorney, and client should discuss any decisions about whether the child or children will remain in the United States or accompany the parent to his or her home country, allowing the expert to be specific in the report. To maximize the report's effectiveness, it should be written with the relevant legal standard in mind. As a report for cancellation of removal is ultimately presented as evidence toward hardship that is "exceptional and extremely unusual," immigration judges are unlikely to consider hardship factors that would apply to any child being forced to depart the United States with a parent. Thus, it is crucial to connect all behavioral and developmental concepts back to the child being evaluated and to his or her specific emotional profile and experience. Although it may provide necessary context, explanation of the effects of relocation or separation on child development in general are not sufficient without application to the child's unique circumstances. Like other reports that professionals prepare, it is the sole product of the clinician's informed opinion. On occasion, an attorney may ask to read the report before it is endorsed by the clinician and may ask for editing that will favor the parent's removal case, but it is essential that the clinician observe the ethical boundaries and not subvert or cloud the findings.

TESTIFYING IN COURT

To restate, the purpose of the clinician as expert witness is to inform the court with fair and unbiased professional opinions, contextualizing the citizen-child's social and emotional life as well as educational and physical condition (Bond & Sandhu, 2005). The role of the expert witness is also to educate the court on other important issues that are relevant to the case, for example, on the features of ADHD or on the fundamental causes for selective mutism. Because of the often long delays between the time of the evaluation and appearance in court, it serves the clinician well to review the evaluation report and the raw data from the evaluation instruments in advance. This provides opportunities to identify gaps in the report or one's knowledge that can be filled by questions to the attorney or the children's parents.

Whenever possible, meeting with the family's attorney ahead of time helps prepare the clinician for the direct examination as well as the cross-examination by the government attorney. Rehearsing the testimony and anticipating the cross-examination can help the clinician prepare for the actual court hearing. Generally, the direct examination starts with a re-statement of the expert clinician witness' credentials. Before the court can accept a clinician's testimony, both the immigration judge and government attorney need to agree—this is, stipulation—that the clinician qualifies as an expert witness, which often requires the clinician to present their professional credentials like education, practice experience, and any specific skills training. The immigrant's attorney might ask relevant questions regarding these credentials, as will the attorney for the government if he or she seeks to discredit the expert's testimony or clarify the extent of his or her expertise. The role of the government attorney in these situations is to test the expert witness' testimony, primarily by challenging the mental health clinician's credentials and pointing mostly to the clinician's limited knowledge and expertise in this area. Despite preparation and anticipation, the expert witness will experience a natural sense of anxiety since the stakes are very high for the family. Seasoned professionals will find their expertise questioned and possibly derided by the government attorney. Government attorneys may also recognize the diffidence of young professionals who are still developing their expertise or understanding of their roles in immigration court, and such attorneys pose difficult and aggressive questions, shaking the clinician's confidence at times or causing the clinician to misspeak.

As the trial attorney proceeds, he or she may attempt to "corner" the mental health professional by asking specific "yes" or "no," answers, or providing less time to respond before asking the next question in order to prove a particular point. In such situations, it is imperative for the clinician to extricate himself or herself from the line of questioning and to return to the issue at hand—why the child would suffer based on his or her unique individual circumstances. Maintaining consciousness of the key points to discuss as well as an awareness of where the trial attorney may be heading will assist in these scenarios.

Once the clinician is accepted as an expert, testimony will move toward an oral re-statement of the findings of the evaluation and the clinician witness' conclusions. In the preparatory sessions, the clinician should pay particular attention to what tactic the government attorney may take in an effort to defeat the request for cancellation of removal. Although it will not cover all possible questions that the government counsel will raise, the rehearsal can help prepare for similar questions or likely points of contention. (I refer you to the cases described in Chapters 7 and 8 for illustrations of the input of mental health professionals in cancellation cases.)

Overall, much of the information elicited during the direct examination may be similar to the information previously submitted in the clinician's report. Particularly during testimony, the clinicians should stay within the realm of their expertise. As with the report, clinicians may describe country conditions, but only if country experts have already offered the information as evidence in the record. As the expert will need to comment on how pre-established country conditions would affect the child's emotional and psychological well-being, citing the country expert's report or testimony in these circumstances will allow the information to be accepted without being discredited by the government attorney. Similarly, it is necessary to be conscious of the "exceptional and extremely unusual" standard while providing testimony. The respondent's attorney will often provide carefully crafted questions to elicit this information, making it important to consistently tie all information and mental health research back to the individual family's case, and explain why this particular child's situation is unique. Remembering to do this is often the most difficult part of the testimony.

The mental health professional may also play a crucial role in supporting the credibility of the respondent. In detailing hardship to a family member, the immigration judge will look for consistency in the information provided as well as the respondent's body language, demeanor, and over-all comportment (Meffert et al., 2010). Due to the nature of trauma, an individual testifying about past abuse or experienced violence may omit details or recite them inconsistently, behaviors that the judge may inter-pret as an attempt to lie or make up details. In such instances, the mental health expert may be called to explain the potential effects of experienced trauma on memory as well to provide an expert opinion on the presence of malingering.

The government attorney may also attempt to "normalize" the case and effectively argue that all children subject to relocations of neighborhoods and schools would experience the same psychological effects. Such is a common argument to prevent the merits of the case from rising to the level of "exceptional and extremely unusual." Similarly, attorneys may propose that children whose parents die or are incarcerated experience the same loss and that this child's situation would be no different. Alternatively, the attorney may challenge that, as long as they accompany their parents, children will be safe and thrive or that children are resilient when living with parents and near extended family regardless of other circumstances they face (e.g., new language, culture, schooling, community). He or she may further support this point by presenting evidence that child transi-tion services are available in the country to which the family returns.

Providing a clear, nonjargonized explanation of the underlying scien-tific theory and techniques for the evaluation that can be understood by the lay person is essential. If the expert builds the assessment of the child on specific theory, he or she must be certain that it is a testable theory, one that has withstood peer review and has been published. Furthermore, the expert should be prepared to demonstrate that the techniques used in the evaluation rely on his or her informed yet subjective interpretation. Scientific reports, especially those published in reputable professional journals, can be presented in the court hearing to bolster the clinician's testimony or the respondent's appeal. Relevance must be established about why the clinician or attorney is introducing this into the discussion. Therefore, research that directly addresses the issue or from which some inferences can be extrapolated can be presented in court. For example, the government attorney may assert that, in the town in Mexico to which a child's parents would be deported, there would probably be services to treat, say, ADHD. An Internet search and contact with professional orga-nizations in Mexico can help reveal whether there are pediatric service or pharmacies in that town to fill prescriptions for the specific medication the child needs. The nearest services may be in the state capital, which might mean a two-hour drive or more.

CONCLUSION

These are just some of the many factors that may arise in immigration court. While the present legal standard imposes a strict burden on families to set apart their cases from others, experts can play a crucial role in keeping families together within the current confines of the system. Each cancellation of removal case is an additional opportunity to protect a citizen-child from additional separation or departure to a foreign country. By understanding the legal framework and associated expectations, mental health professionals are better prepared to contribute their services to immigrant families and, in turn, assist in securing a healthier future for their citizen-children.

NOTE

1. With authority delegated by the US Attorney General, EOIR conducts immigration court proceedings, appellate reviews, and administrative hearings. There are several types of relief for an immigrant who has been issued a removal order. They include adjustment of status, asylum, or other remedies provided by immigration law. For further information visit, http://www.justice.gov/eoir/press/2010/EOIRataGlance09092010.htm

REFERENCES

Aber, J. L., Bennett, N. G., Conley, D. C., & Li, J. (1997). The effects of poverty on child health and development. *Review of Public Health. 18*, 463–483.

Achenbach, T.M., & Rescorla, L.A. (2001). *Manual for the ASEBA school-age forms & profiles*. Burlington, VT: University of Vermont, Research Center for Children, Youth, and Families.

Adam, E. K., & Chase-Lansdale, L. (2002). Home sweet home(s): Parental separations, residential moves, and adjustment problems in low-income adolescent girls. *Developmental Psychology, 38*, 792–805.

Adesope, O. O., Lavin, T., Thompson, T., & Ungerleider, C. (2010). Systematic review and meta-analysis on the cognitive benefits of bilingualism. *Review of Educational Research, 80*, 207–245.

Agency for Healthcare Research and Quality (2009). *National healthcare quality report, 2009*. Washington, DC: U.S. Department of Health and Human Services.

Alarcón, R. (2000). Skilled immigrants and cerebreros: Foreign-born engineers and scientists in the high-technology industry of Silicon Valley. In N. Foner, R. Rumbaut, & S. J. Gold (Eds.), *Immigration research for a new century: Multidisciplinary perspectives* (pp. 301–321). New York: Russell Sage Foundation.

Allen, B., Cisneros, E. M., & Tellez, A. (2013). The children left behind: The impact of parental deportation on mental health. *Journal of Child and Family Studies, 22*, 1–7.

American Immigration Council. (2012). "The 287(g) program: A flawed and obsolete method of immigration enforcement." Retrieved from http://www.immigrationpolicy.org/just-facts/287g-program-flawed-and-obsolete-method-immigration-enforcement

American Psychiatric Association (2000). *Diagnostic and statistical manual of mental disorders* (4th ed., Text rev.). Washington, DC: Author.

Arroyo Rodriguez, N., & O'Dowd, P. (2011, August 20). A rural Guatemalan town with young U.S. citizens. *Fronteras Desk*. Retrieved from http://www.fronterasdesk.org/content/rural-guatemalan-town-young-us-citizens

Ayon, C. (2014). Service needs among Latino immigrant families: Implications for social work practice. *Social Work, 59*, 13–23

Barajas, R., Philipsen, N., & Brooks-Gunn, J. (2008). Cognitive and emotional outcomes for children in poverty. In D. Crane & T. Heaton (Eds.), *Handbook of families and poverty*. Thousand Oaks, CA: Sage Publications.

Batalova, J., & McHugh, M. (2010, July). *DREAM vs. reality: An analysis of potential DREAM act beneficiaries*. Washington, DC: Migration Policy Institute.

Baubock, R., & Honohan, I. (2010). Access to citizenship in Europe: Birthright and naturalization. Brussels: Eudo Dissemination conference, 18–19 November.

Baum, J., Jones, R., & Barry, C. (2010). *In the child's best interests? The consequences of losing a lawful immigrant parent to deportation*. University of California, Berkley, School of Law & University of California, Davis, School of Law. Retrieved from http://www.law.berkeley.edu/files/IHRLC/In_the_Childs_Best_Interest.pdf

Baunach, P. J. (1985). *Mothers in prison*. New Brunswick, NJ: Transaction Books.

Bendall, S., Jackson, H. J., Hulbert, C. A., McGorry, P. D., 2008. Childhood trauma and psychotic disorders: a systematic, critical review of the evidence. *Schizophrenia Bulletin, 34*, 568–579.

Benjet C., Borges G., Medina-Mora, M. E., Zambrano, J., & Aguilar-Gaxiola, S. (2009). Youth mental health in a populous city of the developing world: Results from the Mexican Adolescent Mental Health Survey. *Journal of Child Psychology and Psychiatry, 50*, 386–395.

Betts, A. (2013). *Survival migration: Failed governance and the crisis of displacement*. Ithaca, NY: Cornell University Press.

Bhabha, J. (2009). The "mere fortuity" of birth? Children, mothers, borders, and the meaning of citizenship. In S. Benhabib & J. Resncik (Eds.), *Migration and mobilities: Citizenship, borders, and gender* (pp. 187–227). New York, NY: New York University Press.

Bhabha, J. (2014). *Child migration & human rights in a global age*. Princeton, NJ: Princeton University Press.

Bialystok, E., Craik, F. I. M., Green, D. W., & Gollan, T. H. (2009). Bilingual minds. *Psychological Science in the Public Interest, 10*, 89–129.

Birmaher, B., Brent, D.A., Chiappetta, L., Bridge, J., Monga, S., & Baugher, M. (1999). Psychometric properties of the Screen for Child Anxiety Related Emotional Disorders (SCARED): A replication study. *Journal of the American Academy of Child and Adolescent Psychiatry, 38*(10), 1230–1236.

Blair, C., & Raver, C. C. (2012). Child development in the context of adversity: Experiential canalization of brain and behavior. *American Psychologist, 67*, 309–318.

Bolaño, R. (2011). Exiles. In *Between parentheses: Essays, articles and speeches (1998–2003)* (Edited by I. Echevarria; N. Wimmer, Trans.; pp. 49–60). New York, NY: New Directions. (Original published 2003).

Bond, T., & Sandhu, A. (2005). *Therapists in court: Providing evidence and supporting witnesses*. London, England: Sage Publications.

Boss, P. (1991). Ambiguous loss. In F.Walsh & M. McGoldrick (Eds.), *Living beyond loss: Death in the family* (pp. 237–246). New York: Norton.

Boss, P. (1999). *Ambiguous loss: Learning to live with unresolved grief*. Cambridge, MA: Harvard University Press.

Boss, P. (2002). Ambiguous loss in families of the missing. *The Lancet, 360*, 39–40.

Boss, P. (2007). Ambiguous loss theory: Challenges for scholars and practitioners. *Family Relations, 56*, 105–111.

Bauback, R., & Honohan, I. (2010). *Access to citizenship in Europe: birthright and naturalization*. Brussels: European Union Democracy Observatory.

Bowlby, J. (1982). *Attachment and loss: Vol. 1. Attachment*. New York: Basic Books. (Original work published 1969).

Brabeck, K., & Xu, Q. (2010). The impact of detention and deportation on Latino immigrant children and families: A quantitative exploration. *Hispanic Journal of Behavioral Sciences*, 32, 341–361.

Briere J. (1996). *Trauma symptom checklist for children: Professional manual.* Lutz, FL: Psychological Assessment Resources.

Bush, G. H. W. (1990). *Statement on signing the Immigration Act of 1990.* The American Presidency Project. Retrieved from http://www.presidency.ucsb.edu/ws/index.php?pid=19117.

Bush, G.W. (2007). *State of the Union.* Accessed at http://georgewbush-whitehouse.archives.gov/stateoftheunion/2007/

Cambria, N. (2012, July 19). Judge gives Missouri couple custody of illegal immigrant's child. *Saint Louis Post-Dispatch.* Retrieved from http://www.stltoday.com/news/%20local/crime-and-courts/judge-gives-missouri-couple-custody-of-illegal-immigrant-s-child/article_8d7ca32d-94e9-54f4-91a8-7512476da753.html

Capps, R., Castañeda, R. M., Chaudry, A., & Santos, R. (2007). *Paying the price: The impact of immigration raids on America's children.* Washington, DC: Urban Institute for National Council of La Raza.

Capps, R., Rosenblum, M. R., Rodríguez, C., & Chishti, M. (2011). *Delegation and divergence: A study of 287(g) state and local immigration enforcement.* Washington, DC: Migration Policy Institute.

Capps, R., & Fortuny, K. (2006). *Immigration and child and family policy.* Paper presented for the Urban Institute and Child Trends Roundtable on Children in Low-Income Families, January 12.

Carcamo, C. (2013, March 19). Accidental foreigners: America's forgotten citizens. *Equal Voice for Families.* Retrieved from http://www.equalvoiceforfamilies.org/accidental-foreigners-americas-forgotten-citizens/

CBS News (2010, May 19). *Second grader to Michelle Obama "My mom doesn't have any papers."* Retrieved from http://www.cbsnews.com/news/second-grader-to-michelle-obama-my-mom-doesnt-have-any-papers-video/

Chaudry, A., Capps, R., Pedroza, J., Castañeda, R. M., Santos, R., & Scott, M. (2010). *Facing our future: Children in the aftermath of immigration enforcement.* Washington, DC: Urban Institute.

Chavez, J. M., Lopez, A., Englebrecht, C. M., & Viramontez Anguiano, R. P. (2012). Sufren los niños: Exploring the impact of unauthorized immigration status on children's well-being. *Family Court Review*, 50, 638–649.

Child Welfare Information Gateway (2012). *Determining the best interests of the child.* Washington, D.C.: U.S. Department of Health and Human Services. Retrieved from https://www.childwelfare.gov/systemwide/laws_policies/statutes/best_interest.pdf

Clarkin, J. F., Lenzenweger, M. F., Yeomans, F., Levy, K. N., & Kernberg, O. F. (2007). An object relations model of borderline pathology. *Journal of Personality Disorders*, 21, 474–499.

Clifton, J. (2012). *150 million adults worldwide would migrate to the U.S.: Potential migrants most likely to be Chinese, Nigerian, and Indian.* Washington, DC: Gallup.

Clinton, W. J. (1996). *Statement on the executive order on illegal immigration.* The American Presidency Project. Retrieved from http://www.presidency.ucsb.edu/ws/?pid= 52396

CNN (2011, January 27). Missouri court rules immigrant's adoption rights terminated illegally. Retrieved from http://www.cnn.com/2011/US/01/25/missouri.immigrant.child/

Coles, R. (1961). A young psychiatrist looks at his profession. *Atlantic Monthly, 208,* 108–111.

Cook, J. T., Frank, D. A., Berkowitz, C., Black, M.M, Casey, P.H., Cutts, D.B., . . . Nord, M. (2003). Food insecurity is associated with adverse health outcomes among human infants and toddlers. *Journal of Nutrition, 134,* 1432–1438.

Congressional Research Service (2010). *Birthright citizenship under the 14th amendment of persons born in the United States to alien parents.* Retrieved from http://www.fas.org/sgp/crs/misc/RL33079.pdf

Cousineu, M. R., Farias, A. J., & Pickering,T. (2009). *Preventable hospitalizations among children in Los Angeles County and the impact of the CHI.* Los Angeles, CA: University of Southern California Center for Community Health Studies.

Creswell, J.W., Clark, V.L.P., Gutman, M.L., & Hanson, W.E. (2003). Advanced mixed method research designs. In A. Tashakkori, & C. Teddlie (Eds.), *Handbook of mixed methods in social and behavioral research* (pp. 209-240). Thousand Oaks, CA: Sage.

Cristancho, S., Garces, D. M., Peters, K. E., & Mueller, B. C. (2008). Listening to rural Hispanic immigrants in the Midwest: A community-based participatory assessment of major barriers to health care access and use. *Qualitative Health Journal, 18,* 633–646.

Crosnoe, R. (2006). *Mexican roots, American schools: Helping Mexican immigrant children succeed.* Palo Alto, CA: Stanford University Press.

De Genova, N. (2010). The deportation regime: Sovereignty, space and the freedom of movement. In N. De Genova & N. Peutz (Eds.), *The deportation regime* (pp. 33–65). Durham, NC: Duke University Press.

Degboe, A., BeLue, R., & Hillemeier, M. (2012). Parental immigrant status and adolescent mental health in the United States: Do racial/ethnic differences exist? *Child and Adolescent Mental Health, 17,* 202–215.

Delva, J., Horner, P., Martinez, R., Sanders, L., Lopez, W.D., & Doering-White, J. (2013). Mental health problems of children of undocumented parents in the United States: A hidden crisis. *Journal of Community Positive Practices, 13,* 25–35.

Dettlaff, A. J. (2012). Immigrant children and families and the public child welfare system: Considerations for legal systems. *Juvenile & Family Court Journal, 63,* 19–30.

Dower, J. (1986). *War without mercy: Race and power in the Pacific War.* New York, NY: Pantheon Book.

DREAM Act Portal (2010). Accessed at http://dreamact.info/

Dreby, Joanna (2012). The burden of deportation on children in Mexican immigrant families. *Journal of Marriage and the Family, 74,* 829–845.

Enforcement and Removal Operations. (2013). *ERO annual report:FY 2013 ICE immigration removals.* Washington, DC: Immigration and Customs Enforcement. Retrieved from file:///X:/Research/BOOK%20on%20Exiles%20and%20Orphans/Chapter%20by%20Chapter%20PENULTIMATE/New%20Literature/2013-ice-immigration-removals.pdf

Engel de Abreu, P. M. J., Cruz-Santos, A., Tourinho, C. J., Martin, R., & Bialystok, E. (2012). Bilingualism enriches the poor: Enhanced cognitive control in low-income minority children. *Psychological Science, 23,* 1364–1371.

Erikson, E. H. (1950). *Childhood and Society.* New York, NY: Norton.

Evans, G. W. (2006). Child development and the physical environment. *Annual Reviews, 57,* 423–51.

Evans, G. W., & Kim, P. (2013). Childhood poverty, chronic stress, self-regulation, and coping. *Child Development Perspectives, 7*, 43–48.

Farrell, A. D., & Sullivan, T. N. (2004). Impact of witnessing violence on growth curves for problem behaviors among early adolescents in urban and rural settings. *Journal of Community Psychology, 32*, 505–525.

Ferguson, T. J., Stegge, H., Miller, E. R., & Olsen, M. E. (1999). Guilt, shame, and symptoms in children. *Developmental Psychology, 35*, 347–357.

Finley, B. (2013, July 28). Court rules against Hazleton immigration law. *The Philadelphia Inquirer*. Retrieved from http://articles.philly.com/2013-0728/news/40834380_1_ hazleton-immigration-law-joe-yannuzzi-u-s-court

Foley, E. (2010, December 18). DREAM Act vote fails in Senate. *Huffington Post*. Accessed at http://www.huffingtonpost.com/2010/12/18/dream-act-vote-senate_n_798631.html

Ford, G. (1976). *Statement on signing the Immigration and Nationality Act amendments of 1976*. The American Presidency Project. Retrieved from http://www.presidency.ucsb.edu /ws/?pid=6495

Friedler, E. Z. (1995). From extreme hardship to extreme deference: United States deportation of its own children, *Hastings Constitutional Law Quarterly, 22*, 491–556.

Gonzales, R. (2011). Learning to be legal: Undocumented youth and shifting legal contexts in the transition to adulthood. *American Sociological Review, 76*, 602–619.

Gregory, R. J. (2011). *Psychological testing: History, principles, and applications* (6th ed.). Upper Saddle River, NJ: Pearson.

Grubaugh, A. L., Zinzow, H. M., Paul, L., Egede, L. E., Frueh, B. C., 2011. Trauma exposure and posttraumatic stress disorder in adults with severe mental illness: A critical review. *Clinical Psychology Review, 31*, 883–899.

Gullone, E., & King, N. J. (1993). The fears of youth in the 1990s: Contemporary normative data. *The Journal of Genetic Psychology, 154*, 137–153.

Gustafson, J. (2013, December 5). *U.S. Immigration policy leaves behind "Orphans of Deportation. Oregon Public Radio*. Portland, OR: Oregon Public Broadcasting. Available at http://www.opb.org/news/series/immigration/us-immigration-policy-leaves-behind-orphans-of-deportation/

Hagan, J.M. (2008). *Migration miracle: Faith, hope, and meaning on the undocumented journey*. Cambridge, MA: Harvard University Press.

Hale, E. E. (1863). The man without a country. *The Atlantic Monthly, 12*, 665–680.

Hall, G. S. (1897). A study of fears. *American Journal of Psychology, 8*, 147–249.

Haskins, R., Greenburg, M., & Fremstad, S. (2004). Federal policy for immigrant children: Room for common ground? *Future of Children, 14*, 1–6.

Hausmann-Stabile, C., Zayas, L. H., Runes, S., Abenis-Cintron, A., & Calzada, E. (2011). Ganando confianza: Research focus groups with immigrant Mexican mothers. *Education and Training in Developmental Disabilities, 46*, 3–10.

Heidbrink, L. (2014). *Migrant youth, transnational families and the state: Care and contested interests*. Philadelphia: University of Pennsylvania Press.

Henderson, S. W., & Baily, D. R. (2013). Parental deportation, families, and mental health. *Journal of the American Academy of Child and Adolescent Psychiatry, 52*, 451–453

Hernandez, D. J., Denton, N. A., & Macartney, S. E. (2008). Children in immigrant families: Looking to American's future. *Social Policy Reports of the Society for Research on Child Development, 22*, 1–22.

Human Rights Watch (2009). *Forced apart (by the numbers): Non-citizens deported mostly for nonviolent offenses*. New York, NY: Author.

Huntington, S. P. (2004). The Hispanic challenge. *Foreign Policy, 44*, 30–45.

Immigration and Customs Enforcement. (2012a). *ICE total removals through February 20, 2012. United States Department of Homeland Security*. Retrieved from http://www.ice.gov/ doclib/about/offices/ero/pdf/ero-removals1.pdf.

Immigration and Customs Enforcement. (2012b). *Removal statistics. United States Department of Homeland Security*, Retrieved from http://www.ice.gov/removal-statistics.

Immigration and Customs Enforcement. (2014a). *Fact Sheet: Delegation of immigration authority section 287(g) Immigration and Nationality Act*. Retrieved from http://www.ice.gov/ news/library/factsheets/287g.htm.

Immigration and Customs Enforcement. (2014b). *Secure Communities*. Retrieved from http://www.ice.gov/secure_communities/.

International Organization for Migration (2013). Facts and figures. Retrieved from http://www.iom.int/cms/en/sites/iom/home/about-migration/facts--figures-1.html.

Johnson, L. B. (1965). *Remarks at the signing of the immigration bill, Liberty* Island, NY. Retrieved from http://www.lbjlib.utexas.edu/johnson/archives.hom/%20speeches.hom/651003.asp

Jones, M. (2012, July 11). Postville, Iowa, is up for grabs. *The New York Times*. Retrieved from http://www.nytimes.com/2012/07/15/magazine/postville-iowa-is-up-for-grabs.html?pagewanted=all&_r=0

Jose-Kampfner, C. (1995). Post-traumatic stress reactions in children of imprisoned mothers. In K. Gabel & D. Johnston (Eds.), *Children of incarcerated parents* (pp. 89–102). New York, NY: Lexington Books.

Kahn, C. (2010, August 5). Republicans Push to Revise 14th Amendment. *National Public Radio*. Retrieved from http://www.npr.org/templates/story/story.php?storyId=129007120

Kaehler, L. A., & Freyd, J. J. (2012) Betrayal trauma and borderline personality characteristics: Gender differences. *Psychological Trauma: Theory, Research, Practice, and Policy, 4*, 379–385

Kaitz, M., Levy, M., Ebstein, R., Faraone, S. V., Mankuta, D. (2009). The intergenerational effects of trauma from terror: A real possibility. *Infant Mental Health Journal, 30*, 158–179.

Kalashnikova, M., & Mattock, K. (2014). Maturation of executive functioning skills in early sequential bilingualism. *International Journal of Bilingual Education and Bilingualism, 17*, 111–123.

Kalil, A., & Chen, J.-H. (2008). Mothers' citizenship status and household food insecurity among low-income children of immigrants. *New Directions in Child and Adolescent Research, 121*, 43–62.

Kalil, A., & Crosnoe, R. (2009). Two generations of educational progress in Latin American immigrant families in the United States. In E. Grigorenko & R. Takanishi (Eds.), *Immigration, diversity, and education* (pp. 188–204). New York, NY: Routledge.

Keating, D. P. (1999). Developmental health as the wealth of nations. In D. P Keating & C. Hertzman (Eds.), *Developmental health and the wealth of nations: Social, biological, and educational dynamics* (pp. 337–347). New York: Guilford.

Keating, D. P., & Hertzman, C. (1999). *Developmental health and the wealth of nations: Social, biological, and educational dynamics*. New York: Guilford.

Kelly, J.B. (1994). The determination of child custody. *Children and Divorce, 4*, 120–142.

Kemper, E.A., Stringfield, S., & Teddlie, C. (2003). Mixed methods sampling strategies in social science research. In A. Tashakkori, & C. Teddlie (Eds.), *Handbook of mixed methods in social and behavioral research* (pp. 273-296). Thousand Oaks, CA: Sage.

Kochanska, G., Barry, R. A., Jimenez, N. B., Hollatz, A. L., & Woodard, J. (2009). Guilt and effortful control: Two mechanisms that prevent disruptive developmental trajectories. *Journal of Personality and Social Psychology, 97*, 322–333.

Kovacs, M. (2003). *CDI children's depression inventory. Technical manual update.* North Tonawanda, NY: Multi-Health Systems, Inc.

Kohlberg, L. (1973). Continuities in childhood and adult moral development revisited. In P. B. Baltes & K. W. Schaie, K. W. (Eds.), *Life-span development psychology: personality and socialization.* New York, NY: Academic Press.

Kohlberg, L. (1981). *Essays on moral development, Vol. I: The philosophy of moral development.* San Francisco, CA: Harper & Row.

Kohm, L. M. (2008). Tracing the foundations of the best interests of the child standard in American jurisprudence. *Journal of Law & Family Studies, 10*, 337–376.

Kozol, J. (2000). *Ordinary resurrections: Children in the years of hope.* New York, NY: Broadway Books.

Kremer J. D., Moccio, K. A., & Hammell, J. W. (2009). *Severing a lifeline: The neglect of citizen children in America's immigration enforcement policy.* Minneapolis, MN: Dorsey & Whitney.

Kullgren, J. T. (2003). Restrictions on undocumented immigrants' access to health services: The public health implications of welfare reform. *American Journal of Public Health, 93*, 1630–1633.

Lamberg, L. (2008). Children of immigrants may face stresses, challenges that affect mental health. *Journal of the American Medical Association, 300*, 780.

Lincoln, Y.S., & Guba, E.G. (1985). *Naturalistic inquiry.* Beverly Hills, CA: Sage

Luk, G., Green, D., Abutalebi, J., & Grady, C. L. (2011). Cognitive control for language switching in bilinguals: A quantitative metaanalysis of functional neuroimaging studies. *Language and Cognitive Processes, 27*, 1479–1488.

Luster, T., Qin, D.B., Bates, L., Johnson, D.J., & Rana, M. (2009). The lost boys of Sudan: Ambiguous loss, search for family, and reestablishing relationships with family members. *Family Relations, 57*, 444–456.

Lynch v. Clarke (1844). *New York Legal Observer, 3*, 236-260. Accessed January 25, 2014 from http://tesibria.typepad.com/whats_your_evidence/Lynch_v_Clarke_1844_ocr.pdf

Mackie, D., & Hamilton, D. (1993). *Affect, cognition, and stereotyping: Interactive processes in group perception.* San Diego, CA: Academic.

Martinez, O. (2013). *The beast: Riding the rails and dodging narcos on the migrant trail.* New York, NY: Verso Books.

Matthews, H., & Ewen, D. (2006). *Reaching all children? Understanding early care and education participation among immigrant families.* Washington, DC: Center for Law and Social Policy.

McDonnell, P. J. (1997, November 15). Prop. 187 found unconstitutional by federal judge. *Los Angeles Times.* Retrieved from http://articles.latimes.com/1997/nov/15/news/mn-54053

McDonnell, P. J. (1999, July 29). Davis won't appeal Prop. 187 ruling, ending court battles. *Los Angeles Times.* Retrieved from http://articles.latimes.com/1999/jul/29/news/mn-60700

McKay-Semmler, K., & Kim, Y. Y. (2014). Cross-cultural adaptation of Hispanic youth: A study of communication patterns, functional fitness, and psychological health. *Communication Monographs, 81*, 1–24.

McLoyd, V. C. (1989). Socialization and development in a changing economy: The effects of paternal job and income loss on children. *American Psychologist, 44*, 293–302.

McLoyd, V. C. (1998). Socioeconomic disadvantage and child development. *American Psychologist, 53*, 185–204.

McLoyd, V. C., Kaplan, R., Purtell, K., Bagley, E., Hardaway, C., & Smalls, C. (2009). Poverty and socioeconomic disadvantage in adolescence. In R. Lerner & L. Steinberg (Eds.), *Handbook of adolescent psychology* (3rd ed, pp. 444–491). New York, NY: Wiley.

Meffert, S. M., Musalo, K., McNiel, D. E., & Binder, R. L. (2010). The role of mental health professionals in political asylum processing. *Journal of the American Academy of Psychiatry and the Law, 38*, 479–489.

Mendoza, M., & Olivas, E. (2009). Advocating for control with compassion: the impact of raids and deportations on children and families. *Oregon Review of International Law, 11*, 111–122.

Morse, J.M. (2003). Principles of mixed methods and multimethod research design. In A. Tashakkori, & C. Teddlie (Eds.), *Handbook of mixed methods in social and behavioral research* (pp.189-208). Thousand Oaks, CA: Sage.

Morton, J. (2011). *Exercising prosecutorial discretion consistent with the civil immigration priorities of the agency for the apprehension, detention and removal of aliens.* U.S. Department of Homeland Security. U.S. Immigration and Customs Enforcement. Retrieved from http://www.ice.gov/doclib/secure-communities /pdf/prosecutorial-discretion-memo.pdf

Moss, E., Rousseau, D., Parent, S., St.-Laurent, D., & Saintong, J. (1998). Correlates of attachment at school age: Maternal reported stress, mother-child interaction, and behavior problems." *Child Development. 69*, 1390–1405.

Muris, P., Merckelbach, H., Schmidt, H., & Mayer, B. (1999). The revised version of the Screen for Child Anxiety Related Emotional Disorders (SCARED-R): Factor structure in normal children. *Personality and Individual Differences, 26*, 99–112.

Napolitano, Janet (2012, June 15). *Exercising prosecutorial discretion with respect to individuals who came to the United States as children.* Washington, DC: U.S. Department of Homeland Security. Retrieved from http://www.dhs.gov/ xlibrary/assets/s1-exercising-prosecutorial-discretion-individuals-who-c ame-to-us-as-children.pdf

Nazario, S. (2006). *Enrique's journey: The story of a boy's dangerous odyssey to reunite with his mother.* New York, NY: Random House.

Nickerson, A., Bryant, R. A., Aderka, I. M., Hinton, D. E., & Hofmann, S. G. (2013). The impacts of parental loss and adverse parenting on mental health: Findings from the National Comorbidity Survey. *Psychological Trauma: Theory, Research, Practice, and Policy, 5*, 119–127.

Niedenthal, P. M., Tangney, J. P., & Gavansky, I. (1994). "If only I weren't" versus "if only I hadn't": Distinguishing shame and guilt in counterfactual thinking. *Journal of Personality and Social Psychology, 967*, 585–595.

Nolo (2014). "Issues faced by detained applicants applying for asylum." Retrieved from http://www.nolo.com/legal-encyclopedia/issues-faced- detained-applicants- applying-asylum.html

Nowrasteh, A. (2013). Immigration reform is not amnesty. Cato Institute. Retrieved January 16, 2014 from http://www.cato.org/blog/immigration-reform-not-amnesty.

Obama, B.H. (2011, January 25). *Remarks by the President in the State of the Union address*. Washington, DC: The White House. Retrieved from http://www.whitehouse.gov/the-press-office/2011/01/25/remarks-president-state-union-address.

Obama, B. H. (2013, January 21). *Inaugural address by President Barack Obama*. Washington, DC: The White House. Retrieved from http://www.whitehouse.gov/the-press-office/2013/01/21/inaugural-address-president-barack-obama.

Obama, B.H. (2010, June 21). *Remarks by the President on a Father's Day event*. Washington, DC: The White House. Retrieved from http://www.whitehouse.gov/the-press-office/remarks-president-a-fathers-day-event

Obama, B.H. (2013, February 15). *Remarks By The President On Strengthening The Economy For The Middle Class*. The White House. Retrieved from http://www.whitehouse.gov/the-press-office/2013/02/15/remarks-president-strengthening-economy-middle-class

Open Society Foundations (2013). Dominican Republic court ruling raises mass statelessness threat. Retrieved from http://www.opensocietyfoundations.org/press-releases/dominican-republic-court-ruling-raises-mass-statelessness-threat

Organization of American States (1969). *American convention on human rights*. Washington, DC: Organization of American States.

Ortega, A. N., Fang, H., Perez, V. H., Rizzo, J. A., Carter-Pokras, O., Wallace, S. P., & Gelberg, L. (2007). Health care access, use of services, and experiences among undocumented Mexicans and other Latinos. *Archives of Internal Medicine, 26*, 2354–2360.

Ortega, A. N., Horwitz, S. M., Fang, H., Kuo, A. A., Wallace, S. P., & Inkelas, M. (2009). Documentation status and parental concerns about development in young US children of Mexican origin. *Academic Pediatrics, 9*, 278–282.

Patton, M.Q. (1990). *Qualitative evaluation and research methods* (2nd Ed.). Newbury Park, CA: Sage.

Perez-Diaz, S. (2012, November 9). US citizen among Guatemala earthquake victims. *Associated Press*. Retrieved from http://bigstory.ap.org/article/us-citizen-among-guatemala-earthquake-victims

Phillips, S., Hagan, J., & Rodriguez, N. (2006). Brutal borders: Examining the treatment of deportees during arrest and detention. *Social Forces, 85*, 93–110.

Piaget, J., & Inhelder, B. (1950). *The psychology of the child*. New York, NY: Basic Books.

Piers, E.V., Harris, D.B., & Herzberg, D.S. (2002). *Piers-Harris Children's Self-Concept Scale*, 2nd Edition. Los Angeles, CA: Western Psychological Services.

Reasoner, W. D. (2011, July). *How immigration enforcement works (or doesn't) in real life*. Washington, DC: Center for Immigration Studies. Retrieved from http://cis.org/deportation-basics

Ramos, J. (2005). Dying to cross: The worst immigrant tragedy in American history. New York: Harper.

Roos, S., Hodges, E.V.E., & Salmivalli, C. (2014). Do guilt- and shame-proneness differentially predict prosocial, aggressive, and withdrawn behaviors during early adolescence? *Developmental Psychology, 50*, 941–946.

Ryo, E. (2013). Deciding to cross: Norms and economics of unauthorized migration. *American Sociological Review, 78*, 574–603.

Rumbaut, R. G., & Ewing, W.A. (2007). *The myth of immigrant criminality and the paradox of assimilation: Incarceration rates among native and foreign-born men.* Washington, DC: Immigration Policy Center.

Sapolsky, R. M. (1994). *Why zebras don't get ulcers: A guide to stress, stress-related diseases, and coping.* Boston: Freeman.

Satinsky, S., Hu, A., Heller, J., & Farhang, L. (2013). *Family unity, family health: How family-focused immigration reform will mean better health for children and families.* Oakland, CA: Human Impact Partners: Oakland, CA.

Schwerdtfeger, K. L., Larzelere, R. E., Werner, D., Peters, C., & Oliver, M. (2013). Intergenerational transmission of trauma: The mediating role of parenting styles on toddlers' *DSM*-related symptoms. *Journal of Aggression, Maltreatment & Trauma, 22,* 211–229.

Security Weekly (2013, January 17). *Mexico's drug war: Persisting violence and a new president.* Stratfor Global Intelligence. Retrieved from http://www.stratfor.com/.

Select Commission on Immigration and Refugee Policy (1981). *U.S. immigration policy and the national interest: The final report and recommendations of the select commission on immigration and refugee policy with supplemental views by commissioners.* Washington, DC: Congress of the U.S.

Shamdasani, R. (2013). *Briefing notes on Libya/torture in detention, Dominican Republic.* Geneva, Switzerland: UN High Commissioner for Human Rights, 1 October.

Shear, K., & Shair, H. (2005). Attachment, loss, and complicated grief. *Developmental Psychology, 47,* 253–267.

Stewart, S. (1956). *Give us this day.* New York: W. W. Norton.

Styron, W. (1979). *Sophie's choice: A novel.* New York: Random House.

Suárez-Orozco, C., & Suárez-Orozco, M. (2001). *Children of immigration.* Cambridge, MA: Harvard University Press.

Talavera, V., Núñez-Mchiri, G. G., & Heyman, J. (2010). Deportation in the U.S.–Mexico borderlands: Anticipation, experience and memory. In N. De Genova & N. Peutz (Eds.), *The deportation regime* (pp. 166–195). Durham, NC: Duke University Press.

Tangney, J. P., & Dearing, R. L. (2002). *Shame and guilt.* New York: Guilford.

Taylor, P., Lopez, M. H., Martinez, J. H., & Velasco, G. (2012). *When labels don't fit: Hispanics and their views of identity.* Washington, DC: Pew Hispanic Center.

The Telegraph (2010, May 26). *Girl who asked Michelle Obama immigration question becomes star in Peru.* Retrieved from http://www.telegraph.co.uk/news/world-news/northamerica/usa/7769282/Girl-who-asked-Michelle-Obama-immigration-question-becomes-star-in-Peru.html

Thompson, A. (2008). *A child alone and without papers: A report on the return and repatriation of unaccompanied undocumented children by the United States.* Austin, TX: Center for Public Policy Priorities.

Thompson, G. (2009, April 22). After losing freedom, some immigrants face loss of custody of their children. *The New York Times.* Retrieved from http://www.nytimes.com/2009/04/23

Thompson, R. A., & Hoffman, M. L. (1980). Empathy and the development of guilt in children. *Developmental Psychology, 16,* 155–156.

Thronson, D. D. (2005-2006). Choiceless choices: Deportation and the parent-child relationship. *Nevada Law Journal, 6,* 1165–1214.

Thronson, D. B. (2008). Creating crisis: Immigration raids and the destabilization of immigrant families. *Wake Forest Law Review, 43,* 391–418.

Thronson, D. B. (2011). Clashing values and cross purposes: Immigration law's marginalization of children and families. In J. Bhabha (Ed.), *Children without a state: A global human rights challenge* (pp. 237–254). Cambridge, MA: The MIT Press.

Transactional Records Access Clearinghouse (2013). *Judge-by-Judge Asylum Decisions in Immigration Courts, FY 2007-2012.* Syracuse, NY: Syracuse University. Accessed at http://trac.syr.edu/immigration/reports/306/include/denialrates.html

Truman, H. (1952). Public papers of the president of the United States. Washington, DC: Government Printing Office.

United Nations Population Fund and International Organization for Migration (2013). *International migration and development: Contributions and recommendations of the international system.* Geneva: United Nations.

U.S. Department of Health and Human Services. (2011). *Frequently asked questions related to the poverty guidelines and poverty.* Retrieved from http://aspe.hhs.gov/poverty/faq.shtml#developed

U.S. Department of Homeland Security (2006). *Treatment of immigration detention at enforcement facilities.* Washington, DC: US Department of Homeland Security. Office of the Inspector General.

U.S. Department of Homeland Security (2013). *Yearbook of immigration statistics: 2012* Washington, DC: Office of Immigration Statistics, Department of Homeland Security.

U.S. Department of Justice (2014). *The immigration judge benchbook.* Washington, DC: Executive Office for Immigration Review, U.S. Department of Justice. Retrieved from http://www.justice.gov/eoir/vll/benchbook/

U. S. Government Accountability Office. (2007). *Immigration enforcement: ICE could improve controls to help guide alien removal decision making.* (Report GAO-08-67) Washington, DC: U.S. GAO.

Urrea, L. A. (2004). *The devil's highway: A true story.* New York: Little, Brown and Co.

Vishneski, J. (1988). What the court decided in Dred Scott v Sandford. *The American Journal of Legal History, 32,* 373–390.

Wessler, S. (2012, November 28). A deported father wins a long, painful fight to keep his kids. *ColorLines.* Retrieved May 18, 2013 from http://colorlines.com/archives/2012/11/nc_judge_reunites_deported_father_with_three_us_citizen_children.html

Wessler, S. (2011). *Shattered families: The perilous intersection between immigration enforcement and the child welfare system.* New York, NY: Applied Research Center.

Wilson, T. D. (2000). Anti-immigrant sentiment and the problem of reproduction/ maintenance in Mexican immigration to the United States. *Critique of Anthropology, 20*(2), 191–213.

Wilson, W. (1915, January 28). *Veto message to the House of Representatives.* Accessed at http://www.presidency.ucsb.edu/ws/?pid=65386

Wing, N. (2010, September 13). Arizona Immigration Law Architects Turn Sights On 14th Amendment, Birthright Citizenship. *The Huffington Post.* Retrieved from http://www.huffingtonpost.com/2010/09/13/arizona-14th-amendment_n_714524.html

Woltjen, M. (2014). Unaccompanied immigrant children are most vulnerable. *Chicago Tribune,* June 27. Retrieved from http://theyoungcenter.org/stories/chicago-tribune-op-ed-by-director-maria-woltjen/

Women's Refugee Commission. (2013). *Avoidable adverse impacts on children of ICE enforcement practices*. Retrieved from http://womensrefugee commission.org/programs/detention/807-avoidable-adverse-impacts-on-children-of-ice-enforcement-practices

Word, D. L., Coleman, C. D., Nunziata, R., & Kominski, R. (2000). Demographic aspects of surnames from census 2000. Washington, DC: U.S. Bureau of the Census. Retrieved from http://www.census.gov/genealogy/www/data/2000surnames/surnames.pdf

Wray, H. (2013). The psychology of exile. *Huffington Post*, July 16. Retrieved from http://www.huffingtonpost.com/wray-herbert/the-psychology-of-exile_b_3604720.html

Xu, Q., & Brabeck, K. (2012). Service utilization among undocumented Latino immigrant families. *Social Work Research, 36*, 209–221.

Yoshikawa, H. (2011). *Immigrants raising citizens: Undocumented parents and their young children*. New York, NY: Sage.

Yoshikawa, H., Aber, J. L., & Beardslee, W. R. (2012). The effects of poverty on the mental, emotional, and behavioral health of children and youth: Implications for prevention. *American Psychologist, 67*, 272–284.

Young Center for Immigrant Children's Rights (2013). *Our mission*. Accessed at http://theyoungcenter.org/about/mission/

Zayas, L.H. (2004, July 17). Letter to the Editor: "The learning curve: One language or two?" *The New York Times*, p. A12.

Zayas, L. H. (2010). Protecting citizen-children safeguards our common future. *Journal of Health Care for the Poor and Underserved, 21*, 809–814.

Zayas, L. H. (2011). *Latinas attempting suicide: When cultures, families, and daughters collide*. New York, NY: Oxford University Press.

Zayas, L. H., & Bradlee, M. (2014). Exiling children, creating orphans: When immigration policies hurt citizens. *Social Work, 59*, 167–175.

Zigler, E. F., & Hall, N. W. (2000). *Child development and social policy*. McGraw-Hill.

ABOUT THE POET: KANE SMEGO

The excerpts that open this book are taken from *Super Mario* by Kane Smego. Copyright © 2012. The excerpts are reprinted with the poet's permission.

Kane Smego is a spoken-word poet and hip-hop artist, a National Poetry Slam finalist, and the co-founder and former artistic director of the award-winning youth arts nonprofit, Sacrificial Poets. A native of North Carolina, Kane has performed, taught, and realized poetry and hip-hop projects throughout the United States, and abroad in Central America, Europe, and Africa. He has a BA in Spanish Language from the University of North Carolina at Chapel Hill and has run poetry, literacy, and arts programs with Latino youth in his local community. He is the primary author of the *YouTh ink. Curriculum* that uses poetry and hip-hop to help youth and adults tell their own stories, and challenges them to transform themselves and their communities through the use of the spoken and written word.

I express my sincerest thanks to Kane for permitting his words to grace this book.

CREDITS

INDEX